CW01082443

THE NEW SOCIOLOGY OF AGEING

The New Sociology of Ageing seeks to explore the challenges and opportunities of Ageing as a global force in its own right working alongside globalisation, urbanisation, new technology, and now both climate change and global pandemics, in transforming life in the 21st century.

Through the eyes of a young sociology student and her multigenerational family, this book seeks to sketch out a new sociological framework to interpret this societal shift and to explore how the "New Old" – the baby boomer generation – might be mobilised as an agency of social change in transforming later life. It also explores the possibility of this generation as the co-architects of a new intergenerational social contract for the era ahead rather than just remaining the recipients of a post-war 20th-century social contract that society can no longer support.

This book therefore seeks to fill a significant gap in current textbook provision by raising the profile and providing a broad overview of the emerging discipline of the sociology of ageing. With Britain as a case study and societies across the world as examples, it seeks to explore the emerging revolutions in work and retirement, the potential crises in pensions, healthcare and housing, and the transformations in both family life, and in our attitudes to sex and death in later life. It seeks to introduce students to the dynamics of demography as a sociological force of the future, as well as to alert them – as the younger generation – to the perils and the promises of longevity as societies across the world approach the 100-Year Life. Japan is nearly there; Europe and South East Asia are close behind and eventually even Africa will follow. This book will be of interest to undergraduate students and early scholars in sociology, social sciences, gerontology and social policy.

Martin Slattery is a retired Sixth-Form College Principal and Senior Education Officer who has previously written a number of introductory and specialist texts in Sociology including *The ABC of Sociology* (1985), *Key Ideas in Sociology* (2003), *Urban Sociology* (1985) and *Official Statistics* (1986). Since retiring, he has focused on the emerging topic of Ageing and Longevity in the 21st century with the publication of *The Ageing of Great Britain* in 2019.

Routledge Advances in Sociology

For more information about this series, please visit: https://www.routledge.com/Routledge-Advances-in-Sociology/book-series/SE0511

THE NEW SOCIOLOGY OF AGEING

Martin Slattery

LONDON AND NEW YORK

First published 2022
by Routledge
2 Park Square, Milton Park, Abingdon, Oxon OX14 4RN

and by Routledge
605 Third Avenue, New York, NY 10158

Routledge is an imprint of the Taylor & Francis Group, an informa business

British Library Cataloguing-in-Publication Data
A catalogue record for this book is available from the British Library

Library of Congress Cataloging-in-Publication Data
Names: Slattery, Martin, author.
Title: The new sociology of ageing / Martin Slattery.
Description: Milton Park, Abingdon, Oxon; New York, NY: Routledge,
   2021. | Includes bibliographical references and index.
Identifiers: LCCN 2021033157 (print) | LCCN 2021033158 (ebook) |
   ISBN 9780367465377 (hardback) | ISBN 9780367465384 (paperback) |
   ISBN 9781003029373 (ebook)
Subjects: LCSH: Older people—Social conditions. | Older people—
   Government policy. | Population aging.
Classification: LCC HQ1061 .S522 2021 (print) | LCC HQ1061 (ebook) |
   DDC 362.6—dc23
LC record available at https://lccn.loc.gov/2021033157
LC ebook record available at https://lccn.loc.gov/2021033158

ISBN: 978-0-367-46537-7 (hbk)
ISBN: 978-0-367-46538-4 (pbk)
ISBN: 978-1-003-02937-3 (ebk)

DOI: 10.4324/9781003029373

Typeset in Bembo
by KnowledgeWorks Global Ltd.

This book is dedicated to my family, my grandchildren and especially to my wife, Jacqueline, for her enduring patience & loving support.

My thanks to Emily Briggs, my editor and especially to Lakshita Joshi, my editorial assistant, and Harshita Donderia, my project manager, whose advice & support even during the worst of COVID-19 went well beyond the call of duty.

CONTENTS

LIST OF FIGURES

AN INTRODUCTION TO THE AGEING WORLD AHEAD

> Old Age is like everything else. To make a success of it, you've got to start young.
> *Theodore Roosevelt*

This quote from Theodore Roosevelt sums up much of this book. Ageing may sound like a topic for old people only. It may sound like the final stage of life; may sound like the most boring and unsexy topic for sociological study but as this reader hopefully shows, it is potentially one of the most fascinating and life changing topics on the planet; and one of the most critical for young people today. We are entering a new age of longevity. We are entering what Lynda Gratton and Andrew Scott have called the ***100-Year Life***. We are embarking on the start of a Second Life for older people, the start of a 50-Year Career for younger people and the start of a multistage life for children born today. Age and stage no longer align and some believe that we may be moving towards super-ageing or even ageless societies in the future. All that and now we have coronavirus; a global pandemic that has hit all ages but the older ages the hardest with a global death toll of COVID-19-related deaths of over 2.5 million as of March 2021, over 70% of which were in the older age groups.

Ageing, today, is a global force; a mega force that sits alongside globalisation, urbanisation, new technology, climate change – and now global pandemics – in terms of its potential impact on life in the 21st century:

- **For the first time in human history**, the old – the over 60s – will out-number the young – those aged 15.
- **For the first time in human history**, the Old Age Dependency Ratio (OADR) ratio will shift from 4:1 to 2:1, from four workers to every pensioner

DOI: 10.4324/9781003029373-1

to less than two in Europe and the advanced economies whilst developing nations such as China are likely *to grow old before they get rich.*

• **For the first time in the post-war period**, populations in developed countries such as Russia and Japan are threatening to "implode" or shrink as their birth rates sink below replacement levels and their older populations explode by 20% or more of their national populations.

The world, the whole world, is going through a demographic revolution that eventually even Africa will experience; a seismic shift in the world's population structure, the likes of which and the speed of which has never been seen before. As the *Economist* explained in 2012, "In the 20th century, the planet's population doubled twice". In the 21st century, "the over-65 age group is set to double within 25 years" – all on its own! Not only that but also the Old Old, those aged 85 and above, are the fastest growing sector of the world's population with centenarians, those over 100, expected to multiply from just over 300,000 today to 3.2 million by 2050; a 10-fold increase in less than 40 years. As the Centre for Strategic and International Studies explained in 2014, "We live in an era of many challenges, from global warming to global terrorism. But few are as certain as Global Aging and few are as likely to have such a large and enduring impact on the size and shape of government budgets, on the future growth in living standards, and on the stability of the global economy".

The world is going through a demographic revolution that will transform the future – your future – but doesn't seem to know it. The world is going through a sociological revolution that is about to turn societies – East and West – on their demographic heads as an age wave, a grey wave sweeps across every continent except Africa in the next 30 years with extraordinary speed and extraordinary effect. It will overturn traditional social and political structures and in partnership with new technology and artificial intelligence unleash such new social phenomena as the multigenerational family, the silver economy, sexbots and even a new style death industry. Some scientists today are even predicting the possibility of everlasting life, of humanoid life as humans merge and marry AI and robotic machines of the future. The world is equally facing an ageing crisis, an economic time-bomb, an age avalanche as two billion older people, aged 60 and over, pour on to the "shores of retirement", living not for a few more years of quiet relief but for decades to come and threatening in the process to drain the younger generations of taxes, jobs, housing and their own future pensions. No government, no society before has had to deal with the challenges of mass ageing; of having waves of retirees pouring onto the shores of welfare states already under huge strain after the financial crises of 2008/2009 and now the COVID-19 pandemic of 2020/2021. The older ages are now threatening to outnumber the young and threatening to live longer than ever before. This is a massive challenge for wealthy first world countries with infrastructures that should cope. For emerging nations with embryonic health and social care services, the challenge of ageing is potentially overwhelming and possibly catastrophic.

However, ageing, like global warming, potentially contains the seeds of its own salvation. It holds the promise of a brighter, longer and potentially happier human future not just for the elderly but for all ages; for Young and Old; for generations now and in the future; for grandchildren to come. Beneath the *grey cloud* of ageing lies the *silver lining* of the 100-Year Life; of children born today living well into the next century, of new technology not only liberating the Old physically but liberating the elderly socially as communication aids and robots become their companions. The Sociology of Ageing is no longer just about the Old getting older. It is about human life getting longer and, in the process, generating a silent sociological revolution as human societies reshape their social structures to better meet the needs and aspirations of the age-friendly or even ageless societies of the future. A fundamentally new type of society is emerging in the 21st century as the result of dramatic and permanent changes in longevity and lifestyle; the ageless or at least age-friendly society, multigenerational in length and multi-national in breadth. A new age and a new stage in man's evolution towards a higher civilisation and a higher state of mind with the opportunity not just for extra life but for a multistage life, a **second or even third life** even after retirement with the time to follow new careers, start new businesses, adopt new lifestyles, engage in community volunteering and to continue to support your family through childcare – and even eldercare as grandparents live into much "riper old age"; a *Silver Heaven on a Silver Earth* with the potential for humankind in the 21st century to become a higher order of being. This all sounds ridiculous – fantastical even – but as Laura, the student at the centre of this reader, found as she read more widely such fantasies about future life are not just the fictions of mad scientists but the new horizons for Amazon, SpaceX and the billionaires who have already conquered Planet Earth and are now aiming for the Moon and Mars. As Professor Rudi Westendorp (2014) summed it up: "Less than a hundred years ago, the average Western life expectancy was 40; now it is 80. And there is no end in sight: the first person who will reach 135 has already been born".

You would think that with all this wonderful longer life before us, ageing would be the subject of great public debate, great public celebration and intense sociological study. ***But it is not***. Ageing barely ever "hit the headlines" and now, when it has, it has been because of the onslaught of COVID-19 or as an economic or social "time-bomb" that is about to devastate our welfare state, escalate taxes and plunge the economy into "downfall" as governments struggle to cope with a *population explosion* of older people that it cannot control; a nightmare scenario to rival the blockbuster film Mad Max, of the "grey and gloomy" world that apparently lies ahead in which disability, dementia and death haunt the streets and care homes and hospitals struggle to contain millions of elderly literally on their "last legs". Despite the warnings of the UN, WHO and EU, few national governments outside South East Asia and Scandinavia are seriously planning for the ageing world ahead and even fewer, for the inherent promises of longer, better life that lie beneath.

Even the New Old, the baby boomers who were part of a population explosion after WWII, one that tore up the age playbook, challenged every tradition and age restriction in sight and demanded a brave new world of freedom and personal expression, seem unaware that they are now in the midst of a revolution in *old age*, that many of them are now living *a second life* and that they have the wealth and the political power, if they choose to use it, to transform the future for their grandchildren and for generations to come. No century before, no generation before has had the gift of *reflection,* the gift of *generativity,* the gift of having the time and the temperament to be able to look back on life to-date and still have the time and the opportunity to do something different or better. The New Old – the baby boomer generation – have that opportunity. They have the opportunity to turn ageing into an asset rather than a liability. But do they still have the energy, the attitude, the ambition to take on yet another social revolution; "break down" barriers, challenge traditional images and expectations about old age in the same way as they did when they were younger. Or are they passed it, content to carry on spending their children's inheritances whilst "basking in the sun" abroad or roaming the golf courses and shopping malls at home with money and time to burn.

But, longevity isn't just creating longer older life. It is creating longer stages of a longer life for all ages. It, therefore, needs a new sociological paradigm to describe and inform it. It needs a new philosophy of life to realise its true promise for all ages and for humankind at large. The 100-Year Life is here to stay and as you will see, Japan, the oldest nation in the world, is already living with and grappling with the challenge of converting a mushrooming elder population from an economic liability into a sociological asset; of converting this *Land of the Rising Sun* into a *Beacon of Silver Light* that other nations might follow. Ageing is here to stay. It will not go away. By 2050 all continents except Africa will be beginning to *Go Grey.* The sooner national governments across the world face up to this new force of nature and plan ahead, the sooner the debate about how best to use and exploit this monumental gift of extra life can begin. And time is running out – 2050 is barely 30 years away and over **two billion** older people are amassing on the social, economic and political horizon even as we speak.

So, these are the main themes of this reader. This is the emerging shape of the New Sociology of Ageing that this book seeks to describe in four main parts:

Firstly, the global context of ageing in the 21st century and the global challenges ahead.
Secondly, ageing in modern Britain and its emerging impact on virtually all Britain's traditional social structures from retirement and pensions, through to health, housing, family and even sex, death and dying.
Thirdly, the New Old – the baby boomer generation – and their potential to yet again be a force for sociological change and, in doing so, revive Karl Mannheim's concept of Generation as a force capable of driving

paradigm change and generating a new intergenerational social contract for the century ahead.

Fourthly, what a new sociology of ageing – or even a new-age sociology – might look like, how it might inform a new-age manifesto and a new intergenerational social contract; how a new sociology of ageing might offer a new and exciting paradigm or theoretical framework for understanding the ageing world ahead; one that the paradigms of the late 20th century now seem ill-equipped to provide. And finally, how well the world is preparing for ageing and what an ageing or ageless society might look like, as *super-aged* Japan leads the way with Europe in hot pursuit, ageing Asia not far behind and America still "wallowing" in middle-age. Meanwhile, Africa is still undergoing a population explosion of its own; a population explosion of its young but this time of young people, not just young children; a *demographic dividend* of youth and an "explosion" of young labour that might make this young continent; or break it.

So, this reader seeks to offer a broad sociological sweep of the ageing world ahead, its threats and its opportunities written, however, not from the perspective of an ageing academic but from that of a young sociology student, Laura. It is after all the young who will inherit this grey nightmare or this silver sun. It is they who will enjoy the full fruits of longevity or suffer the agonies of ageing. Seen from this perspective, ageing becomes an even more urgent issue, a more political even moral challenge that needs an intergenerational response not a generational one. It needs the energy of the young as well as the wisdom and political clout of the old or else the Young will be left with the "bill" for an aged world that they had no say in creating and that fails to provide the future they need. Few young people will have thought of Ageing in this way but for the purposes of this book, Laura has.

Laura is an undergraduate student in Sociology and Politics, who originally intended that her dissertation be about the exploitation and abuse of women in developing nations but who, on the advice of her tutor Jonathan, was persuaded to see ageing as a more original and underdeveloped topic. Like so many of her age group, Laura initially saw ageing as an "old people's" issue; a boring and sexless topic with little relevance to her age group or her ambitions for the future. However, once she did some background reading, not only did she warm to the subject but also became enthralled by it, not only because she could now see its potential as the possible PhD thesis she was hoping for but also because it inflamed her passion for social justice and human rights. How could the society that created the British Welfare State treat the elderly in some of its hospitals and care homes so badly and so abusively? How could any civilised society afford to shunt its elderly off into retirement homes and isolation where "waiting for death" – and more recently "waiting for COVID-19" – seems to be the main pastime rather than celebrating the life that had been; and that with proper support, might still be? How could society ignore her nan's generation – the silent genera- tion – after all that it had suffered in the Second World War on behalf of freedom and all that it had left behind for future generations, not least the British Welfare State. What a legacy they left but do we still remember and appreciate them? No, not while Ageism is as rampant as sexism, racism or homophobia; not while we live in a world in which Youth is revered and Old Age feared; in which newness and novelty trump tradition and experience. What a stark contrast to pre- industrial societies where the Elders ruled and were revered as fonts of wisdom and were regarded as the Godfathers and Godmothers of the future.

So, this was a hugely ambitious project for any student but one that Laura took up with relish once she had discussed it in more detail with her own mul- tigenerational family; a multigenerational family that included grandparents still working respectively in politics and the NHS, a mother with expertise in mass media and a range of relatives engaged in developing new businesses or new technology while her memories of her great grandmother Christina drove her on whenever her academic curiosity and inspiration faltered. So, Laura's degree dissertation became a family project and eventually a post-graduate thesis as she progressed from exploring the ageing challenges facing the United Kingdom and governments elsewhere, to investigating the super-ageing societies of tomorrow and the need for a new social contract for the 21st century and the 100-Year Life beyond; a personal voyage of discovery from academic theory into real world practice. So, this is Laura's story and her journey into the ageing world ahead; a world of grey or silver; gloom and doom or hope and happiness; peril or prom- ise. So, just imagine too what ageing today might mean for you; just imagine planning a future life of 100 years or more; just imagine living in a super-ageing society like Japan or an "imploding society" like Russia, just imagine living in a world where grandparents outnumber grandchildren and where robots are just as likely to be your workmates and companions as fellow human beings.

The sociology of ageing is potentially one of the new sociologies of the 21st century; if not the new sociology of the 21st century, yet it still sits outside the bounds of most introductory sociological textbooks; outside even the sear- ing insights of Founding Fathers such as Marx, Durkheim and Weber and their followers in the late 20th century. The sociology of ageing needs to be brought "in from the sociological cold" and not only take its place at the high table of the social sciences but be considered as the basis of a new sociological paradigm; a new academic and policy framework designed to investigate the 100-Year Life ahead, the transition to a more ageless or age-free society in the future and to inform the new political agenda and manifesto needed to liberate the Old from the traditional stereotypes of age, restoring them to active life in the mainstream of society ahead and encourage and enable them to support younger generations in successfully navigating the chaotic world that is fast emerging in the years ahead.

Finally, no sociology textbook or reader today can ignore the immense and profound impact coronavirus has had, is having and will have on every society and government today and in years to come. In death toll alone, it has hit the oldest hardest and ruthlessly exposed weaknesses and inequalities in our health and social care systems. On the positive side, it has elevated health and healthy living to the forefront of every government agenda, accelerated the progress and integration of new age technology into human life and forced everybody, every family, community and society to reflect on and rethink their priorities and current lifestyles; trends that not only might help extend human longevity but dramatically enhance its quality as well as its quantity.

Welcome to the World of Ageing. Welcome to the Life of Longevity that is now all around you and ahead of you, once coronavirus has run its route.

Welcome to the 100-Year Life ahead and to the insights that the sociology of ageing hopefully has to offer for its future and for yours. *Enjoy the Journey.*

Bibliography

Centre for Strategic and International Studies (CSIS): *GAP Index* (2014)

Gratton, Lynda; Scott, Andrew: *The 100 Year Life: Living and Working in an Age of Longevity*: Bloomsbury (2017)

The Economist: Franklin D, Andrews A (eds): *Megachange: The World in 2050*: Profile Books (2012)

Westendorp, Rudi: *Growing Older Without Feeling Older*: Scribe (2014)

PART I

The global challenge of ageing and the global response

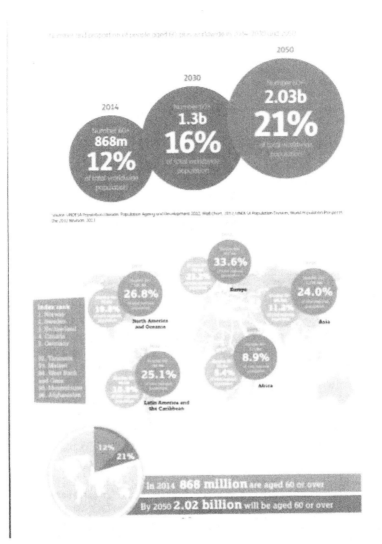

FIGURE I.1 Map of global ageing (GlobalAge)

Source: Global Ageing: HelpAge International/UNDESA (2015)

1

THE GLOBAL CHALLENGE OF AGEING AND THE GLOBAL CONTEXT

"The Ageing are Inheriting the Earth" declared the Global Agenda Council on Ageing Society in 2012: Ageing is both a Peril and a Promise, a global phenomenon "that is both inevitable and predictable. It will change society at many levels and in complex ways, creating both challenges and opportunities".

It is a global "time-bomb", a megatrend that is:

- **unprecedented** and without parallel in the history of humanity
- **pervasive**, affecting all the countries of the world
- **profound**, having major consequences and implications for all facets of human life – economically, socially and politically
- **enduring** as it is here to stay as the percentage of older people on the planet is set to treble within the space of just one millennium from 8% in 1950 to 22% by 2050.

> **By 2030** the world's population is projected to rise by more than 1 billion bringing the total to over eight billion. 97% of this population growth will come from emerging or developing countries. Equally significantly, people in all regions are living longer and having fewer children. The result is that the fastest growing segment of the population will be the over 65s–there will be 390 million more of them in 2030 than in 2015.
>
> *PWC: 2020*

According to the UN 2019 *World Population Prospects* Report, we are all living longer – much longer. Globally life expectancy at birth is projected to rise from 72.6 years in 2019 to 77.1 years by 2050 – an astonishing rise of nearly 5 years; a rise of nearly 13 years in all since 1990 as illustrated in Figure 1.1 on the next page.

DOI: 10.4324/9781003029373-3

	1990	2019	2050
World:	**64.2**	**72.6**	**77.1**
Europe & N. America	73.5	78.7	83.2
Eastern & S.E. Asia	68.8	76.5	80.8
Latin America & Caribbean	66.1	75.5	80.9
Sub-Saharan Africa	49.4	61.1	68.5

FIGURE 1.1 Life expectancy at birth

Source: Sample selected from World Population Prospects (WPP): UNDESA Table 4 (2019)

- **By 2050**, the total world population is predicted to rise to 9.7 billion from 7.7 billion in 2019 with over half of this projected increase concentrated in the countries of sub-Saharan Africa and India. At the very same time, the populations of most of Asia, Latin and North America and Europe are projected to peak and decline.
- **By 2050**, the world's median age is projected to be 36 years, 5 years up from 2019 and 12 years or some 33% up from 1950, with Europe the highest today at 42 years and Africa the lowest at 18 years: a Global Age Gap of some 24 years.
- **By 2050**, the world's elder population aged 65 and over is projected to double to 1.5 billion from 703 million in 2019: from 6% of the world's population today to 16% by 2050 with the largest increases in Asia (+901 million), Europe and North America (+296 million). By 2100, 23% – nearly a quarter of the world's population – is projected to be aged 65 and over.
- **By 2050**, there will be more older people aged 65 years and above in the world than children and young people aged 15–24 years.

The most rapidly rising older population, though, is the *oldest old*, those aged 80 years and above. It is projected to more than triple from 143 million in 2019 to 426 million in 2050, and then double again to 881 million by 2100 – a 16-fold increase in just over 100 years and nearly 10% of the world's population by the beginning of the 22nd century. In fact, we will soon have *three ages* of oldness – the **new old**, aged 65 plus; the **older old**, aged 80 plus; and top of the "pops", the **oldest old**, the centenarians dancing and dating into the 22nd century, having exploded from just over 300,000 today to 3.2 million by 2050 – a truly astonishing ten-fold increase.

The world is going grey at sonic speed. It is undergoing a ***global age shift*** as the older populations outnumber the young with Japan leading the way and South Korea in "hot pursuit" with an *average* life expectancy of 84 years for baby boys and a whopping 91 years for baby girls. Europe is not far behind with

	2019 %	2050 %
World:	**9.1**	**15.9**
Europe & N. America	18.0	26.1
Eastern & S.E. Asia	11.2	23.7
Latin America & Caribbean	8.7	19.0
Sub-Saharan Africa	3.0	4.8

FIGURE 1.2 Percentage aged 65 years in developing & developed worlds: 2019 & 2050

Source: Sample selected from World Population Prospects (WPP): UNDESA Table 2 (2019)

French women and Swiss men predicted to have the highest life expectancies at 88.6 and 84 years, respectively by 2030 (WHO/Imperial College London: 2017). Longevity – or life expectancy – in Great Britain, however, is somewhat weaker and the United Kingdom languishes currently at number 29 in the UN 2019/20 rankings, somewhat behind other wealthy, advanced nations but above the United States, Croatia and Mexico.

But as illustrated in Figure 1.2 below, ageing is not just **a western** phenomenon, it is **a global phenomenon**. By 2050, 80% of those aged 60 and over will live in the developing world. Asia already has 54% of the world's older people compared to Europe's 21% and North America's 8%, whilst Latin America and the Caribbean area is expected to undergo an age reversal from being one of the world's youngest populations in 1950 to becoming one of the oldest by 2100. By the middle of the century, China alone could have one-third of its population over 60 and up to 100 million people over 80 years of age – a phenomenal increase from the 14 million 80-year olds on the entire planet only a century ago. And global ageing has only just begun. Like a runaway train, the world is soon to "hyper-age". What took France 115 and Sweden 85 years will now take China only 26 years, Brazil 21 years and Columbia 20 years.

As Professor Sarah Harper has succinctly described it (ILC-UK Conference: 2016), "By 2030 half the population of Western Europe will be over 50, one quarter of the population of the developed world will be over 65 and one quarter of the population of Asia will be over 60. This is historically unprecedented. It will make the 20th century the last century of youth; the 21st century heralds a new demography – that of maturity".

But world populations are not only exploding with older people but also "imploding" as their younger populations shrink through fertility rates so low that they no longer replace the older ages dying out. There will, therefore, soon be an explosion of "super-aged" nations, those with 20% or more of their population aged 65 years or older, from 3 in 2013 to 34 in 2030. Countries like Russia, Germany, Greece, Italy and even China are now part of what George Magnus (2009) has rather dramatically called *the demographic death row* as their

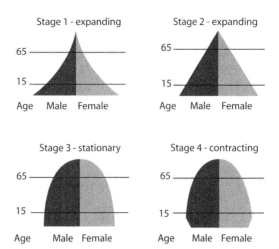

FIGURE 1.3 Global population pyramids

populations "implode" and shrink. So, as illustrated in Figure 1.3 above, this Demographic Revolution, this is Global "Age Wave is quite literally 'Turning the World on its (Demographic) Head', turning societies, new and old, from the 'population pyramids' of the 20th century into the beehives and pillars of the 21st".

As the rating agency Standard & Poor declared in 2010, "**global ageing (is) an irreversible truth**: No other force is likely to shape the future of national economic health, public finances and national policies as the irreversible rate which the world's population is growing older".

The causes of ageing

So, what is causing this seismic change in the balance of the ages and why are we all living longer? According to the World Economic Forum (WEF: 2012), there are five potential drivers of population ageing:

1. **Dramatic falls in birth rates** – the world's total fertility rate, the number of children born per woman, has fallen from 5 children per woman in 1950 to roughly 2.5 today, and it is projected to drop to 2.2 by 2050 and 1.9 by 2100. The fertility rate in Europe and North America is already below the natural replacement level of 2.1 at just over 1.7 and likely to remain so for most of the 21st century. So, most of the future fall is likely to occur in the developing world with fertility rates even in sub–Saharan Africa projected to plummet from 4.6 live births per woman in 2019 to 3.1 by 2050 and 2.1 by 2100.

2. **Dramatic falls in death rates** – both infant mortality and old age mortality rates have fallen dramatically across the world but a child born in sub-Saharan Africa "is (still) 20 times as likely to die before his or her fifth birthday as a child born in Australia/New Zealand".

3. **Dramatic increases in life expectancy** – *Two thousand years ago, the average Roman could expect to live 22 years. Those born in 1900 could only expect to live 47.5 years; by 1960 this was 69.7 years and today it is approaching 80 years.* The average life expectancy for a girl born in 2020 is 79.6 years and for baby boys is 76.2 years. A third of the babies born today are projected to live up to 100 years or more – well into the 22nd century. The differences across continents, across countries, across developed and developing nations, however, are huge. Whilst a typical girl in Singapore might expect to live more than 97 years, a typical boy born in Sierra Leone is projected to live just 58.5 years – almost 40 years less.

4. **Dramatic increases in healthy life expectancy** – in "adding life to years not just years to life", a ***Longevity Bonus*** that means that across the world women aged 65 today can now expect on average to live a further 18 years and men a further 16 years with both sexes enjoying 2 more years by 2050. Moreover, the ***compression of morbidity and mortality*** means that the age – and stage – at which we are likely to suffer from chronic illness and disability in our final few years of life is being dramatically reduced.

5. **Dramatic shifts in world populations through global migration** – global migration clearly makes a significant impact on countries both receiving and losing large numbers of migrants. According to the 2020 World Migration Report, the total number of international migrants in 2019 was 272 million or 3.5% of the world's population coming mainly from India (17.5 million), Mexico (11.8 million) and China (10.7 million) and migrating mainly to the United States (50.7 million) – an astonishing number of people on the move and nearly twice that of 2000. A "human tide" of global migrants, as Paul Morland (2019) has called them, is now flowing across the planet at an accelerating rate, disrupting and transforming national population profiles and age distributions in its path as migrants fly towards higher standards of living, personal freedoms and "bright lights" of the West or flee the civil wars, corruption, crime and profound poverty that is destroying life in their own country. The current crises in countries such as Syria, Ethiopia and now Afghanistan, the wars in the Middle East and the resultant impact on Europe has brought the size and rate of global migration to the forefront of public attention but international migration has become a highly contentious and political issue that has led many wealthier countries, including the European Union, United Kingdom and the United States to close their borders in recent years. Global migration, though, is equally being driven by the global economy and digital revolution. It is part of the global recruitment strategy of multi-national corporations, keen to recruit the best talent in the world irrespective of country of origin aided by the growth and ease of global

transport in moving millions of people around the world daily for business or pleasure. Global migration, however, is no longer a "one-way" street from the emerging East to the wealthier West. A "reverse migration" is also underway as the multinationals of the emerging economies seek to attract not only their own young talent but also those who left earlier, leaving *Death Row* countries facing a "double-dilemma" as their own youth migrate abroad and they are unable to attract "new blood" from elsewhere.

So, the world appears to be entering the fifth – or possibly sixth – stage of the demographic transition set out years ago by theorists such as Warren Thompson (1929) and Frank W. Notestein (1945). Whilst societies in the past evolved demographically from the high birth and high death rates typical of pre-industrial society to the "population explosions" of the mid-20th century as the birth rate exploded after WWII, so the world now seems to be entering a period of relative demographic stability as both birth and death rates go into decline. According to the UN, the world's population is expected to peak at 10.9 billion later this century and then fall thereafter.

The impact of ageing

The potential impact of global ageing is therefore profound and as the UN predicted in 2012, potentially permanent and all-pervasive; as Philip Longman and Paul Hewitt neatly summarised it back in 2002/03:

For governments and public services, the implications are:

- vast increases in the cost of pension and health benefits programs
- large and destabilising deficits
- pressure to reduce benefits, raise taxes or "crowd out" spending for programs such as education, defence and infrastructure

For employers, businesses and workers, the implications are:

- increased taxes, shrinking markets and slow growth
- tight labour markets making it difficult to retain top-quality personnel and creating incentives to move jobs and production abroad
- falling stock and housing prices as the baby boomers age and start selling their financial assets en masse to the next generation so reducing prices and "creating a great depreciation" for the stock market

For retirees, the implications are:

- fewer caregivers as the younger generations fall in size and so is less able to care for an expanding elderly population
- less secure access to healthcare as the older elderly live longer than ever before thus threatening the collapse of healthcare systems that currently exist

- possible "generational backlash" and increased ethnic tensions as migration increases the population flow from poorer to wealthier countries leading to increased xenophobia and a possible backlash against ethnic groups living and working in wealthy countries

For the global balance of power:

- **Economically**, the dramatic shift in global dependency ratios from 4:1 to less than 2:1 in many advanced economies (OECD: 2019) is likely to generate a dramatic increase in dependency spending on pensions and healthcare with the heaviest burdens falling on the "oldest" nations. By 2050, Japan, the world's oldest nation, may "have almost as many dependents as working age adults. No society has seen such a thing before" (Economist: 2012 Megatrends study). And, as Paul Hewitt predicted back in 2004: "we are going to see the decline of Europe and Japan as economic powers … as the economies of the West start to shrink and the economies of the emerging markets rise". We will also see the "spread of middle-age" to developing countries like China, India and Mexico, although these countries may *get old before they get rich* as the speed of their ageing outstrips the pace of their economic growth and their political stability.
- **Politically**, the "younger" nations of Asia and Africa will outgrow the superpowers of America, Russia and China. Nigeria, for example, is projected to grow from 57 million to 374 million by 2050 and India is expected to replace China as the most populous country in the world with a projected population of some 1.6 billion people. China's ambition, though, is not to become a demographic superpower but an economic and political one; the global centre of the artificial intelligence (AI) universe, the trade hub of a "Silk Road" that stretches right across Asia and a leader in space exploration.
- **Socially**, we may be looking at the rise of a **global generation gap** as the developed nations age and the poorer countries become adolescent on a scale and at a speed never seen before: *in 1950, the difference in the median age between Japan and Yemen, the worlds' oldest and youngest countries, was just 2.7 years. Today, it's about 27 years, and by 2025 it will be 35 years.* It is in the very young and often very poor countries such as Iraq, Yemen and Afghanistan where civil conflict is rife and the typical person is a teenager. As Paul Hewitt put it, if you want to know where the worlds' future conflicts are likely to be "look at the youthful countries".

So, over the next 30 years, the world will potentially be facing a **demographic double whammy**; a simultaneous population explosion of both young and old:

- **A population *explosion* of young people** in Africa and in the poorer, emerging nations as the planet's population continues to escalate from 7.7 billion today to 9.7 billion by 2050. Sub-Saharan Africa alone is projected to double its population from 1.1 billion today to 2.4 billion in 2050 and to 4.2 billion by 2100 with countries such as Indonesia, Tanzania, Ethiopia, Uganda and Niger exploding to over 200 million by the end of the century.

- **A population *explosion* of older people aged 65** from just over 700,000 in 2019 to over 1.5 billion and growing by 2050. Europe is already the oldest continent on the planet, Japan the oldest society and large parts of Asia, notably China, are ageing as we speak.

Together, these simultaneous population explosions have the potential to generate "a negative demographic momentum", as the "natural population replacement rate" of 2.1 children collapses, contracting generations of young women of childbearing age, making a population resurgence potentially impossible and a *demographic implosion* highly likely. This is what is happening in Japan, where its population is projected to fall from 127 million people in 2012 to 94 million by 2050 while Russia is predicted to go "from red to grey", from 149 million in 1990 to 111 million by 2050. This is likely to have a devastating effect on Russia's economy as well as on its military power in the world. Maybe, thought Laura, this explains President Putin's apparent determination to expand the Russian Federation and take ex-Soviet States – and their populations – back into its fold.

Secondly, what is fundamentally different to population explosions today to those in the past is the speed of change. The *population explosion* in the 20th century from 2 billion to 6 billion took 72 years between 1927 and 1999. The *population explosion* of older people projected for the 21st century of some 700 million today to over 1.5 billion in 2050, is projected to take half that time – a mere 30–40 years. This *leap in later life* and this leap in lifespan can be attributed to the monumental advances in medicine and environmental health as well as the dramatic fall in infant mortality rates. Life expectancy across the world has *leapfrogged* in the late 20th century by a massive 20 years and the human race has doubled its lifespan in less than 150 years. Truly an astonishing human achievement, truly the Ninth Wonder of the World, one that coronavirus may well set back but is unlikely to halt.

The global context of ageing

Ageing, however, is not operating in isolation. Rather, according to Richard Dobbs and his colleagues at the McKinsey Global Institute (2015;2021), ageing is operating in tandem or possibly in partnership with three of the most powerful forces the world has ever seen – globalisation, urbanisation, and new technology and the internet; and they in turn now face the challenges of global warming and global pandemics such as coronavirus. The world of the 21st century is changing at a rate and in a form that is way beyond our previous experience, and it is operating within a global economy that now stretches across both the developed and the developing worlds.

Globalisation is clearly reshaping the *world economy*, integrating the world into a global capitalist system beyond any governments control, and in the process it is creating a new breed of "superpower", the mega corporation of the 21st century and a new breed of global entrepreneur that some writers perceive as a new power-elite – a power-elite with ambitions of world domination, not through military power as in the past but through economic and technological power today; power based on the internet and power to control world markets and global finance. The tech giants, Amazon, Apple, Facebook and especially Google see the world as their oyster and they are in the process of creating their own mini-states and centres of power. And behind these *masters of the universe* are waves of new competitors from the developing nations – the "Ali-Babas" of Asia soon to be followed by those from Africa and South America. The older mega-corporations of the late 20th century are under immense pressure from the new younger entrepreneurs with the ambition and technology not only to replace them but also to transform the very nature of the way businesses now operate. The banks don't just fear competition from other banks or even such new forms of currency such as bitcoin; they fear Amazon and the tech giants and their ability and ambition to transform the banking industry and cream-off such lucrative services as credit card transaction. Online delivery is transforming the whole basis of every retail business from food and clothing through to entertainment and finance whilst digitalisation is transforming every mode of human communication. Google's DeepMind software, for example, is soon to be embedded in the United Kingdom's national grid collecting data on all of us; Alexa is already at home in millions of households across the world whilst the Amazon boss, Jeff Bezos, is now competing with Elon Musk to conquer space – a galactic rivalry that in the past only superpowers like America and the Soviet Union could possibly have afforded.

So, a new world order has emerged, a new type of global economy has been created and a new generation of entrepreneurs from both the developing and developed nations is challenging, changing and disrupting the global economy in a fight for control of the markets ahead. Facebook, Amazon and even Google did not exist 25 years ago. They represent a new form of capitalism; a *Capitalism Without Capital* according to Haskel & Westlake (2018) in which the ownership of intellectual property and innovative ideas seems to have replaced the ownership of land and physical property as the basis of wealth and economic power. Alibaba, the world's largest retailer, owns no warehouses; Uber, the world's largest taxi company, owns no cars; and Airbnb, the world's largest accommodation provider, owns no hotels. So, whilst there may be evidence according to writers such as Stephen King (2017) and Gervais Williams (2016) that globalisation is slowing down as a result of the 2008 financial crisis, Brexit and most immediately the impact of coronavirus, it seems highly unlikely that the underlying trend towards global integration will stop completely or go into reverse.

Rather, as W. Brian Arthur of McKinsey Associates (2017) has argued, digital technologies seem to be creating a ***second economy*** – a virtual and autonomous economy that through algorithms and various forms of artificial intelligence is creating a new form of business intelligence; an automated form of intelligence and decision-making that is external to modern business rather than within it; one that is increasingly rendering human intelligence and decision-making obsolete. Modern computers and software are even now capable of *inter-association*; of communicating amongst themselves, of using their sensors and processors to correlate and interrogate vast banks of data in milliseconds and make sense of patterns that human beings alone cannot even see. As modern computer systems become increasingly capable of collective communication and decision-making independent of human action, then the implications of this shift from internal to external intelligence for the human race as a species are monumental. Autonomous intelligent systems are increasingly capable of taking over the organisation and running of vast swathes of the global economy – from transport and banking through to warfare and healthcare – and transforming them. Jobs may disappear as many fear, or simply be transformed and relocated within the virtual economy. Jobs may no longer even be the way that humans earn their living and the 20th-century economic debate about the creation of material wealth may shift to a 21st-century debate about the distribution of that wealth – shift from an economic debate to a political one – one about what on one hand is just and fair and on the other about what the planet can sustain; a debate that W. Brian Arthur predicts will bring the free market philosophy of the United States into sharp contrast with the more collectivist style of government found in Scandinavia and the State capitalism evident in China and elsewhere.

So, are we now in the Fourth Industrial Revolution – a Globalisation 4.0, as Richard Baldwin (2019) has described it, where through communication technology, tele-migration enables workers living in their home countries to work across the world; one where AI-driven automation takes over both the manufacture of goods and the administration of services; one where waves of new technological advances, more sophisticated algorithms and much greater technological integration not only disrupt existing industries and traditional models of business but also generate whole new ones that both reduce costs and lessen today's unsustainable pressures on the planet's natural resources; one where smart technology will soon light up and heat our homes much more efficiently, seawater desalination create huge new supplies of clean water and electric vehicles supersede the petrol engine; one where digitech and AI-driven automation are transforming the production of goods, threatening to wipe out whole swathes of the manual and service sector as robots replace human labour and globots replace human brains, potentially leaving human beings to concentrate on providing creativity, intuition and emotional intelligence.

Such hyper-globalisation, however, seems to be creating a world where human beings feel increasingly insecure, isolated and left behind and one that is increasingly unequal, divided and disrupted as China and America engage in a guerrilla-style trade war, Europe and western democracies strain under the polarising effects of populist politics and a world that is only just recovering from the financial recession of 2008 is now reeling from the viral tsunami that is COVID-19. The economic "tigers" of southeast Asia seem to have pushed ageing nations in Europe into the global background while globalisation and automation are reshaping the global economy, denuding whole areas of industrial and local production, leaving whole communities bereft of jobs for the unskilled and the young and bereft of hope for the future. This has stimulated the anti-globalisation backlash and surge in distrust of national governments reflected in the United Kingdom's Brexit vote, and in Donald Trump's US election in 2016. As David Goodhart (2017) has argued western societies seem increasingly to be divided between the *Anywheres* who have enjoyed high levels of material success and mobility in today's open and liberal societies and so who are confident about the future and happy to think and live globally; and the *Somewheres*, who feel threatened by globalisation and what they feel that it has done to their jobs, countries and their future prospects. They feel overwhelmed and powerless against the pace and impact of global change and especially global migration, on themselves and their communities. As a consequence, they distrust the liberal elites in capital cities who have run their countries since 2008; they are instinctively nationalist in outlook and highly sceptical of global change. The post-war structures of largely western leadership are tottering and adopting almost a siege mentality in trying to cope with the new global forces banging on their door and although the election of the new American President Joe Biden, after the turbulence of Donald Trump, may help restore calm to world leadership, unless the West reasserts its moral as well as its political authority, the rising powers of the East may well soon take over. We now live in what the McKinsey Global Institute (Jan. 2019) has called "an era of disruption": a disruption that is intensifying, exacerbating the *digital divide*, polarising global inequality more starkly and overtly and "splintering" the long-held social contracts that have kept business, the economy and society bound together.

So, has globalisation and the unfettered free trade of 21st century capitalism now had its time and sown both the seeds of its own destruction and the populist backlash predicted over a 100 years ago by such radical critics as Karl Marx? Has globalisation, in the words of Dani Rodrik (1997) *Gone Too Far*? And has the financial collapse of 2008 and the gross inequalities in the distribution of world wealth not only led to populist uprisings and the breakdown in trust of government and political elites across the developed world, but also led to an existential questioning of capitalism, American world leadership and even of liberal democracy itself. Has 'Globalization been Unmasked' as Petras and Veltmeyer claimed in 2001 and is a rebalancing of the world order underway as power and wealth shift from West to East, creating the new multipolar world order described by writers like Michael O'Sullivan (2019) of three or four superpowers, with China and India soon sitting alongside the EU and the United States.

New technology and the internet are clearly at the heart of globalisation in the 21st century and in turn transforming world communication and generating revolutions of their own; revolutions of interconnectivity, virtual reality and cyberspace previously unheard of and undreamt of; revolutions in science and technology that will transform human life and both the way we live and how long we live. AI and the rise of the robot have the potential to transform working life and the world economy; biotechnology to transform our bodies and how long we live; algorithms to transform our financial world and the power of the global corporations to know us better than we know ourselves, predict our inner secrets and control the way we live, vote and buy. The **Internet of Things**, the growth of Big Data and the data-gathering revolution resulting from the proliferation of data collecting devices and data services all round us, from GPS, CCTV and physical sensors in our cities and on our roads through to the explosion in market intelligence about what we buy, what we want, what we think and how we behave is creating "game-changing" opportunities for businesses, big and small, to satisfy our every need, our every whim – even before we know it – and transforming not only modern manufacturing and retail but impacting on every other sector too – even the "weather of things". Even our cities and our transport systems are affected as they seek to accommodate, service and mobilise ever increasing masses of people from across the world. Increasingly, we live in what Marshall McLuhan, back in the 1960s, called the "global village" with face-to-face communication "zoomed" across the planet irrespective of where you live. Through social media such as Facebook, Twitter and Skype or Zoom, personal relationships and communications are no longer confined by national boundaries and even the most powerful of dictators can no longer exclude the outside world completely – though China, Russia and North Korea continue to try to do so. One venture capital firm in Hong Kong, Deep Knowledge Ventures, has even gone as far as to appoint a "decision-making algorithm" to its board of directors. So, if AI and algorithms can run companies more efficiently than humans, what do we need CEOs and senior managers for?

However, the internet also has its "dark" side; a Wild West that seems completely out of control by real-life politicians and security forces in what Yuval Harari (2015) has described as "a free and lawless zone that erodes state sovereignty, ignores borders, abolishes privacy and poses perhaps the most formidable global security risk. Whereas a decade ago, it hardly registered on the radars, today hysterical officials are predicting an imminent cyber 9/11. Any day now we might wake up to discover that the power grid is down, the local refinery is up in flames, and crucial financial data has been erased so that nobody knows who owns what". Just think how close, and how often, such threats now come close to home as your bank gets hacked, your airport goes on terrorist alert and even your very identity gets stolen. Organised crime has thrived on the "dark net" while terrorists have "weaponised" social media in recruiting new members and waging global jihad. Meanwhile, *Big Data* – your personal details and preferences – is being harvested by virtually every company that you now deal with and sold onto others in an open market while GPS and CCTV mean that every move you make can be monitored and tracked. *Big Brother* is alive and very well in the world of the 21st century with Google and Facebook watching our every move – and predicting the next one – whilst Amazon has even managed to install Alexa in millions of homes not just as a voice-box but as a "family friend". Data protection is becoming a hope rather than a reality and at times, even these Tech Giants don't seem to be in control of their content, let alone governments or parents. Fake news and post-truth seem to have taken over objective reporting and debate with terrorist and foreign security organisations using social media to distort political elections and even young minds. "Big lies" are now much easier to communicate than "Big Truths" and *Big Government* seems increasingly unable to control, let alone tax the Tech Giants while the social and psychological repercussions of their activities on human communication and social relationships are only just beginning to emerge. Whilst the smart phone is a miraculous invention, it has generated a whole new economic system designed to exploit people's human vulnerability and hold their attention 24/7. Whilst Mark Zuckerberg's original grand vision of Facebook might have been that it would open up human connectivity across the world, many observers now see it as having helped create a more anti-social and inward-looking global society as texting and Facebook become a 21st-century addiction that has not only intruded into people's homes but into their children's minds. As Frank Foer (2018) has speculated, have these Tech Giants become a new form of world power or worse a new form of tyranny and in the process, begun to distort, if not derail democracy, as it is claimed happened in the 2016 American Presidential election. Are we sleepwalking into a world where *we're constantly watched and constantly distracted* with Mark Zuckerberg and Co. watching over us and subtly and surreptitiously influencing or changing voter turnout or our consumer purchasing when it suits them. The tech giants, according to writers such as Ronald J. Deibert (2021), have hijacked the internet and the whole world is now sliding towards "info-tyranny" as smart technology spreads and becomes more sophisticated. This is a crisis potentially worse than any global pandemic because of the degree to which corporate power now rests on the *unprecedented and extraordinary visibility of everyone's personal lives right down to the genetic and possibly sub-conscious levels*; levels we all collude in and happily submit to apparently blithely unaware of potential consequences. Governments may now be reacting and calling Big Tech to account, but until they tighten regulations and make them accountable for their content – by say redefining them as publishers not platforms – then they will continue to just pay the fines and out-manoeuvre the regulations. Meanwhile, hackers are having a field-day and even such technological fortresses as Sony, Yahoo and the National Lottery have proved vulnerable to internet infiltration. Meanwhile, the Chinese Government appears to be creating what Kai Strittmatter (2019) has described as the perfect "Surveillance State"; a colourful mix of George Orwell's 1984, Aldous Huxley's Brave New World and Steven Spielberg's Minority Report based ultimately on self-surveillance through new technology; a new Social Contract whereby in return for ever growing economic prosperity, 1.4 billion Chinese citizens submit to having every one of their actions and transactions recorded through their smartphones so that in effect they are willingly self-censoring and self-sanctioning themselves. And being rewarded or sanctioned by a State that not only knows what all its citizens are doing at any one time but also that through its algorithms can potentially predict what they are likely to do in the future; particularly those who may express dissent or opposition to the State or Communist Party. Hence too, the growing fear in many western nations that companies like Huawei are not independent companies but arms of the Chinese state.

So profound are these changes that the European Futures Observatory – a highly respected academic organisation not normally given to fanciful specu-lation – was moved to raise the possibility of a new *Singularity*; of a new and unparalleled stage in the scale of social and economic transformation compa-rable to the agrarian and industrial revolutions of the past but with far more dramatic and devastating effect; far greater speed and scale with the potential for international disruption on a global, even planetary scale. We may, accord-ing to Dr Stephen Agillar-Millan of the World Future Review be entering a new stage, a *Sixth Wave* in the progression of technological and social para-digms; one that Professor Klaus Schwab of the WEF (2016) has called a Fourth Industrial Revolution. The WEF (2017) now has AI and Robotics amongst its Top Ten Global Risks, writers such as Mark Connell (2018) have raised the spectre of a post-human future populated by humanised machines and Jamie Bartlett has claimed that *The Internet is Killing Democracy* (2017) as Big Tech becomes the 21st century's Big Brother, relentlessly invading our daily lives and undermining elections in both the United States and the United Kingdom through the activities of foreign hackers and companies such as Cambridge Analytica.

The Age of Man (Anthropocene), therefore, seems to be giving way to the Age of the Machine (Technocene), to what Brynjolfsson and McAfee (2014) have called a Second Machine Age; an age where machines can think for them-selves and develop their own network of communication. Robots are apparently already making music and writing poetry, and Amazon's Echo has even been called as a witness in a murder trial while some believe that "killer robots" are being developed in North Korea. Whilst all this may sound very 1984 and Brave New World, possibly the scariest point is that AI may already be out of control – rampaging, for example, through recent stock market surges – and even Silicon Valley researchers are beginning to admit that even they don't know exactly how Deep-Learning works – only the Robots do. Meanwhile, the Genome and the revolution in DNA are raising not only the prospect of DNA editing to cut out rogue genes but creating CRISPR, the means to redesign life. CRISPR, apparently, has already created tomatoes that never rot, double-muscle dogs capable of patrolling crowds and cows without horns. What's next? Children without parents and Super Humans with superpowers? Whilst such immense and invasive technology is putting untold wealth and power in the hands of a tiny Global Elite, it may equally be leaving Super-Robots ruling our world for us. Shoshana Zuboff (2019) suggests that we are now living in the Age of Surveillance Capitalism with the "Big Others", Google and Facebook watching ominously over all of us in the West – out of sight and out of control. As Stephen Hawking commented in his final publication (2018) "Creating AI would be the biggest event in human history. Unfortunately, it might also be the last unless we can learn how to avoid the risks".

Urbanisation

Ageing is not working in demographic isolation. Ageing is working alongside urbanisation in reshaping the *geography of the world*, sweeping away traditional ways of life and instigating a tidal shift of human populations from the country to the city in numbers and at a pace never seen before in developing countries. As the World Urbanization Prospects Report (2019) declared, "The future of the world's population is urban and by 2050 "roughly two thirds (68%) of the world's population will be living in urban areas" as some 3 million people a week move from villages to towns and cities. Nearly 90% of this spatial shift is likely to be concentrated in Asia and Africa whilst megacities of over 10 million inhabitants are set to grow from 33 in 2018 to between 41 and 53 by 2030 as the emerging economies of China, India and Nigeria grow and expand. These mega-cities are becoming the nerve centres of a global economy that is fast beyond the control of national or even international government. They now control *nearly half of global GDP growth* (McKinsey: 2015) and according to the 2019 Global Cities Index, generate intense city-state competition for people and business as western giants such as London, New York and Paris face growing pressure from eastern challengers such as Beijing, Shanghai and Mumbai and – in recent years – an influx of Silver Surfers as baby boomers world-wide seek urban life-styles in later life.

The global world of the 21st century, therefore, offers both immense oppor-tunity and equally immense uncertainty. The world is becoming a much smaller, much more integrated place, economically and socially, but it is equally becoming a very "disrupted" place; disrupted by the forces above, operating at phenom-enal speeds, *10 times the speed and 300 times the impact of the Industrial Revolution* (McKinsey: 2015). These forces, however, are not operating in harmony, nor are they under anyone's control. They are not part of some grand plan – human or heavenly. Rather, they are forces of the 21st century's apocalypse, sit-ting now alongside climate change and global pandemics, transforming life as we know it and creating a radically different world in the century ahead, a world of "cascading catastrophes" that through "error or terror" will send "shock-waves" across the planet. Hence, the escalating fears that globalisation is outstripping itself, outstripping the globe's sustainability and threatening the survival of the planet. Hence, the fear about ***inequality*** and its global backlash. Hence, what Pope Francis claimed in his 2015 Lent Sermon, the "global indifference" to the suffering of millions, if not billions, across the world as their plight is projected daily onto our television screens, be they in Syria and Aleppo or on the shores of the Mediterranean, attempting to escape war and poverty. Hence, the rise of

anti-immigrant and anti-globalisation political movements and such global terrorist movements as Al-Qaeda, ISIS and White Power in reaction to the sense of
powerlessness, alienation and loss of local and national culture and control that
many feel today? Do we need a new form of globalisation, a *smart globalisation*,
based on new values – sustainable values that encapsulate inclusion, equity and
human rights and new forms of governance that are more genuinely democratic
and representative of people themselves not just the international and national
political elites currently in power? Do we need a New International Social
Contract as proposed by McKinsey Global Institute (Jan/Dec. 2020) whereby
international co-operation supersedes national rivalry in the face of such powerful common foes; a new Social Contract that ironically Covid-19 might have
also instigated as governments across the world act to protect their populations
on a scale never seen before outside wartime; over $10 trillion amongst the G20
countries alone; 30 times the size of the Marshall Plan that helped rebuild Europe
after WWII?

So, what part will **ageing play in this global – or rather Google – battle
of power?** Will demography be a "drag" on global growth, or will demography
actually accelerate it by creating whole new markets; new silver markets and silver cities seeking to serve the explosion of older people around the world. "The
developed retiring and elderly will be extraordinarily important to global consumption from 2015 to 2030", predicted the McKinsey Report on Urbanisation
Global Consumers in 2016, generating $4.4 trillion and accounting for nearly
60% of consumption growth in Western Europe and North East Asia alone; an
age-shift in global consumption that can only be executed harmoniously if ageing operates in partnership with new technology to offset the catastrophic falls
in the dependency ratios predicted for 2030 and beyond. Germany's working
population, for example, is projected by the European Commission to shrink
from 54 million to 36 million by 2060 with cataclysmic results for its economy and its people, especially the young, while Japan is investing heavily in a
Robot Revolution that it hopes will revive its stagnant economy and liberate it
from its own *demographic nightmare* of millions of ageing people left dependent
and isolated; nightmare scenarios made all the more real and immediate now
by coronavirus. Are the new old though a source of new hope and new life?
Will the baby boomers, the post-war generation that became notorious for its
capacity to question and challenge the Establishment, demand personal freedom
and create new lifestyles, now regenerate life in the 21st century, recharge the
global economy through Silver Markets everywhere and challenge the apparently unstoppable forces above? They now have longer life; renewed life but
does this extraordinary generation still have the power and potential to lead
a New Age Revolution, to check and challenge the global forces above and
the global elites behind them; and in the process, shape them to their own
ambitious demands for an active, engaging and fulfilling later life and for an
Intergenerational Agenda that might leave their grandchildren a legacy to
remember?

Bibliography

Aguilar-Millan, Stephen: *World Future Review* (May 2014)

Arthur, W. Brian: *The Second Economy*: McKinsey Quarterly (2017)

Baldwin, Richard: *The Globotics Upheaval: Globalization, Robotics and the Future of Work*: W&N (2019)

Bartlett, Jamie: *The People Vs Technology: How the Internet is Killing Democracy*: Penguin (2017)

Brynjolfsson, Erik; McAfee, Andrew: *The Second Machine Age*: W.W. Norton & Co. (2014) *Machine, Platform, Crowd-Harnessing Our Digital Future*: W.W. Norton (2017).

Deibert, Ronald J: *Reclaiming the Internet for Civil Society*: September Publishing (2021)

Demographic Transition Theory developed by Warren Thompson (1929) and Frank W. Notestein (1945). See Kirk, D: *Demographic transition theory*: *Population Studies*: (Camb) (1996)

Dobbs, R; Manyika J; Woetzel J: *No Ordinary Disruption*: Public Affairs/Perseus (2015)

Foer, Frank: *World Without Mind*: Penguin/Random House (2018)

Franklin, D; Andrews, J (eds): *Megachange: The world in 2050*: The Economist/Profile Books (2012)

Global Ageing Council on Ageing Society: *Global Population Ageing: Peril or Promise?*: WEF (2012)

Goodhart, David: *The Road to Somewhere*: Penguin (2017)

Harari, Yuval Noah: *Homo Deus: A Brief History of Tomorrow*: Penguin/Vintage Books (2015)

Haskel, J; Westlake, S: *Capitalism without Capital*: Princeton University Press (2018)

Hawking, Stephen: *Brief Answers to the Big Questions*: John Murray (2018)

Hewitt, P: *Global Aging and the Rise of the Developing World*: Geneva Papers, Vol. 27, pp.477–485 2002; Longman, P: *Think Again: Global Aging*: Foreign Policy News (October12, 2010)

ILC-UK Conference: *Tomorrow's World: The Future of Ageing in the UK* (2016)

IOM (UN Migration): *World Migration Report* (2020)

King, Stephen D: *Grave New World: The End of Globalisation*: Yale University Press (2017)

Magnus, George: *The Age of Ageing*: John Wiley & Sons (2009)

McKinsey Global Institute (MGI: *Navigating a World of Disruption*: Briefing Note for WEF (January 2019)

McKinsey Global Institute (MGI): *The Social Contract in the 21st Century* (February 2020; *Covid-19 has revived the social contract in advanced economies-for now* (December 2020)

McKinsey Global Institute Report: *Urbanisation and Global Consumers* (2016)

McLuhan, Marshall; Powers, BR: *The Global Village*: OUP (1992)

Morland, Paul: *The Human Tide*: John Murray (2019)

O'Connell, Mark: *To Be a Machine*: Granta Books (2018)

O'Sullivan, Michael: *The Levelling: What's Next after Globalization*: Public Affairs (2019)

OECD: *Pensions at a Glance* (2019)

Petras, J; Veltmeyer, H: *Globalization Unmasked: Imperialism in the 21st Century*: Zed Books ltd. (2001)

PWC: *Demographic and Social Change* (2020)

Rodrik, Dani: *Has Globalization Gone Too Far?*: Peterson Institute for International Economics (1997) or *The Globalization Paradox*: OUP (2012)

Schwab, Klaus: *The Fourth Industrial Revolution*: Crown Publishing Group (2017)

Standard & Poor: *Global Ageing* (2010)

Strittmatter, Kai: *We Have Been Harmonised*: Old Street Publishing (2019)

The Kearney: *Global Cities Report & Index: A question of talent*: (2019)

UN (DESA): *World Urbanization Prospects Report* (2019)

UNO (Dept. of Economic and Social Affairs: Population Division): *World Population Prospects Report* (2019)

WHO/Imperial College London: *International Longevity Study: Future Life Expectancy in 35 countries* (2017)

Williams, Gervais: *The Retreat of Globalisation*: Harriman House (2016)

World Economic Forum (WEF): *Global Population Ageing: Peril or Promise* (2012)

World Economic Forum (WEF): *Global Risks Reports* (2017/2018)

Zuboff, Shoshana: *Age of Surveillance Capitalism*: Profile Books (2019)

2

THE INTERNATIONAL CHALLENGE OF AGEING AND THE INTERNATIONAL RESPONSE

Introduction

So asked Laura, if Ageing is such a Global Challenge, such a *Global Peril or Promise,* why isn't it an international headline and a national debate that sits right alongside globalisation, global warming and now global pandemics? Why have we heard nothing about it when the grey tsunami is on everyone's doorstep and about to transform every nation, community and family across the world?

How well prepared is the world for:

- the enormous challenges of populations ageing right across the world and the costs involved to government and families?
- the restructuring of society, the reordering of government priorities and the refocusing of industry and the global markets to meet the needs and demands of a world in which over 22% of the world's population will be over 60 by 2050?
- the longer life, possibly the 100-Year Life that the UN proclaimed back in 2012 is "one of humanity's greatest achievements"?

The answer is:

- At an international level through the UN, WHO, EU and associated think-tanks, global awareness is high and planning is underway;
- At a national level, government responses and preparation range from far foresight and forward planning to woeful ignorance and tragic neglect.

DOI: 10.4324/9781003029373-4

At an international level

The UN and the World Health Organization (WHO) have led the *Ageing Way*. They heralded the coming of ageing before the millennium and actively sought to present it as an opportunity rather than a threat. They have sought to lead the ageing debate and they have adopted *Active Ageing* as both the vision for the 21st century and as the strategy for developing "an inclusive society for all ages" (Madrid Conference: 2002). Their underlying aim has been to try and "reinvent" ageing and liberate the full potential of the old by setting national governments a series of priority actions that:

- **Ensure that all the older persons can live** with dignity and security, independence and autonomy, enjoying access to essential health and social services at a minimum income.
- **Support communities and families in developing support systems** to facilitate "ageing in place".
- **Invest in young people today** by promoting healthy habits, educational and employment activities whilst also integrating older people back into the labour market.

The 2012 report argued for "a new rights-based culture of ageing and a change of mind-set and societal attitudes towards ageing and older persons from welfare recipients to active, contributing members of society".

In other words: **Help the Aged** and they help *themselves:*

Help the Aged and you help *yourselves.*

The 2012 Report identified ageism and inequality as two of the root causes of the ageing challenge ahead. The WHO's solution was on one side, *age-inclusiveness*, a vision of an ageless future that is fairer, more just and more open for both young and old alike. And on the other side, intergenerational engagement and the power of the *intergenerational legacy*, that older citizens might wish to leave their children, grandchildren and generations in the future; a legacy far beyond any financial wealth they might still have left but rather the soft, less tangible values of health and humour that tend to precede property and money in the West and religion in the East.

In the WHO's view, the key to a full-scale ageing strategy lies in "mainstreaming" ageing, in prioritising ageing as a political priority to be put high up on the international agenda and integrated into all national policy programmes as part of the shift towards the "Ageless, Age-Inclusive Society" that in their view is critical to human development in the 21st century. Ironically, as the WHO Report commented, it is often the poorer and developing nations, such as Brazil and Bolivia, who have led the ageing way rather than the rich, more powerful nations of the developed world; a perspective beautifully illustrated by Maria Gabriela, aged 90. When the Law for the Rights of Older People (Estatuto do Idoso) was passed in Brazil in 2003, we started to live; "older people abandoned their sandals and their rocking chairs and started having a life. Now we are supported by the law. We can demand our rights. We need to end the separation between older and younger people. We can share experiences with each other, which is very exciting….and they are learning that we also have the right to sing, to dance, to talk".

In 2019, the WHO launched its Decade of Healthy Ageing 2020–2030; a strategic framework designed to link healthy ageing to the UN's Sustainable Development Goals (SDGs) and embed and integrate ageing within these SDGs as a means to put ageing at the forefront of global economic planning rather than leave it as a footnote as in the past; a global priority upon which partnerships might be built, innovation inspired and progress measured but this time from the bottom-up rather than just the top-down.

The European Union (EU) has been equally active and enthusiastic in promoting active ageing and in turn it has added its own particular brand of age-inclusiveness – *intergenerational solidarity* – "solidarity between generations"; a European vision that was reflected in the EU's European Statement in 2012; "Europe can only meet the challenges of demographic change through active ageing; its future prosperity and social cohesion depend on it". As Laszlo Andor, European Commissioner for Employment, Social Affairs and Inclusion explained back at the Dublin Conference of the Third Age in Oct. 2012: "Older people depend on the success of younger people if they want to enjoy good social protection and social services; so it is in their best interest to invest in the future of the young….We can and must avoid confrontation between generations". The EU is therefore keen to promote a "multi-dimensional" approach to ageing, one that offers an integrated and comprehensive strategy based on the whole "**life-course**" rather than focusing just on the ageing of the old.

The EU's 2020 strategy and its **vision for ageing in Europe in the 21st century** have instigated numerous programmes in support of smart ageing ranging from assisted living and eHealth to the 2020 Health for Growth programme while its Active Ageing Index (AAI) illustrated in Figure 2.1 has been designed

Cluster	Country	Overall Score
1: Green	Greece	27.7
2: Red	France	38.6
3: Blue	Germany	39.6
4: Yellow	U.K.	41.3
	Netherlands	42.7
	Sweden	47.2
	EU average	**35.7**

FIGURE 2.1   2018 AAI

Source: Sample from: UN/EC: 2018 Active Ageing Index (Oct. 2019)

not just to plot progress on such specific issues as pensions and healthcare but to identify how well countries are managing to realise "the untapped potential of older people for more active participation in employment, in social life and for independent living". As the architects of the Index emphasise, it is only by fully "mobilising the potential of both older women and men" that the prosperity for all generations in ageing societies will be achieved. Mobilising this "elder dividend", however, is an immense challenge and one that even the more proactive Scandinavian countries have, at times, struggled to fulfil.

As the 2018 AAI has shown, while the Scandinavian nations and the Netherlands have been developing comprehensive ageing strategies, have opened up a dialogue on ageing with the public at large and begun to develop comprehensive and age-inclusive national plans that are economically sustainable, many other EU nations lag somewhat behind, caught up in the aftermath of the 2008 financial crisis, the migrant crisis of 2015, Brexit and the departure of Great Britain, and now a global pandemic that has hit Europe especially hard and seemed at times to be threatening the very existence of the EU itself, let alone the future peace and prosperity of its members.

At a national level, progress on active ageing and developing comprehensive ageing strategies has generally been quite slow and variable.

The Global AgeWatch Index (GAWI), for example, sought to create a *Global Index of Elder Wellbeing*, designed to measure the *quality of life and well-being* of older people around the world based on four key measures: income security, health, capability and enabling environment. As illustrated in the 2015 edition below (Figure 2.2), Switzerland came top with Norway and Sweden close behind whilst the UK was 10th, high up on "enabling environment" in terms of access to transport and civic freedom but only 20th and 27th respectively in terms of the health, employment and educational opportunities for older people, well below such counterparts as Canada, the Netherlands and Germany.

1. Switzerland

2. Norway

3. Sweden

6. Netherlands

9. USA

10. United Kingdom

FIGURE 2.2 GAWI: 2015 ranking

Source: Sample ranking from Global Age Watch Index (2015)

The National Longevity Development Plans Global Survey launched in 2019, however, found that in the intervening years, significant progress has been made and numerous initiatives for promoting healthy longevity have since sprung up from Japan's lifestyle and fitness programmes to Singapore's age-tech projects for smart homes for the elderly, Switzerland's financial innovation program for retirees and the Netherland's Deltaplan for dementia. However, whilst this latter-day survey still found no evidence yet of a full-blown Longevity Development Strategy, it did perceive the rudiments of one in Seoul's "2020 Master Plan for the Aged Society" and in the UK's Industrial Grand Strategy within which ageing is a core strand. On that basis, it ranked the UK No. 1 in its 2019 review – summarised in Figure 2.3 below – and declared it to be "well positioned to become a leader in Healthy Longevity".

1.   United Kingdom

2.   Netherlands

3.   Singapore

4.   South Korea

5.   Israel

FIGURE 2.3   National Longevity Development Plans: Global Survey Ranking: 2019

Source: Sample from Global Landscape Overview (2019: 1st edition)

The World Happiness Index, however, goes a step further, claiming that the *happiness* of all ages is the key to "improving the world well-being and its sustainability". As shown in Figure 2.4 below, in its 2021 Global Survey, Finland, Denmark and Switzerland were the top three rankings while the UK came 17th, an improvement on previous years but still below Israel and Costa Rica and only just above the USA. The World today, generally, is an unhappy place, positive ageing is still sadly under-developed, and the 2008 economic crisis – and now COVID-19 – hang like shrouds over the world economy and the worldview of the future.

1.   Finland

2.   Denmark

3.   Switzerland

15.   Ireland

16.   Costa Rica

17.   United Kingdom

FIGURE 2.4   World Happiness Index: 2021

Source: Sample Ranking: World Happiness Report (2021)

Conclusion: The World Economic Forum (WEF:2021) has declared that the growth in global ageing "will be one of the greatest social, economic and political transformations of our time"; one that will force changes in systems, impact families and require new solutions in which collaboration among policy-makers, civil society, academia and the private sector is crucial if this surge in adults age

65 and over to 1.6 billion by 2050 is to be a "booming opportunity" rather than a "looming crisis". There are now signs in the international surveys and indices of ageing above, of hope that the challenges and opportunities of ageing are at last being recognised and that *healthy ageing and age-friendliness* are now priorities. Some governments, such as Norway, are developing ageing strategies, some have appointed Ministers for ageing while others such as Ireland have considered adopting smart ageing as part of their economic strategy for promoting growth in such fields as functional and healthy food, health, assisted living, adaptable housing and even tourism (Technopolis Report: 2015). However, overall, these initiatives are still just *silver shoots* in what is fast becoming a *grey world* in which there is no international movement to embrace ageing globally beyond the pleas of the UN and the EU. Moreover, just as the world is entering an era of unprecedented global risks and an era of unprecedented ageing, it is now facing a global pandemic that has swept the world, almost overran many of the world's health services, shut down the global economy and locked down "normal" human life. COVID-19 has represented an existential as well as a physical and economic challenge to human life. But it may, just may, have a silver-side; an opportunity to look afresh, not just at healthy living and our current healthcare services but at active ageing and healthy longevity as part of a new global vision post-coronavirus; and part of a new international and national drive towards a healthier planet. However, if governments fear or fail to take the lead, then as Dr Alexandre Kalache (2012), the WHO Director of Ageing and Health until 2008, has argued, it may fall to the New Old, the Baby Boomer generation, to lead the way. "We (Baby Boomers) must fight the stereotypes. We have to change the attitude toward ageing… (We) have to force society to accept that older people can continue to contribute. I am 65. At this age my grandfather had a walking stick, and was walking towards his tomb. I have a completely different prospect ahead of me". The generation that created adolescence now has the opportunity to create *'elderescence'*; a New Age of Ageing and a New Age Agenda. And no index to date, no national or international plan yet, seems to have factored in the power of the Old, the New Old and the power of the Baby Boomer Generation into their analysis of the future; a conclusion that set Laura wondering whether her thesis now had a new dynamic, a new agency of sociological change; one where the Old themselves, the New Old drive the shift from an ageing world towards a more healthy and age-friendly, or even ageless, one.

Bibliography

EU Commission: *Europa: A New Vision for Old Age* (2012)
EU Commission: *Active Ageing Index* (AAI) (2018)
EU Commission: *Ageing Europe* (2020)
EU Commission: *Impact of Demographic Change* (2020)
Global AgeWatch Index (GAWI) (2015)

Helliwell, J; Layard, R; Sachs, J: *World Happiness Report & Index*: Sustainable Development Solutions Network (2021)

Kalache, Alexandre: *How the Baby Boomers Are Reinventing Old Age*: Huffington Post (April 2012)

National Longevity Development Plans: Global Overview (2019)

Sethumadhavan, A; Saunders, M: *Ageing: Looming Crisis or Booming Opportunity?*: World Economic Forum (March 2021)

Technopolis Report: *A Mapping of Smart Ageing Activity in Ireland and an assessment of the Potential Smart Ageing Opportunity Areas* (April 2015)

The UN and the World Health Organization (WHO): *Active Ageing: A Policy Framework*: Second World Conference: Madrid (2002)

The UN and the World Health Organization (WHO): *Ageing and Health* (2015)

The UN and the World Health Organization (WHO): *Transforming Our World*: *The 2030 Agenda for Sustainable Development* (2019)

The UN and the World Health Organization (WHO): *Decade of Healthy Ageing* (2020–2030): (2019)

PART II

The national challenge of ageing and the national response

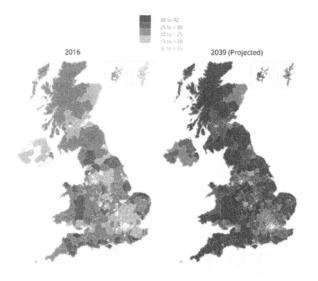

FIGURE II.1 Age maps of UK: 2016 and 2039

Source: 2016 mid-year population estimates for UK, Office for National Statistics, 2014-based subnational population projections for UK, Office for National Statistics, Welsh Government, National Records Scotland and Northern Ireland Statistics and Research Authority, contains OS data © Crown copyright 2018

3

THE DEMOGRAPHIC CHALLENGE AND THE GOVERNMENT'S RESPONSE

The national challenge

So, if Part I has set out the global challenge of ageing, what does ageing Britain look like? What is this age-shift that is so fundamentally and permanently changing the demography of Great Britain?

According to the Office of National Statistics (ONS: 2021)

- **The total population** of the UK is set to rise from 66.8 million in 2021 to 72 million in 2041, and would have become the largest country in the EU/EFTA area if Great Britain had stayed in the EU (Figure 3.1).
- **The New Old in the UK are set to rise dramatically**. Those aged 65 years and over were just under 12.0 million in 2016. They are projected to rise to 19.8 million by 2069 or 24% of the total population whilst the **Middle Old**, those aged 85 and over, are projected to treble from 1.6 million in 2018 to over 5 million by 2066. Meanwhile, the **Oldest Old**, those aged 100 and over are projected to leap from 13,330 in 2019 to over 21,000 by 2030; an astronomic increase of nearly 200% from the 7,600 centenarians living in 2002; only 20 years ago.
- **The New Young are set to fall dramatically.** In 2012, the total fertility rate (TFR) fell from 1.9 children on average per woman in the UK to 1.68 in 2018. Around 100,000 fewer children were born in that period and unless this birth rate changes dramatically, the UK's younger populations will continue to shrink in size and number.
- **The "Balance of the Ages" is being turned on its head** as the under-16-year-old age group shrinks from 19% of the population in 2019 to 16.9% in 2039 while the 16–64 age group falls from 62.5% of the total population to 59.2% in the same period.

DOI: 10.4324/9781003029373-6

Age	% increase
0-19	+3%
20-34	-1%
35-49	+2%
50-64	+2%
65-79	**+36%**
80+	**+69%**

FIGURE 3.1   Projected population change: 2016–2036

Source: Adapted from Centre for Ageing Better: The State of Ageing in 2019

- Today, there are more people in the UK aged 60 and over than there are under 18; *more pensioners than children under 16.*
- Today, there are four people of working age supporting each pensioner in Britain; *by 2050 this will have fallen to two.*
- By 2083, it is estimated about one in three people in the UK population will be over 60 and *nearly one in five people currently living in the UK will live to 100 years plus.*

As illustrated in the Age maps in Figure II.1 at the beginning of this section and in Figure 3.2, **Great Britain is becoming *Grey Britain*;** the British Isles are becoming the "Silver Isles" and the UK is facing a demographic revolution; *a leap in longevity as, on* average, we are now living 35 years longer than we would have done 100 years ago. In 1901, baby boys were expected to live for 45 years and baby girls 49 years. Boys born in Britain in 2018 are predicted to live to nearly 80 years and girls to 83 years, rising to 86.4 and nearly 89 for new-born baby boys and girls by 2066. This is truly amazing. Our life span, on average, has nearly doubled in just over a hundred years and nearly a third of

Year	LE: Male	LE: Female
1841	40	42
1900/1910	48	52
1930	58	62
1950/52	68	72
2000/02	76	80
2026	81	84
2066	86	89

FIGURE 3.2   Life expectancy (LE): England & Wales: 1840–2010

Source: Adapted from CMO Annual Report (2020): ONS (2018)

	Years in Good Health	Years Not in Good Health	Total L.E. at age 65
Females	11.2 (53.6%)	9.7	20.8 years
Males	10.4 (56.0%)	8.2	18.6 years

FIGURE 3.3   Healthy life expectancy (LE) at age 65: UK (2014–2016)

Source: Adapted from ONS: Fig. 31 (2018)

children born today are expected to live to 100 years and beyond. We now enjoy life spans that previous centuries could only dream of. We are now enjoying the Gift of Longevity; the gift of extra life- and yet we take it all for granted!

But that is not the end of it. As illustrated in Figures 3.2 and 3.3, not only is **life expectancy** in the UK today longer and healthier than ever before but it actually "Goes Up with Age"; *the longer you live, the longer you are likely to live.* According to the ONS (2020):

- **Life expectancy** at birth in the UK is currently 79.4 years for men and 83.1 years for women rising to 85.7 years and 87.6 years, respectively by 2030.
- **Life expectancy** at age 65, however, is 18.8 years for men and 21.2 years for women with 60% of this longer life in good health.
- **Life expectancy** at age 85 is 5.8 years for men and 6.8 years for women.

The key to living longer though is good health. Living longer in good health is heaven; living longer in pain and disability is hell! According to the ONS, healthy life expectancy at birth – the number of years of life in good health one can expect to live – has now risen in England to 63.5 years for men and 63.9 years for women in the UK. We can now expect to live over 80% of our total life span in very good or good health and even at age 65, we can expect nearly 60% of our remaining 18–21 years to be in good rather than bad health. We are pushing back the boundaries of morbidity and compressing it by living healthy lives free from such modern "killer diseases" as obesity and smoking. Healthy living earns us extra life, even later on in life. Healthy living since 1950 has already earnt British males aged 60, seven extra years on average with more to come for those staying healthy, active and frisky. What a gift; what an amazing achievement for the NHS and the welfare state; what a post-war legacy after two World Wars killed millions of young men and women; and now millions more live on into ripe, old age. As Professor Sarah Harper summed it up (2016) death is steadily losing its dominion. "In 1850 half the population in England were dead before they reached 46. Now half the population in England are alive at 85; and 8 million people currently alive in the UK will make it to 100 years or more". The two oldest men in Britain are now 110 years of age, and according to Professor Rudi Westerndorp (2015), the first person to reach 135 years of age has already been born.

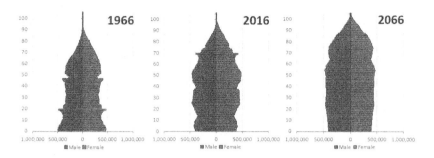

FIGURE 3.4   Population pyramids: UK 2015 and 2035

Source: Population estimates, Principal population projections, 2016-based, Office for National Statistics

On the downside, though, the UK's Dependency Ratio is predicted to double from roughly 4:1 workers to every one dependent child or OAP today to 2:1 by 2050, unleashing a "demographic earthquake" over the next ten years that will severely strain the British Welfare State, drain British industry of a whole generational of highly educated, highly skilled and experienced workers and managers and flood an inadequate housing market with Baby Boomers seeking to downsize from family homes to retirement accommodation well beyond the current provision and choice. The UK's age ratio is also "tipping-over" and soon the number of grandparents will begin to outstrip the number of grandchildren and a "super wave" of silver centenarians, of great-grandparents, even great-great grandparents, will begin to emerge; half a million by 2066 according to the ONS (2018); a 40-fold increase on the 14,000 today and likely to escalate even further as 1 in 3 babies born in 2012 are expected to reach their 100th birthday; a **"demographic miracle"** and a demographic rainbow as the British Isles gradually goes grey or possibly grey-brown as Britain's ethnic minorities also begin to feed into old age. As illustrated in Figure 3.4 above, the UK is transforming from a pyramid to a pillar and may possibly tip-over in the future.

By now Laura was mesmerised by demographic data. Where previously, she had had a sort of number-blindness with statistics, she could now see a seismic shift in Britain's demography; an age-shift that, as her tutor Jonathan advised her, was almost certainly shifting if not shattering the sociological structure underneath exposing fault-lines such as:

Class and longevity

As the ONS (2018) identified, there is a deep and dark chasm in the UK's demographic landscape; a gap in Life Expectancy between the least and most deprived areas of England today of over 7 years for baby girls and over 9 years for baby boys, and worse, a gap in healthy life expectancy of just over 19 years between the better-off and most deprived males in England and a gap of 18.8 years for females – a gap that is apparently is still growing. A gap graphically and tragically illustrated in Kensington and Chelsea, the richest borough in London and the site of the Grenfell Towers disaster where the gap in average life expectancy between the richest and poorest residents of this exceptionally wealthy area is now some 16 years. As the ONS explains: "Based on 2010-2012 death rates, 79% of new born baby boys in the most deprived areas will survive to their 65th birthday compared with 92% in the least deprived areas" a 13% gap in male life expectancy that is not only socially divisive but economically damaging. A 'loss of life' that is far greater than in other advanced countries and one that could be avoided".

Geography and longevity

Equally, where you live in the UK, not only seems to affect how you live but how long you live. For example, your chances of living a long and healthy life are better in England than Scotland or Wales; better in the South of England than the North. In England 2017–19, both male and female life expectancies at birth were highest in Westminster at 84.9 and 87.2 years, respectively and lowest in Blackpool at 74.4 and 79.5 years, respectively. In terms of healthy life expectancy, the highest male HLE was in Richmond-upon-Thames at 71.9 years and lowest for females was in Nottingham at 54.2 years. As the 2017 study by Public Health England showed, the North-South divide is alive and well. While life expectancy in the South of England now ranks amongst the best in the world, life expectancy in parts of the North ranks amongst the worst; partly the result of poor diet, obesity and smoking; partly the result of social and economic inequalities that according to Professor John Newton "are deep-rooted and persistent and lie largely outside the health system". Britain is also facing a geographic "age-divide" as the older generations move out to the country and the coast whilst the younger ones converge on the inner cities and the university towns. By 2036, over half of local authorities are projected to have ageing populations with 25% or more of their communities aged 65 and over with all the dependency costs that this *silver shift* will inevitably bring.

Better abroad than in the UK

Finally, as Figure 3.5 below illustrates, the Japanese, Scandinavians and the Mediterranean countries are still "years ahead" of us in the Longevity League tables for both men and women–and Scotland still "trails" behind all of us. As Sir Steve Webb, former Lib-Dem Pensions minister summed it up *"The UK has slumped from being one of the top performers when it comes to improving life expectancy to bottom of the league."*

Immigration might have mitigated some of the impact of ageing in Great Britain and provided the sort of *young blood* any ageing society needs. However, with the Brexit decision, the UK seems to have closed its borders to open immigration from the EU, despite studies such as that by the OBR in 2013 and UCL in 2014 that immigrants, whether from the EU or beyond, have overwhelmingly had a positive effect on the UK's economy and British society, contributing over

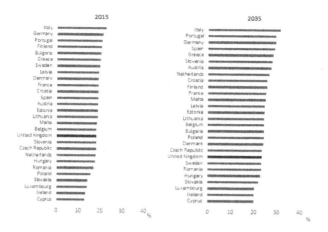

FIGURE 3.5 International life expectancy: UK & EU

Source: ONS 2018 and World Population Prospects the 2017 revision, World Population Prospects the 2017 revision, custom data acquired from website, United Nations Department of Economic and Social Affairs Population Division

20 billion to public finances, supporting the ever-growing needs of the UK's health and social care services as well as staffing our financial and technical sectors. It is therefore, somewhat ironic, that despite the Brexit decision, immigration to the UK has remained relatively the same as in 2016, the year of the Referendum, at 313,000 albeit with a shift from EU to non-EU immigrants (ONS: 2021)

Coronavirus has, is and is likely to continue to have a profound effect on longevity in the UK and on the ageing of Great Britain, particularly as shown below, the vast majority of COVID-19-related deaths have been in the 70+ age groups, particularly in the care homes of the most elderly and most vulnerable. As the Centre for Ageing Better (2020) puts it: "Three in every four people who died for COVID-19 related reasons have been age 75 or older". How this pandemic will affect ageing and longevity in the UK in the longer-term is as yet unclear, but in the immediate and short-term the effect has and will be devastating for the families involved, for businesses closed down and for youngsters now facing lengthy catch-up in their education and careers. In the long-term, with new vaccines and a health service now on high alert against further global pandemics and promoting prevention as well as treatment, then it is possible that Britain's older population will be better protected, "boom" once again and live even longer.

The new old

So, Laura's next question inevitably, was who are the **"Old"** in the UK today and what do they look like? According to the Office of National Statistics (ONS: 2019) and Age UK (2019), the over-age-65 population of England and Wales comprises some 12 million residents representing over 18% of the population and an increase of almost one million since 2001. Of this age group:

- 60% were married or in a civil partnership; 10.5% were divorced; 2.8% were cohabiting (almost double the figure for 2001 of 1.6%) and 31% were living alone; some 3.8 million older people; 70% of whom are women.
- 86% were retired and 10% still economically active, double that for 2001.
- 50% of residents aged 65 and over living in households reported that their health was good or very good compared to 88% of those under age 65.

In addition:

- About 14 million people are grandparents; 1.5 million of whom are under 50.
- Some one in three households are now headed by someone over 60.
- 1.8 million pensioners are still living in poverty, a high proportion of whom are Black Caribbean, Bangladeshi or Pakistani in origin.
- 25% of older households live in what is classified as non-decent housing.

So, as Figure 3.6 illustrates, Britain is undergoing a silent but seismic demographic revolution; a revolution in longevity that is likely to fundamentally change our way of life and the social structure under which we live; a generational revolution amply illustrated in the chart below:

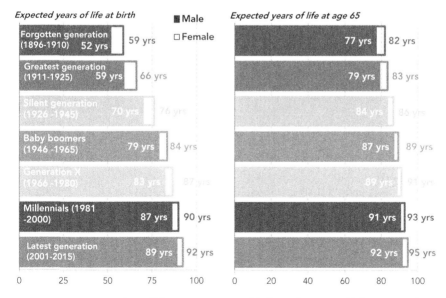

FIGURE 3.6 Mean cohort life expectancy at birth and at age 65 by generation: England & Wales.

Notes: Cohorts born prior to 1956 cover England and Wales only, cohorts born after cover the UK

Source: ONS, UK lifetables 2014-based, and ONS, England and Wales lifetables 2014-based

As Laura now realised, Great Britain is slowly but inexorably being trans-formed into *Grey Britain* and this demographic transformation is as much about the young as the old; as much about life in the future for her generation as that of her parents and grandparents. This was a light bulb moment; one that trans-formed her academic interest in ageing into a personal passion; one that made her realise that an ageing Britain is the future ahead for her generation as much as that for the older age groups. The more, therefore, that the young know and understand about ageing, the more that they can influence and steer it; the more that they can help Britain become the silver society that many commentators hope for rather than the grey nightmare many fear. But, before venturing into life in ageing Britain, Laura asked her grandmother, Polly the politician, what the UK Government is doing about ageing and how well prepared the UK is for the social, economic and political revolution ahead.

The government response

Nearly ten years ago in 2013, the Chair of the House of Lord's Select Committee on Ageing, Lord Filkin, declared government response to the emerging chal-lenge of Ageing as *woeful* and later on in 2016 as *wilful* in its neglect and failure to plan ahead. In a scathing report, the Filkin Committee highlighted the complete absence of any government forward planning for the ageing world ahead and it recommended that a national strategy on ageing be drawn up as a matter of urgency based on two central pillars, namely that:

A **new deal – a new fairer social contract** be drawn up *between* the generations that fully reflects the changing needs of Britain in the 21st century rather than the much more limited needs of the post war era. The 1944 British Welfare State was designed as a *safety net* for a post-war population of some 5.5 million pensioners living on average just a few years in retirement. It was not designed to cope with the needs and demands of a burgeoning pensioner population approaching 12 million today and projected to increase to 20 million or more by 2037 with retirement lifespans approaching 20 years or more. The post-war social contract between the State and the Individual, between the Young and the Old needs to shift and the wealthier amongst the older generation now need to contribute as well as receive.

A **new fairer deal** be struck *within* generations, between social classes, genders and ethnic minorities. Poorer people arrive in old age lack-ing wealth, with poorer pensions and having accumulated health dis-advantage throughout their lives. Women, in particular, arrive in old age with lower pensions through career breaks caring for children and elderly parents or through divorce. Compared to men, older women are much more likely to be single or disabled, even if they still live longer. Over time, as inequalities in working life are likely to be replicated in retirement, Britain remains one of the most unequal societies in the western world and many of the old today are as unequal as the young – and as unhappy.

Given the average age of the British House of Lords, these were quite radical and forward-thinking conclusions designed to "jump-start" a national debate on ageing in the UK and drive government planning for an ageing population from one of "crisis management" and knee-jerk reaction onto a new, forward-looking national strategy based on a new social or "silver" contract that celebrates longer life rather than fears it. The 2010–2015 Coalition Government responded in part by promoting the recruitment and retention of older people through the recommendations of "Fuller Working Lives-A Framework for Action", establishing the Care Act as the framework for the biggest change in the Care System since 1948 and committing to implementing the social care funding reforms recommended by the Dilnot Commission. Its major reform, however, was the 2014 Budget Statement and the "liberation" of retirement pensions from the prescriptive and restrictive rules of the past to give pensioners far greater control over their future finances and to encourage long-term planning, saving and investment. This step alone massively raised the profile of ageing and pension planning and it represented a clear recognition by the Government of the power and importance of the "silver vote" – as well as the inadequacy and inflexibility of the range of financial products available in the retirement market at that time. By putting "pension power" back in the hands of pensioners, the government hoped to shake up the financial markets and highlight the growing responsibilities of the individual for financial planning in an ageing society – as well as securing the pensioner vote prior to the 2015 General Election. However, as valuable though these changes undoubtedly were, they did not in the Committee's view constitute a national plan nor provide the integrated and comprehensive framework for addressing the escalating challenges of an ageing Britain. As Lord Filkin, commented in 2016 "Our Committee-the Filkin Committee-found our society 'woefully underprepared' for ageing; with this response the Government appears to be **wilfully** underprepared"; at a time when the government's austerity programme was underway and the Brexit debate about to take off.

So, for more than 15 years, with the exception of the New Labour Manifesto in 2009 and the Coalition Government reforms above, no British government since 1945 has seriously addressed the spectre of ageing nor developed a national plan comparable to that of the Scandinavians or even such poorer countries as Bolivia and Costa Rica. Even as recently as 2019, the Lord's Select Committee on Intergenerational Fairness highlighted the "lack of political will" to confront the realities of ageing and "the failure of successive governments to plan for the future and prepare for (the) social, economic and technological changes" implicit in the idea of a 100-Year life. As John Harris commented in the Guardian in Feb. 2018, we still "seem to have a collective aversion to focusing on the realities of an ageing society. Successive governments have shied away from the changes that might ease a mounting sense of dread about the future". Instead, "Our visions of later life are in danger of collapsing into despair" at a time "when we ought to be building them on imagination and hope" for the future.

The EU's 2018 AAI Index and the 2019 National Longevity Development Planning Survey cited in Chapter 2, however, both present a more positive and proactive picture of UK government planning; a significant step-change in government thinking and forward-planning. The AAI placed the UK in its yellow cluster alongside the EU's top performers in Scandinavia whilst the NLDP identified the government's Grand Industrial Strategy as a potential model for other countries to follow in integrating ageing with industrial & green planning. Certainly, the current government now has a grand vision for ageing Britain as an integral part of its industrial strategy sitting alongside artificial intelligence, clean growth and the future of mobility with a mission to "ensure that people can enjoy at least 5 extra healthy, independent years of life by 2035, while narrowing the gap between the experience of the richest and poorest"; a mission designed to help:

- support people to remain at work for longer.
- build markets for consumer products and services that better meet the needs of older people.
- drive improvements in public health and innovation across the social care sector including £130 million allocated for investment in healthcare innovation.

This strategy is to be led by Andy Briggs as Business Champion, supported by a UK Longevity Council. A joint UK-Japanese competition for a new generation of assisted living products harnessing the powers of AI and robotics is underway, alongside a House of 2030 design and innovation competition, the creation of a new National Innovation Centre for Ageing in Newcastle and the publication of Greater Manchester's local industrial strategy as part of its WHO age-friendly city strategy. This is all part of Boris Johnson's vision for a Post-COVID Britain; a *New Jerusalem* in which "levelling-up" will be at the front of national planning, green energy development will be world class, housebuilding will be boosted and the injustice of care-home funding fixed. This may not be the all-inclusive strategy nor the intergenerational social contract that the House of Lords had been arguing for but by aligning healthy ageing with digital development, the government does appear to have taken a significant step forward and may, with the public attention generated by COVID-19 and the death rates of the UK's elderly populations, help drive forward a full-scale ageing strategy in the UK in years to come. The litmus test, however, Polly reminded Laura, will be whether these grand promises and this Grand Vision are actually delivered so that Great Britain becomes a great place to grow old in – and grow young in- rather than the Grey Britain, the House of Lords feared. Otherwise, these grand promises, this Grand Vision will not only be "woeful or wilful" but empty and hollow too.

Bibliography

Age UK Monthly Briefing (2019)

Centre for Ageing Better: *The State of Ageing* (November 2020)

Harper, Sarah: ILC-UK Future of Ageing Conference (November 2016)

House of Lord's Select Committee: *Public Service and Demographic Change: Ready for Ageing* (March 2013)

House of Lord's Select Committee: *Tackling Intergenerational Unfairness and Provision* (April 2019)

ONS: 2018–2021 Demographic Reports

Resolution Foundation (IGC Report): *Live Long and Prosper* (2017)

Westendorp, Rudi: *Growing Older Without Feeling Older*. Scribe (2015)

4

THE ECONOMIC AND SOCIAL CHALLENGES OF AGEING IN THE UK TODAY

Introduction

So, in the absence of a government grand plan for ageing Britain, Laura under-took her own grand tour; a sociological survey of a British Isles that is about to go *Grey*; Dark Grey if there is no national plan; Silver Grey, if at last, government leads the way and opens the national conversation. She started in the obvious place with retirement, journeyed on through work, pensions, health and housing and ended back with family, death and dying with even "sex at 60" getting a look-in. Truly a Grand Tour of the Grey Britain emerging today.

4.1 THE RETIREMENT REVOLUTION AND LONGER, LATER LIFE

Retirement would not have been top of Laura's sociological agenda. It was hardly the coolest or sexiest of topics for a young woman in her 20s and with the state age of retirement fast disappearing into the distance for her age group – and with COVID-19 lurking over every care home in the UK – retirement for Laura was an issue at least 50 years away. What possibly did retirement have to do with her; what did it have to do with sociology? Quite a lot as she soon discovered from her initial background reading. Quite a shock as Laura came to appreciate that ageing is not all about the old but that it is fundamental to the future of the young too; that retirement today is not the end of life but opens up the possibility of a new life, an active life, a second life in which her true self might come to the fore and make a continuing difference to the world around her. Suddenly, she was quite envious of her grandparents, jealous of their new freedoms and their new opportunities to be themselves away from the drudgery and discipline of family and work in the 21st century. Suddenly, she now wanted to retire too – even

DOI: 10.4324/9781003029373-7

though she hadn't yet started work; she wanted to explore this new *Garden of Eden* and its sociological potential for finally explaining the meaning of life, now and in the future?

According to the ILC-UK report *When I'm 64* (2017), the numbers of retirees today are far more numerous and are living far longer lives than any previous generations of OAPs. The number of retirees aged 55–69 has increased rapidly from 8.4 million in 1995 to 11 million in 2015 and is projected to rise to 18 million by 2050. Meanwhile average life expectancy at age 65 is 18.6 years for men and nearly 21 years for women. Today's British retirees are no longer a minority population shrinking with age into the sidelines of society but a booming generation, larger than many EU countries and both healthier and wealthier with it. The history of retirement in western societies can be dated back to the introduction of a state pension by Otto von Bismarck, the German Chancellor in the 1880s and to the Liberal government in the UK in 1909. The creation of a state pension was a major step forward in providing social security in Western Europe and it represented the beginnings of a Social Contract between the generations that has existed ever since. However, as the Aegon Retirement Survey explained in 2013, "Retirement was never meant to be expensive. In 1889, when the first modern state retirement system was put in place in Germany, the age of retirement was 70 years, well beyond the age at which the average employee died. Today most countries set their retirement age closer to 65 years, and, having retired, employees can expect to live for another twenty years or more. Retirement has changed from being a rarity into a right". Moreover, as the Royal London Life insurance company argued in 2016, in stark contrast to the mythical image of idyllic old-age on a cruise ship, golf course or couch at home, modern retirement is likely to be as fraught with challenges and strains as it is with happiness and hobbies. "As the population ages, the baby boomer generation face a future in which they are likely to be more financially burdened than ever before as they provide for parents who live longer and children who may be financially dependent into adulthood. This financial burden goes alongside having greater ambitions than any other generation for their future post 65".

This is a devastating conclusion and represents the view that "Retirement, as we know it is Dead". Not only has the traditional model of retirement outlived its use in meeting the needs and demands of retirees, it seems to have outlived its usefulness and sustainability as an economic or social framework for government policy:

- **It cannot cope with mass retirement**; it cannot easily cope with the retirement of one of the largest generations in British history, a "baby boom" generation that exploded onto British society when it was growing up and now threatens to overwhelm it as it retires. The numbers alone – some 600,000 baby boomers per annum over the next 20 years, some 17–18 million pensioners aged 60 to a 100-years plus – appear to be unsustainable; let alone that they are living longer than ever before.

- **It cannot cope economically or financially with the costs of pensions, housing and healthcare** on this scale being funded solely from public taxation; a pensions *time-bomb; a* Global Retirement Savings Gap of some $70 trillion rising to $400 trillion by 2050 according to the WEF in 2017 with the UK deficit alone rising from $8 trillion to $33 trillion in that time.
- **It cannot cope with the challenges involved or the forward-planning so desperately needed**. Numerous surveys by banks and insurance companies such as HSBC, Scottish Widows and Aviva have highlighted the massive lack of preparedness by older Brits for retirement – more so apparently than many other countries. The post-2008 shift by employers out of defined benefit pensions into defined contribution schemes has left employees even more vulnerable than before and the *Retirement Dream* today is even more elusive than in the past. Yet, the 2019 Aviva survey still found 8.9 million employees aged 45 and over who do not know how much they will need to save for a comfortable retirement and the Great British Retirement Survey (GBRS) in 2020 found growing anxieties about the impact of stock market fluctuations on savings, an intensifying fear of financial scams, of future care costs and the increasing demands on the savings of older generations from adult children struggling with unemployment and housing costs. Many still deeply distrust financial advisers and schemes such as equity release after the mis-selling scandals and scams earlier this century. Dreams of a happy retirement are fast disappearing for younger generations too. According to the ILC-UK 2020 Survey, young people today are a "forgotten generation", sleepwalking into retirement disaster and whilst auto-enrolment has been something of a "game changer" for all workers, women are still especially vulnerable with average pension pots of £25,000 – half that of men – and shorter retirement lives than their female counterparts in Europe and Australia. The 2014 OECD study Society at a Glance described British women as "the poor relations' in retirement" compared to their counterparts elsewhere.
- **It cannot cope with the modern, multi-generational family.** Just as the state and the employer are stepping back from pension and welfare support, the family is having to step forward. Just as retirees were about to fly off to pastures new, free now of all family responsibilities, many instead are caught in an Intergenerational "care sandwich" trapped by responsibilities for their ageing parents on one side and the continuing needs for support of younger family members on the other, whether it be "boomerang children" needing help with student debt or younger couples trying to save for housing deposits or needing help with childcare. This is the potential nightmare facing many 21st-century retirees. They are "the meat in the family sandwich, the banker of last resort and the childcare champion" – all rolled into one; this is the darker – or greyer – side of retirement today as family disputes, break-ups and restructuring threaten the anticipated peace

and tranquility of modern retirement and leave families unable or unwilling to plan future financial planning "for fear of causing conflict".

- **It cannot cope with describing retirement in the 21st century, nor its retirees.** The language is all wrong. The very notion of retirement as a defined and legislated stage in life – a final stage – distinctly different and segregated from normal or mainstream life, no longer makes sense. We are moving towards a new notion of retirement, a more flexible transition based increasingly on personal choice and circumstance, health and aspirations rather the regimented model of the past-a second stage, a "third age", even a "second life" during which retirees may just as easily embark on a new "silver" career or business venture as embark on a cruise ship or golf course. Moreover, the "retiree of today" is not the retiree of the past; they are a different breed of retiree, a baby boomer generation demanding active engagement not the passive withdrawal taken by their parents, the Silent Generation. Baby boomers are a **Freetirement Generation** as the SIRC/Friends Provident study called them back in 2007, with high levels of disposable income, keen consumers, technologically engaged, online and "young at heart" and adamant about staying so. This new generation of retirees is not only out to transform retirement as we have known it but, according to Clive Bolton of Aviva (2013), they are out to create "a new model for later life" and to get "the most out of their improved physical health and the freedom to continue working for longer". They may be enjoying the "cradle to cruise" lifestyle portrayed in many adverts and enjoying a "golden era" of retirement, according to the Institute for Fiscal Studies (IFS: 2016), but few retirees in the future will be so well-endowed.

So, the individual today needs a personal retirement plan and maybe the support of a "retirement coach" or lifetime adviser whilst the Government needs a new approach, a new model of retirement, a new paradigm capable too, of informing government policy and long-term planning in such fields as diverse as finance, housing and health. The Country, argued Lord Wei in the 2015 Demos study "Next Steps: Life Transitions in the 21st Century", needs a new all-age, all-inclusive national retirement service to support and advise not only those retiring but youngsters like Laura just starting out on their working lives. Pension-wise and the idea of a Pension Dashboard are just a start if the UK pension system is to leap from its lowly position 17th position in the Global Retirement Index where it currently languishes behind the USA and Czech Republic and way behind Iceland and Ireland.

Towards a new model of retirement

In the absence of government planning, numerous think tanks and consultancies have put forward quite radical ideas not just about retirement itself but about life under longevity. The Centre for Social Justice (CSJ: 2020), for example, has proposed not only that the state retirement age be raised to 75 within the next 15 years, but that life-long Personal Learning Accounts (PLA) be introduced and employers set up mid-life MOT schemes to enable employees to re-plan their careers, training, work-life balance and future retirement. The Aegon Center for Longevity and Retirement has gone even further and called for a *New Social Contract for Retirement for the 21st Century*: a blueprint designed to recognise the fundamental shift in responsibility for planning peoples' financial futures from the state and the employer to the Individual; a blueprint that challenges every assumption of retirement today arguing for automatic savings, financial education and literacy, life-long learning and training, accessible and affordable healthcare and the promotion of an age-friendly world free of ageism. However, as yet, no such blueprint has emerged from government despite its need and urgency and with COVID-19 replacing Brexit as the dominant political debate, no such blueprint is likely to emerge soon. As the IFS reported in 2020, one in eight older workers have already changed their retirement plans as a result of coronavirus and almost a third of older workers believe that their financial situation is worse than before the pandemic. Their lives are at risk; their savings are seesawing dramatically and whilst the more affluent feel relatively secure, those over 50 on low pay or furlough feel extremely vulnerable and exposed.

As Laura's first stop in her tour of ageing, this trip into retirement today was a real eye-opener to the life ahead and the need, even now, for her and her generation to plan ahead if they are to avoid the icy waters already awaiting many of todays' retirees. As a sociologist, she could see both the national car-crash ahead; as a young person, it really brought home the need to plan now for retirement even if it is some 45–50 years away.

4.2 THE FUTURE OF WORK AND THE MULTI-GENERATIONAL WORKFORCE

If the world of retirement is the tail end of life for a young person, work today is the great beginning and now the great unknown; a fourth industrial revolution that is happening at such a speed and with such force that no society, no government can fully prepare for it. If longevity is transforming the world of retirement, globalisation and new technology are revolutionising the world of work and if Laura ever needed a life-plan, she needed one now – not just to plan ahead for retirement but one to help her to navigate the working life ahead. As Charles, Laura's family IFA or financial adviser, explained, the *Future of Work in the 21st Century* is a fascinating array of unbelievable opportunities and technological transformations and an infuriating guessing game as to which "game-changers" will actually change the game.

Firstly, as explained in Chapter 1, the global economy is entering an era of change and disruption never seen before. The internet revolution is going into 'warp speed' claimed the Economist in its report on megatrends in 2012; the world is on an economic rollercoaster and whilst "bumps in the road" such as Brexit in Britain and *America First* under President Trump may delay or divert it, globalisation is here to stay. The impersonal forces of globalisation and new technologies seem to be taking over, shrinking the economic world and leaving the workplace of the future under the control of smart machines, algorithms, technological specialists and a management elite living far away in a super-city or another planet. MGI (2018) has estimated that artificial Intelligence has the potential to grow the world economy by some $13 trillion, generate new jobs and even create whole industries whilst the 2050 International Delphi Forum on The Future of Work (2018) predicted a global unemployment rate up to 24% as automation, AI and robotics accelerate and permeate every sector of employment; a fundamental shift from work today being physical and local to work tomorrow being virtual and taking place in the metaverse or collective virtual space. This New World of Work may see the ending of wage labour and even of working life as we know it over the next 10–20 years. Man and machine may learn to collaborate within some form of symbiotic partnership that to some extent liberates man from mindless labour and allows self-learning machines to take over jobs and tasks that are inherently inhuman and repetitive. The winners of this scenario are likely to be the self-employed and the makers, the creators and the empathetic professions, the specialist engineers in the professions of virtual reality and the metaverse, be they algorithm creators, metaverse janitors or robot repair services. If the world is not to degenerate into a technological race of all against all and a global digital divide of rich and poor, then government at both national and especially international levels will have to take far greater control for the common good in regulating the economy, mitigating inequality, tackling cybercrime and climate change and preparing the individual through education and training for the uncertainties and dangers of the world ahead. The Bain's Macro Trends study of Labor in 2030 predicted a "doomsday" collision of Demographics, Automation and Inequality; "a period of greater macro turbulence and volatility than seen in decades" a period in which extremes become more extreme, technological innovations give rise to new corporate powerhouses, and at the same time, "pervasive insecurity may haunt ordinary families and global enterprises alike". The PWC 2020 study of Megatrends, in turn, predicted the division of the global world between the individualism and highly competitive nature of market economies at one extreme and the more inclusive and holistic approach of collectivist societies at the other; four shades of a 21st-century economic rainbow that ranges from ethical values of the Yellow World of Work through to the environmental priorities of the Green, the digital dominance of the Red and the corporate capitalism of the Blue.

Secondly, the nature and demographic profile of the workforce is stretching and diversifying as never before. The multi-generational workforce has arrived as life has got longer and retirement got later; a new "multigenerational" workforce is emerging, encompassing four, possibly even five generations by 2020; each with their own attitudes, values, priorities and preferred ways of working. Although the baby boomers are still in power in business today as owners, leaders and senior managers, generation X is leading a generational takeover; a transformation of the whole of the workplace and the traditional ways of working. Whereas the baby boomer generation tended to be highly work-centric, highly focused and even workaholic about their jobs and careers, generation X has a very different attitude to work; a more relaxed approach and a work ethic that places a high premium on family time and a strong sensitivity to work-life balance. They dislike rigid work requirements; they expect flexibility in work schedules and they have an entrepreneurial spirit in their approach to working. They value freedom and autonomy and they often prefer to work alone, even at home rather than necessarily in groups or teams. They are much happier using the Internet or social media for group discussions and they detest formal meetings; especially "meetings about meetings". Generation Y, now in their 20s and early 30s, is apparently the "smart generation" – creative, optimistic and highly achievement-orientated – keen to search out creative challenges and eager for personal growth and meaningful careers. They are tech savvy, excellent multi-taskers and they much prefer online communication to face-to-face interaction. As Meister and Williard's 2020 US study (2010) concluded: "Never in the history of the modern world have there been four generations-much less five-in the workplace that bring such vastly different sets of values, beliefs and expectations; Never has a generation entered the workplace using technologies so far ahead of those adopted by its employer".

The immense challenge of managing and motivating this multi-generational workforce is now being compounded by what the Cass Business School has called Talentocalpse (2013); the collapse of senior and middle management as the baby boomer generation retire "en masse" from top jobs leaving a vacuum in corporate leadership and a step change in organisational structure and culture that few companies today seem to be prepared for. The 2018 Mercer Report predicted that by 2025 UK business will face a "workforce crisis" of severe proportions as the labour force shrinks with the mass retirement of older workers. Between 2016 and 2020 the population of those aged 50–65 approaching retirement in the UK is expected to leap from 10.1 million to 13.8 million according to the ONS at the same time that the population of those aged 16–49 is likely to fall by 700,000 – a "demographic time-bomb" that few employers currently seem prepared for. Instead a **global talent war** seems to be underway as companies search the globe for the leaders of tomorrow. Such a competition for talent, predicts the Cass study, may well lead at last to the emergence of a new generation of black and female leaders and the breaking of numerous "glass-ceilings" as this global – and gender – talent race leads to the creation of multinational leadership teams, teams drawn from across the globe to such global cities as London and New York, enjoying lifestyles and living in accommodation distinct from – and separate from – the population at large so becoming part of a new global elite of managers, in service to the current global elite of entrepreneurs and corporate owners described in chapter one, rather than to their own countries of origin.

Talent – Global Talent – will be the workforce of the future whether young or old, male or female, African, Asian or American as Work in the 21st-century undergoes a paradigm shift, a "game change" towards knowledge intensity and creative innovation.

Thirdly, the longevity economy is now coming of age; an economy that according to the WEF (2019) now accounts for over $7.6 trillion in annual economic activity in the USA alone and that potentially may rise globally to $13.5 trillion by 2032. The Silver Economy is emerging as a global economic powerhouse, the third largest in the world after America and China with the Silver Economy in the UK alone predicted to soar from £79 billion to £227 billion. But the Silver Economy is not only about consumers or corporations. It, also, represents a silver trail of older entrepreneurs, many working as part of a small family business; small family businesses that according to the 2018 Report on Work and the Silver Economy employ over 12 million people, earn £1.4 trillion in revenue, contribute £519 billion to the UK economy and £149 billion in taxes to the UK exchequer. The number of family businesses has risen since 2010 by almost 35%, and 21% of family-run businesses are now described as multi-generational. Maximising the longevity dividend, argued the ILC-UK (2019) will help balance the impact of ageing on the economy by boosting overall GDP, increasing tax revenues, stimulating consumer demand, contributing to the informal economy and delay or reduce later life dependency and cost. By 2040 the share of total consumer spending by older households will rise from 54% in 2018 to 63% by 2040; some £550 billion a year whilst consumer spending amongst younger households appears to be falling. Ironically, much of this "silver spending" is likely to be in sectors previously considered strongholds of the young such as technology, hotels and restaurants, and these trends may increase as baby boomers move into their seventies, begin liquidising their assets, potentially adding a further £223 billion to total expenditure by 2040. Realising this longevity dividend, however, means increasing healthy ageing, incentivising longer working and greater silver entrepreneurship, supporting poorer pensioners better and encouraging businesses to become far more age-friendly and age-accessible.

So, the world of work in the 21st century is undergoing a transformation – a revolution in working practices, manufacturing processes, workforce diversity and global markets. There is a "seismic" shift in personnel occurring under the surface of the British economy, a change driven by demography, ageing and attitude as the boomer generation "steps back" and Generations X and Y step forward with women increasingly at the forefront and with global recruitment and so global migration – significant forces on their own. The UK workforce is becoming older, multigenerational and multinational with the average age of the UK's labour force is likely to increase over the next ten years with the largest age band of workers set to shift from 44–46 to 54–56 by 2020. A total of 77% of the rise in employment over the last ten years has apparently been amongst workers aged 50 and over and much of this increase has been amongst older women with the state pension age for them rising from 60 to 65. And with Brexit, this ageing of the British workforce is likely to accelerate as new young blood from the EU may no longer be so readily available.

As the UKCES 2020 Report on the Future of Work, Jobs & Skills in 2030 predicted, the *Digitalisation of Production* is likely to lead to a shift to more localised manufacturing particularly with such innovations as 3D printing, the continued miniaturisation of computing technology, the growth of nano-technology and the spread of Big Data. Automation, AI and robotics and the adoption of Anywhere-Anytime delivery accompanied by the shift in corporate structures from centralised bureaucracies to slimmed down pools of long-term core employees supported by colleagues across the globe and services outsourced to external providers, will become the norm and whilst lockdown has undoubtedly accelerated such changes, the forthcoming Robot Revolution will "game-change" it. According to the WEF 2020 report on the Future of Jobs, the digital shift towards automation and AI may also be creating a new division of labour; but not this time between man and machine but between "man, machine and algorithm" so that soon the time spent on "current tasks at work by humans and machines will be equal". Initially, this may lead to the loss of some 85 million existing jobs, but in the longer run, it may generate some 97 million new roles more adapted to this new division of labour.

Government's response

Most governments are struggling to keep up with such seismic changes. Most governments in the western world have focused primarily on raising the statutory pension age as the main means to combating this "silver brain drain". More progressive governments, however, have sought to encourage and incentivise later-life working. Finland and Norway, for example, are leading the way in developing part-time pension schemes to encourage pensioner working whilst companies such as B&Q in the UK and Lanxess in Germany are examples of companies leading the way in recruiting and retaining older workers. In the UK, the Centre for Social Justice (2019) recommended an Age Confident employer scheme, a National Retraining programme to maximise the employment of older workers 50–64, a Personalised Learner Account (PLA) to support life-long learning and an employee mid-Life MOT scheme to guide career development. More controversially, this report recommended raising SPA to 70 rather than 67 by 2028 and to 75 by 2035 as radical measures to both reduce state pension costs and rebalance the old age dependency ratio (OADR) in light of increasing longevity. The pandemic is "impacting already disadvantaged populations with greater ferocity and velocity" than ever before and whilst COVID-19 has accelerated new technologies and the fourth industrial revolution, it has equally widened existing inequalities in the labour market and begun dividing future workers into three main categories – essential workers, remote workers and displaced workers with all three facing wholesale shifts in working practices and new health and safety risks and social disconnections. "An estimated 88-115m people could fall back into extreme poverty in 2020 as a result of this recession" predicted the WEF

Report in 2020, with women, informal and older workers disproportionately represented. Its call for new jobs in Green and Care Economies is now a matter of urgency and an even greater reason to create the new technical educational qualifications and National Retraining Scheme proposed by the House of Commons report on The Future of Work back in November 2020; and for the British government to invest in a robot and intelligence collaboration between business and universities as advised by the Business, Energy and Industrial Strategy Parliamentary Committee in 2019.

Finally, according to McKinsey & Company (2021), COVID-19 is likely to accelerate three broad trends that may fundamentally reshape the future of work:

- The shift to remote work and virtual meetings with an estimated 20–25% of workforces in advanced economies continuing to work from home between three and five days a week, creating a dramatic drop in city office space and in business travel whilst e-commerce is projected to grow by three to five times the pre-COVID-19 rate.
- The accelerated adoption of automation and AI.
- The mix of occupations with job growth shifting from low wage; low skill occupations to those requiring higher skill levels and offering higher wages; a shift that may affect 25% more workers in advanced economies than before the pandemic with the most disadvantaged workers, those without a college degree, ethnic minorities and women, most at risk.

The role of government and major employers, argues this report, is to support and oversee this dramatic restructuring by significantly upgrading the country's digital infrastructure, especially in rural areas and by supporting workers transit from one job sector to another through reskilling and social protection programmes such as the EU's Pact for Skills programme. The alternative of mass unemployment over the next few years would be economically and socially catastrophic.

Clearly, work in the 21st century is not going to be anything like work in the 20th and whilst globalisation and new technology are the obvious driving forces of the new millennium economy, ageing, in its own quiet way, is having a profound and permanent effect too, offering what the Centre for Ageing Better called in 2018, a possible *Silver Lining for the UK Economy*; the silver lining of the burgeoning silver markets and affluent silver consumers. The Technopolis Report in 2015 similarly advised the Irish government to invest in a *Smart Ageing Strategy*; one where Ireland already had strengths such as functional and health food, connected health, assisted living, adaptable housing and silver tourism; a strategy with a Smart Ageing Leadership Council to lead it and a National (Research) Centre for Smart Ageing to support it; a strategy that would equally fit in well with the UK Government's Grand Vision to combine digital development with healthy ageing. This is exactly the sort of shift in thinking and shift into the silver markets ahead that might well help the emerging *Lost Generation* of young people facing the mass unemployment looming ahead find work and new careers working for and with older generations in the years ahead. Truly a new form of intergenerational contract worth working for.

Laura now had a much better understanding of the world of work in the 21st century; its accelerating technological shifts, its multigenerational nature and the implications not only for her generation but for her whole family in the digital – and post-pandemic – world ahead. While she had long had an interest in economics and the world of work before, she had never appreciated the dramatic – if not seismic – changes underfoot nor that with longevity and ageing, a new Silver Economy is now emerging with massive implications for her generation as well as for the old. The Global economy of the 21st century is going to be fundamentally different to anything before-and so, too, now is Laura's dissertation.

4.3 THE PENSIONS REVOLUTION AND FINANCING LONGER, LATER LIFE

Pensions? What Pensions? What youngster in their right mind at age 21 talks about pensions and later-life financing? What student with loan liabilities of £40,000 plus after completing a degree can possibly think about saving for a pension 50 years in the future? How can any young person today amid the turmoil of COVID-19 and Brexit seriously start planning for retirement when they do not even know if they will have a job let alone a secure career and home of their own?

The global challenge

Mass ageing at any time and in any country would generate an intense debate about the financial costs of ageing in terms of pensions, social security and healthcare. Mass ageing in an era of *extended longevity*, of longer and longer retirements alongside a period of economic downturn and uncertainty following the 2008 credit crisis and now COVID-19 is potentially a "grey apocalypse" as some 17 million British, some 120 million Europeans and millions elsewhere across the western and eastern worlds start to retirement. As Standard and Poor, the highly influential international ratings agency, predicted back in 2010, global ageing is an irreversible truth; "No other force is likely to shape the future of national economic health, public finances, and policy making as the irreversible rate at which the world is ageing" whilst the World Economic Forum (WEF) in 2017 warned governments across the world that they faced a *pensions global time-bomb*; a pensions gap that is set to quadruple from a $70 trillion deficit then to over $400 trillion by 2050 and one that will engulf the six largest pensions – US, UK, Japan, Netherlands, Canada and Australia – as well as the two most populous countries – China and India. The UK, alone, appears to be facing a shortfall of some $8 trillion rising potentially to $33 trillion by 2050 despite having the lowest state pension in the developed world with a work-replacement value of a only 32% compared to the OECD average of 63% and

Country	2020	2050
1. Finland	13.8%	13.2%
2. Germany	10.3%	12.2%
3. Italy	15.6%	17.3%
4. Norway	11.0%	12.0%
5. United Kingdom	7.7%	8.3%
OECD average	8.8%	9.4%

FIGURE 4.1 Projections of public expenditure on pensions: 2020–2050, % of GDP

Source: Sample drawn from OECD Pensions at a Glance: OECD: Table 8 (2019)

a weak record for pensions savings compared to other leading economies. The potential impact of what is called "age-related spending" is enormous and as illustrated in Figure 4.1, appears to be soaring out of control across the EU countries and the G7. And all that is before calculating the aftermath of both Coronavirus and Brexit.

But it is not just the costs of an ageing population that is at risk but the shrinking size of the working population upon which most taxes are based that is most worrying world economists. This Dependency Ratio, this ratio between a country's working population paying taxes and its dependents – the retired and the very young, who are not working and depend on welfare benefits – is at the heart of the ageing dilemma. As the 2019 OECD Fiscal Challenges and Inclusive Growth in Ageing Societies Report highlighted, "Rising old-age dependency ratios will put unprecedented stress on the financing of public pensions, health and long-term care especially in a slow growth environment". Without policy changes, "ageing pressures could increase the public debt burden by an average of 180% of GDP in G20 advanced economies and 130% of GDP in G20 and emerging economies over the next three decades". And worse "Those who are currently young may face higher inequality and poverty risk in their old age than older generations as they are expected to spend more years on retirement income and as the less privileged, accumulate disadvantages over their life course." And now with the COVID-19 lockdown only now beginning to abate that prediction seems something of an underestimate.

Most western pension schemes can be traced back to Otto von Bismarck in Germany and many analysts use Esping-Andersen's (1990) three-fold typology to describe and distinguish their main characteristics:

- The Liberal or Anglo-Saxon model of basic social protection combining low public benefits, topped-up by variable private and occupational schemes so by its nature creating a "have/have not" divide as in the US, UK and Ireland.
- The social-democratic or Scandinavian model of social equity and protection for all citizens with high universal public benefits and low private involvement.

- The Conservative or Continental/European model whereby public benefits are designed to maintain current income and so preserve the existing social stratification and family/household position within the labor market. Mediterranean countries such as Spain, Greece and Portugal have the family and particularly the elderly, as a priority for protection.

Within the Liberal/Anglo-Saxon market model, the individual is now increasingly taking most of the responsibility and the risk that their later life pension and finances will be sufficient. In social democratic insurance systems, the State plays a much greater role in protecting citizens through social insurance whilst under the Continental system, the State is more paternalistic, almost patriarchal in managing risk on behalf of the family and the existing social order. Liberal/ Anglo-Saxon governments generally seek to keep taxes and so public benefits low while encouraging employers and the finance markets to offer attractive occupational and private pension schemes that employees can buy into or take up, encouraged through tax breaks or incentive schemes whilst Scandinavian countries, in contrast, tend to be high-tax/high-benefit nations. However, whatever their philosophy, as ageing has progressed all governments have sought to contain pension costs by incremental changes, reversing incentives for early retirement, raising the pension age and by privatising pensions, particularly during the era of austerity post 2008. The thrust of most reforms has been to decrease future pension entitlements, increase the link between earnings, contributions and future payouts and begin to address the growing public perception of an intergenerational unfairness within the current pension systems. Pensioners today appear to be enjoying a golden era but at the expense of younger generations who are not only facing rising taxes and rising unemployment but who are unlikely to enjoy such generous pensions themselves in their older-age. As ageing approaches a *tipping point* in Europe in 2040 when 25% of the total population of all EU countries are predicted to be age 65 and older, so the issue of pensions will become increasingly urgent and, potentially, a threat to economic sustainability as well as political consensus; a scenario that is already starting to play out in Japan and parts of Eastern Asia.

So, countries across the world face a looming pensions and financial crisis, one that has not only generated an intense debate about the cost of modern pensions and their fairness but one about financial planning throughout the life-course and about the extent to which inequalities in working life are simply replicated in older-age rather than being compensated for or moderated by the state pension scheme. This is particularly so in Anglo-Saxon societies where public pensions tend to be low – more a safety net from poverty than a sustainable standard of living – and occupational pension benefits tend to be highly variable and closely related to previous earnings so perpetuating earlier inequality. Whichever state system is operating, however, women tend to be the pension losers as pension policies have largely been constructed on the basis of male working lives with whole life social security contributions whereas women traditionally face careers broken by child or eldercare and social security contributions reduced by low or part-time pay. Single and divorced women lose out even more as they struggle to work and care often simultaneously and have no partner pension to fall back on in later life. The current tax relief systems on pensions tend to exacerbate rather than mitigate such gender inequalities as well as rewarding the better-off compared to the low-paid. Systems, such as auto-enrolment in the UK, may help offset some of this gender-deficit, but a truly equitable pension policy would give equal weight to women's life-course career as men's and to the importance of caring as compared to working, especially if in an ageing society eldercare becomes as critical a need as childcare. So, pensions aren't just a welfare issue. They are a huge financial and economic issue and a life-course challenge for all generations to come with huge implications for women as well as the less well-off whatever country and whatever pension scheme they live under; a crisis exacerbated by austerity and now facing the *nuclear threat* of a global pandemic generating a world recession.

The national challenge

The British Government faces similar challenges to its European counterparts, moderated only by having a population that is ageing more slowly than Germany or Italy and by having a pension scheme that is one of the least generous in Europe. Nevertheless, the financial challenge of age-related spending is equally awesome. According to the UK Office for Budget Responsibility (OBR) in its July 2019 Fiscal Sustainability Report, state pension costs are projected to rise from 5.5% of GDP in 2018–19 to 7.3% of GDP in 2064–65 as the pensioner population in the UK is projected to rise from 12.2 million in 2014 to over 16 million by 2035 whilst age-related spending is projected to soar from 20.4% of GDP in 2018/19 to 25.1% by 2063/64. Meanwhile, national income is projected in turn to "plummet" as a result of low growth, the uncertainties of Brexit and now the crisis that is coronavirus. The UK faces a "crisis in earnings" to match this "crisis in cost" as the UK's old age dependency ratio (OADR) rises dramatically as the baby boomer generation retire en masse from working and earning and impact instead on old-age spending. The OADR is projected to fall from 4:1 to below 3:1 in the in the period 2010–2060, leaving the UK facing one of the largest *age-related* bills and "among the highest long-term care expenditures by 2050" of any of the 28 countries examined by the OECD back in 2014. Working adults are likely to face the triple blow of higher taxes, longer working lives and less inherited wealth as their parents are forced to sell property to pay for their future care. As long ago as 2013, the National Audit Office identified a potential pensions "car-crash" as people are living longer, spending longer in retirement and yet they are saving less, leaving millions at risk of relying on state pensions alone. If that is how it is now, just imagine what it is likely to be post-COVID-19.

To compound this crisis, not only is Britain's pension scheme increasingly unsustainable but it is outdated and inadequate, designed for an era where pensioners were a small part of the population living for a few short years; not a mass population of millions living 20 years or more. The Liberal government of 1904–1909 and the post-war Welfare State of 1944 created a British pension designed as a basic income, a "safety net" to relieve poverty for the minority population who after a gruelling and usually unhealthy working life managed to survive into old age: most didn't. In 1911, when old-age pensions were first introduced, some 5.2% of population were over 65, state pensions were not paid out until age 70 with the average pensioner living a mere nine years. Today, some 16% of the UK population is aged 65 and over, living on average some 20 years more and projected to rise to 23% by 2033. Successive governments since have built on this hundred year-old pension framework and introduced piecemeal amendments and reforms that have created one of the most complex pension systems in the world, one that the Turner Commission back in 2004/05 described as "not fit for purpose". The Coalition Government of 2010–2015 attempted to dramatically simplify and update the UK pension system in its proposals for "**a State Pension for the 21st century**" published in 2011; proposals that included:

Introducing a new flat rate pension initially of £144 per week to replace the current two-tiered system and so raise basic pension income above the poverty level.

Raising the state pension age (SPA) from age 65 to age 66 in 2020 and to 67 between 2026 and 2028 with an independent review every five years to review national life expectancy rates with the underlying principle that people should now expect to spend on average approximately "one third" of their adult life in receipt of a state pension.

Promoting occupational pensions through "auto-enrolment" schemes, such as NEST.

Releasing non-state pensions from proscribed state regulation and allowing those over 60 (possibly 55) to invest their pension pots as they choose. This radical – and unexpected – "**liberalisation**" of pensions was designed to encourage and reward personal saving and to open up the pensions market to the consumer demand for better returns – particularly from the annuities market where returns since the 2008 crisis that being particularly poor and management costs unacceptably high.

These welcome and substantive reforms did not, however, in the view of many commentators, go far enough and worse may have created even greater problems for the future.

Firstly, in their view, the State Pension remains too low to prevent pension poverty, let alone provide a decent and dignified standard of living. According to the OECD (2019), the UK has one of the lowest state pensions in terms in the developed world. Its "replacement value" is a lowly 32% half that of the OECD average of 63% and well below that of such comparable economies as Denmark, Luxembourg and the Netherlands at 80%. Even Mexico, Poland and

Chile have higher pension levels than the UK. The UK pension is, in many ways a "minimum wage for the elderly". It leaves millions of elderly in the UK "suspended just above the poverty line, dangling there" for the 20–30 years ahead and totally dependent on means-tested benefits – if, that is, they collect them. Auto-enrolment has made a huge difference, but unless the levels of contribution from both employees and employers is raised significantly, the generations of youngsters in the UK are likely to be left with poor pensions well below those of their counterparts in Australia, Singapore and even New York.

Secondly, with employers withdrawing "en masse" out of the guaranteed pensions of defined benefit schemes, employees are left exposed to the risks and uncertainties of defined contribution pension schemes; schemes that have no guaranteed outcome but depend primarily on the ups and downs of the global stock markets for their final payout. The *Pensioner of the Future* is therefore facing an increasingly risky and uncertain future as both the State and the Employer increasingly withdraw from pension provision and leave the Individual exposed and alone to navigate his – and especially her – way through a financial market that is notorious for the complexity of its products, its mis-selling techniques and its poor value for money. The Government's reputation for effectively policing and regulating the banking and insurance sectors suffered badly from the 2008 crash and while its attempts since, through the Financial Conduct Authority (FCA) and the *Pension Wise* scheme have helped, fully restoring public trust in the financial markets after the 2008 collapse, is a massive challenge for all western governments and for the industry itself.

Thirdly, raising the state pension age (SPA) to 66 in 2020 and 67 by 2028 may well seem prudent, fair and save the government some £400 billion over the next 50 years. However, as the ILC-UK study in 2014 pointed out, raising the SPA may in practice prove more regressive than progressive; more beneficial and fair to those in comfortable white-collar occupations with good occupational or private pensions and a healthy life expectancy of some 20+ years of retirement to look forward to, than to those in physically demanding jobs with only a limited span of retirement ahead and already suffering signs of disability and chronic illness. For those in unskilled and manual occupations, in particular, any increase in SPA could be a "death-sentence" as their health continues to decline and their period of retirement shrinks to just a few years.

As Michael Johnson at the Centre for Policy Studies concluded in November 2017, the UK State pension may well be "No Longer fit for Purpose" because:

- **It is unsustainable**. It is paying out more than the National Insurance scheme brings in – £95 billion against £86 billion in 2015/16, so necessitating a £9.6 billion bailout by the Treasury.
- **It is overly complex** and any attempt to personalise pensions to an individual's life expectancy would only twist this tangled web even further.
- **It is unfair** as it is the wealthy who live longer and are effectively being subsidised by the poor who die earlier. Worse, the tax system, until recently,

reinforced and perpetuated social inequity by giving the better-off a generous 40% tax relief on pension saving whilst allowing only 20% tax relief to those on average or below-average earnings. According to the National Economic Foundation (2019), the UK personal allowance system at £111 billion costs more than defence, local government and transport combined and enriches "the highest income households almost seven times faster than the poorest".

- **It is poorly managed.** As the National Audit report identified back in 2013, the UK pension system has no common strategy or integrated approach; no "over-arching programme or single accountability". Rather "Three regulators (for example) have oversight of pension providers but they have no common framework for assessing risk and measuring performance; seven public bodies inform the public about pensions and saving for retirement but, outside the automatic enrolment system, there is no overall strategy or mechanism to make sure they work together".

Meanwhile, the popular perception of British pensioners has shifted dramatically from "Pensioner Poor" to "Affluent Oldie" during what Paul Johnson of the Institute of Fiscal Studies (IFS) has called a *golden era* of retirement (2016). While, many wealthy British pensioners, currently, enjoy comfortable and healthy retirements funded by generous *defined benefit* final salary schemes, rising property values and a portfolio of investments and savings sufficient to put some of them into the millionaire class in terms of total assets, their poorer counterparts – some 1.8 million of them – exist on one of the lowest state pensions in Europe and face a bewildering array of means tested benefits that many do not know about, understand nor collect. Some £3.7 billion to £5.5 billion in potential pension benefits, for example, remain uncollected annually, leaving some 2.7 million pensioners – mostly women – below or just above the poverty line with older women often the *poorest of the poor*, according to the Pensions Advisory Service (2014).

Towards a state pension system for the future?

So, if the current models of state pension created in the early 20th century no longer meet the needs of mass retirement in an ageing society, what, asked Laura, might a model pension system actually look like? Charles' answer was to suggest that the pension principles proposed by the Melbourne Mercer Institute (MMI), one of the world's foremost authorities on international pension schemes, might provide a suitable and sustainable framework; principles that include:

- A clear **vision of ageing** in 21st century for the country involved and the *social aspirations and ambitions* behind it in terms of the future for the Old and Retired and for Intergenerational and Intra-generational Relations.
- A set of **primary aims and objectives** for the overall Pensions and Retirement Income System including the underlying principles of fairness,

equity, adequacy, sustainability; alongside its projected cost and funding, its relationship to the economy at large, its inter-relationship to associated social policies, such as healthcare and housing and its likely effect on the wellbeing of society, its distribution of wealth, its intergenerational relations and the betterment of the young and of family life as well as the elderly themselves.

- An **institutional framework** – or *social contract* – that clearly sets out the mutual benefits and responsibilities between retirees and the working population to ensure equity – and the perception of equity- and to ensure that retirees – and retirees to be – are protected from sudden change, by fair warning of changes in the pension system and their likely impact well beforehand and by a strict, effective and highly accessible regulatory system that enjoys high levels of customer satisfaction.
- A **pension framework** that engages employers and key stakeholders in its design, is seen as an investment, not a cost and one that adds value to employee recruitment, retention and motivation and to employer-employee relations as in the best of such schemes in Scandinavia and elsewhere.
- A **pension structure** that incorporates the lifecycle of saving before and after retirement, the potential for "staged retirement" and a wide choice of high-quality retirement income products that are effective, efficient and trustworthy.
- A set of **taxation rules** to limit the leakage of benefits before retirement and which require that at least two-thirds of the accumulated retirement benefit be converted into sustainable and defined income products.
- Compulsory and/or voluntary **tax incentive** schemes to maximise participation.
- **Impartial and high-quality financial education, advice and guidance** at all ages and at all stages, including that designed specifically for the Young throughout the formative stages of their life cycle.
- **Changes and transitory arrangements** that are clear, publically debated and well explained with gradual and staged arrangements that do not generated unnecessary shocks to pension planning and give substantive warning of change to those approaching retirement and protection for those in it.

In its 2020 Pensions League Table, the MMI ranked the UK 15th overall, a one place improvement on 2019 but still well behind the Dutch, Scandinavians and even Chile. It gave the UK a middling C+ grade, recommended that it raise its rate for low-income pensioners, increase the level and coverage of occupational pension schemes, and dramatically improve retirement and pension savings in the UK overall. As an exemplar for other countries, the MMI yet again cited the Dutch pension scheme given its high replacement rate, one of the highest in Europe, covering 60% to more than 100% of previous earnings when taxes are taken into account; its high coverage with more than 90% of all employees enrolled in occupational pension schemes and the high level of assets used to fund occupational pension schemes and so ensure that all future liabilities are covered.

And most especially the *Social Agreements* that underpin the Dutch pension schemes resulting from high levels of discussion between the key stakeholders – the Employers and the Unions – with the Government acting as "Regulator and Caretaker".

Ultimately, though concluded the Mercer Institute, there is no "silver bullet" solution to today's retirement dilemma. *Retirees in the 21st century* now have to manage their pension themselves as employers and the State withdraw at speed from managing it for them. This dramatic shift in responsibility has huge implications for any ageing society and its ageing population. The **Individual** is no longer simply a passive observer in the international pension drama, particularly the Anglo-Saxon version, but its central character. Pensions are no longer predictable but have to be "managed" by the Individual – and by the household – potentially for a 40–50 year period on the basis of a personal and/or household *retirement financial plan*, properly costed for all eventualities and all aspirations in the 30-year "run-up" to retirement – and potentially afterwards. This is a dramatic and frightening departure from the traditional model of the 20th-century pensioner free of ongoing worries about assets and income and one that the Financial Conduct Authority (FCA) warned in 2018, may leave many floundering unless the banking and financial sectors take rigorous measures to protect older people and safeguard their savings. Technology may well could come to the rescue with some sort of Personalised Pension's Dashboard and the 2019 government's proposals for a new *collective defined* pension contribution scheme and new stronger powers for the Pension Regulator, making wilful or reckless mismanagement of a pension scheme a potentially criminal offence, may well help. Proposed changes to the British tax relief system may similarly help lower earners but none of these changes, even if they are implemented provide the framework for the fundamental overhaul of the UK tax system, many believe is so desperately needed. Meanwhile, the economic aftermath and likely cost of COVID may well see even these modest reforms shelved – yet again.

Pensions, however, are not an item on their own. As Charles explained, pensions today, given their size and impact, are a core element of any nation's economic planning and welfare state. They are a major income stream within the emerging Silver Economy and the prime driver of many of the new silver markets outlined earlier. They, therefore, desperately need some truly radical rethinking and more innovatory ideas if they are not to drag the global economy down. With the shift from austerity after the 2008 crash to levels of state investment and spending not seen since World War II to combat COVID-19, ideas such as a universal basic income (UBI) have again risen to the fore as solutions for post pandemic Britain (ILC-UK: 2020), and the notion of a collective defined pension scheme advocated by the RSA was incorporated into the Oct. 2019 Queen's Speech. The New Economics Foundation (NEF) proposal in 2019 to scrap the current personal tax allowance altogether in favour of a "weekly national allowance" of £48 pw/£2500 p.a. as a way of helping low income families is clearly a much more radical solution to addressing the current inequities within the UK's tax system while the Musgrave Formula of proportionate shares, of a ratio of the per capita earnings of the working population to the per capita benefits (net of taxes) of retirees at a fixed point in time, remains popular among many economists as a potential means to measuring intergenerational equity. Staggered retirement ages and entitlements with the better-off retiring later may be another solution while greater investment by government in childcare and "head start" education would undoubtedly benefit all generations; releasing more women into the workplace to boost the economy and tax system and giving all children a better start in life so possibly reducing future intragenerational inequalities, including those in later life. As the OECD commented back in 2014, pension planning on its own and in isolation is no longer sustainable. "Ageing societies will need much more policy action than just pension reform, and much more strategic thinking: what should our societies of the future look like? How will we deal with the old-age challenge? What will be the fiscal impact of ageing and what will this mean for social protection systems and the sharing of responsibilities between the individual and the state, between public and private providers? And how can we maintain solidarity in a context of rising inequalities between and within generations"? So, pensions and later life financial planning are not challenges just for retirees and baby boomers in their 50s and 60s. They are challenges for all ages, all generations in an age and at a stage when retirement at 70 is likely to be the "new norm". As Scottish Widows warned in 2019, whilst the young are saving substantially more than before due to auto-enrolment, 60% of those under age 30 are still not saving enough for a comfortable retirement and 14% of 22–29-year-olds are not saving anything at all. What is needed is not just an increase in auto-enrolment contributions to say 15% as a minimum by 2030 but the creation of a whole-life savings product not just to support old-age but all the financial challenges in-between, be they education & training, a deposit a new home or savings for a personal health crisis. And as Tom McPhail of Hargreaves Lansdown warned back in 2013 (Telegraph in June 2013), "For a whole generation in their forties and fifties now, it is probably already too late. They are going to have to work to 70 or beyond before they can retire. For people in their twenties and thirties, there is still time to make a significant difference, but only if they can be persuaded to engage with their retirement savings".

Certainly, when Laura started researching pensions, she never imagined that her reading would take her into the worlds of national and global economic planning nor into the whole new world of the *Silver Economy*. She never realised that pensions constitute such a huge financial sector on their own nor that they sit right in the centre of any national plan for an Ageing Society. The global pensions "time-bomb" many commentators regularly refer to is not only about the sheer size of this financial challenge ahead and the economic fallout that it will create if Government gets its sums wrong, but it is also equally about the pensions industry's failure to reform and innovate, failure to transform its public image, regain public trust and create high quality, value-for-money pension products that people can rely on in their old age and feel safe with. It is equally a *personal time-bomb* if people – young and old – fail to plan and save ahead and recognise that in future neither the State nor the Employer is going to bail them out in later life. Alongside healthcare, pensions are the financial "elephant in the ageing room" waiting to wreak untold havoc across every household in the land. Radical and innovative thinking is desperately needed along the lines of the MMI principles and the practices of countries such as Holland, if pensions in the UK are to be affordable, fair and sustainable and a positive contribution to the UK economy rather than become an economic liability – and worse a source of age-anger over who pays. And all this before the full impact of COVID-19 takes effect particularly on the young, low paid, unemployed or those in the gig economy on casual contracts with little or no-inbuilt protection "Many Britons are still risking a retirement in poverty with two in five failing to save adequately and 15% not saving at all" concluded the Scottish Widows Survey in 2020. However, as Charles explained, there is a potential "silver lining" for any young person willing to start saving now. By investing 12.5% of their income in their 20s, a young person today could become a pension millionaire by the time that they retire – and still have 20 to 30 years of life left to enjoy it. From this perspective, pensions suddenly look sexy rather than sad; an investment rather than a liability; a bragging post on social media rather than a sad citation on your CV.

4.4 THE HEALTHCARE CHALLENGE AND ELDERCARE IN LATER LIFE

Coronavirus has brought healthcare and healthy living to the forefront of every agenda, every headline, every conversation across the world, not only as a sinister and silent global disease that anyone could catch but also as one that preys especially on the old, the deprived and those with underlying ill-health conditions. It has been the pandemic of old-age, ill-health and inequality, and it has spread like wildfire with a speed only the most swift and decisive governments have been able to stem or control. It has been a generational disease hitting the health of the oldest hardest and disrupting or destroying the livelihoods and the futures of the youngest in ways as yet unknown for years to come. So, it is a supreme irony that it has taken a global pandemic to put healthy living and robust public health services back to the forefront of modern life and alert all authorities to the need for hugely heightened public awareness about health and safety in every walk of life; and all families about the virtues of healthy living and the dangers of poor diet, obesity and lack of exercise. What a perverse position for humankind to be in; what a reverse position for the age of longer living so many were predicting before; what a generational reminder that even in this age of virtual living, the "dice of life" lurks ever near to bring us crashing back to reality and back to what really matters when our loved ones are under threat.

Despite being a fitness fanatic and something of a food freak, even Laura hadn't felt safe from the pandemic after suffering asthma as a child badly enough to disrupt much of her early secondary schooling and so seriously undermine her teenage self-confidence and academic performance. Worse, she now knew how quickly COVID-19 could kill – ten short days in the case of her uncle Alfred living alone in Knowsley. So, she was especially fearful for the safety of her beloved grandparents, both now in their late 60s and both key workers; and if Laura, ever needed any motivation for researching the sociology and political economy of healthcare in the 21st century, she only had to imagine her great nan Christina imprisoned in a care home under coronavirus and the agony that would have caused. COVID-19 has destroyed or damaged millions of lives across the world, pushed hospitals and emergency systems to the brink of breakdown, tested governments capacity for clear and decisive leadership to the limit-and found many wanting as it left economic and social chaos in its wake. Laura now fully understood that the healthcare challenge for the UK was as much a challenge for her age group as it was for pensioners. She now fully appreciated that even if the government managed to vaccinate the whole world, life would not return to normal anytime soon. There might instead be a new normal – or none at all. As Laura's tutor, Jonathan, pointed out, we are possibly entering a new age of healthcare, a new global era of bioscience and potentially a new zest in living longer, living well with those claiming that they had the key to everlasting life, being ever more enthused. This was not the Sociology of Health that Laura had studied at A-level. This was not the Sociology of Sickness that in the 20th century had focused attention and resources on simply treating ill health and disease. This was the sociology of healthy living and healthy ageing; of promoting good health and preventing bad health not just in western or wealthier societies but also across a global world where today *no one is safe until everyone is safe*; a new sociological paradigm that without global healthcare, there is no global economy nor any normal life.

The global challenge

So, healthcare is at the heart of the Ageing Challenge. As Dr Margaret Chan, Director-General of the World Health Organization (WHO) explained back in 2012: "Good health must lie at the core of any successful response to ageing. If we can ensure that people are living healthier as well as longer lives, the opportunities will be greater and the costs to society less. This great demographic challenge of the first half of the 21st century therefore demands a public health response, and WHO has identified this as a priority for the organisation".

As outlined in Chapter 1, the upside of the ageing revolution is that people across the globe are living longer, much longer. By 2050, the WHO predicts that there will be over 2 billion people alive of age 60 and over; 22% of the world's population and twice the world's *total* population in 1900. On the "downside", the question is who is going to care for all these older people and at what cost as the world's dependency ratio soars and all countries face a healthcare funding crisis of potentially catastrophic proportions. The real paradigm shift, though, is that whilst the global diseases of the past were driven by nature and natural ageing, the global diseases of today and the future are increasingly driven by human lifestyle and the environment. The sources of coronavirus have yet to be officially identified, but it is not the only pandemic facing humankind. Obesity, for example, has now been identified by McKinsey Global Institute (2015) as one of the "top three social burdens" with more than 2.1 billion people – nearly 30% of the global population – overweight or obese with an economic impact of $2 trillion annually or 2.8% of global GDP while dementia was declared by the WEF in 2017 to be "One of the biggest global health crises of the 21st century" affecting some 50 million people worldwide, rising to 150 million by 2050 and costing some 2 trillion dollars by 2030 with women particularly at risk: a sea of ill-health that, in turn, is leaving humankind extremely vulnerable to the next global pandemic.

The Global Response to the healthcare challenge as well as to COVID-19 has largely been led by the World Health Organization (WHO). It has sought to tackle the challenge of global healthcare on two fronts. Firstly, the prevention and eradication of pandemic diseases to combat the spread and impact of "natural" diseases as in the case of small pox or typhoid. And secondly, by promoting active and healthy living for all ages, not just the old. This holistic and *person-centred* strategy was the paradigm shift adopted by the WHO at the Alma Ata Conference back in 1977. It is based on a radical and much broader definition of good health as "a state of complete physical, mental and social well-being, and not merely the absence of disease or infirmity". This **life–course** approach to active ageing is based on four key elements:

> **Promoting** good health and healthy behaviours at all ages to prevent or delay the development of chronic disease; starting in early life and continuing into older age.
>
> **Minimising** the consequences of chronic disease through early detection and quality care (primary, long-term and palliative); including dying with dignity.
>
> **Creating** physical and social environments that foster the health and participation of older people; notably environments that are age-friendly.
>
> **Re-inventing ageing** by changing social attitudes to encourage the participation of older people; moving from attitudes created during the 20th century, when there were far fewer older people, to developing "new models of ageing that will help us create the future society in which we want to live".

This *life-course* approach recognises that ill health in old age is often the result of poor nutrition or unhealthy living earlier in life and appreciates that psychological well-being is as important to good health as the absence of disease or disability. These were quite radical and ground-breaking "step-changes" in thinking and health strategy at this time. They took the ideal of good health out of its narrow medical and biological model and placed it firmly and squarely in the broader political and socio-economic environment of wealth and poverty. It emphasised also the importance of mental and psychological health as much as biological health in promoting personal and community well-being. Moreover – and possibly more crucially – it embraced the ideal of *good health as a human right* and as such part of the UN/WHO broader vision of social justice. The 2002 Madrid International Plan of Action on Ageing (MIPAA) reinforced and strengthened this strategy and equally put responsibility for good health and well-being as much in the hands of the individual and the family as in the hands of doctors or the state. Good health and the compression of morbidity are now as much "in our hands" as in the doctors and, as Daniels et al. explained in 2002, it now requires life-time management: "By the time a sixty year old heart attack victim arrives at the emergency room, bodily insults have accumulated over a lifetime, such that for this person, medical care is, figuratively speaking, the 'ambulance waiting at the bottom of a cliff'".

The 2015 WHO Report on Ageing and Health took this strategy to another level by firstly introducing the concept of the **age friendliness** within the surrounding environment and by promoting the ideal of the *Age-Friendly City.* Secondly, by attacking **age discrimination**, highlighting its insidious and widespread nature and its profound impact on the elderly and on society at large; and thirdly, by declaring active ageing to be a human right. By drawing up a **charter for the rights of the older person**, the WHO declared that the rights of the old in the 21st century were now as important as the rights and welfare of the young had been in the 20th. Most importantly, this declaration sought to promote active ageing as an economic blessing rather than an economic threat, highlighting the economic benefits of older workers, their actual and potential contribution to the national economy and their importance to sustainable future development.

By definition, this active ageing health strategy also highlighted the correlation between health and wealth. It contrasted the health and longevity of the wealthier, developed nations with the poverty and ill-health endured in the developing world; a contrast poignantly illustrated by Professor Sarah Harper in 2006: "While a baby girl born in Japan today can expect to live about 85 years, a girl born at the same moment in Sierra Leone has a life expectancy of 36 years. The Japanese girl will receive vaccinations, adequate nutrition and good schooling" and "high quality maternity care" while "the girl in Sierra Leone has little chance of receiving immunization and a high probability of being underweight throughout childhood. She will probably marry in adolescence and go on to give birth to six or more children without the assistance of a trained birth attendant. One or more of her babies will die in infancy, and she herself will be at high risk of death in childbirth". Medical treatment throughout the rest of her short life will be limited and "she will die prematurely".

Healthcare is, therefore, now very much part of *wealth-care* and as much an international issue as a national one. The WHO "Decade of Health Ageing" report (2019), therefore, set out to align this health strategy with the UN's 17 Sustainable Development Goals (SDGs) for economic prosperity. It set out the "transformational pathways" and action framework that the WHO believes is necessary for combatting Ageism, developing age-friendly cities and communities, designing person-centred integrated care for older people, developing long-term care systems, developing communication platforms and global partnerships for promoting the voice of older people, connecting stakeholders, fostering research and measuring accountability. As the WHO's follow-up document "Implementing a Health 2020 Vision" emphasised, this is not a strategic objective simply for national healthcare departments. It is a whole of government, whole of society imperative that requires wholesale government commitment and the utmost political will, engaging all departments and all people in a coordinated drive towards healthy ageing over the next ten years. Recent lapses in the rate of healthy ageing in countries such as the UK and EU and the ongoing threat to world health and the global economy of pandemics such as SARS, MERS and most recently COVID-19 have not only reinforced the WHO's message but hopefully also converted it into a global mission; a mission that not only involves the health and longevity of older people but that of the whole population throughout their life-course-a generational legacy for any ageing person to be proud of.

This world health-wealth debate has also brought into sharp focus the interrelationship between the financial decisions of such international institutions as the World Bank and the IMF and their impact on national health; an impact starkly illustrated by the austerity drives that followed the 2008 economic crisis when health budgets across the western world were slashed and ill-health and social depression escalated, particularly in countries experiencing the worst of the downturn, such as Greece and Spain. Healthcare today is therefore is as much about wealth-care as it is about good health; as much about the distribution of global wealth as it is about the distribution of global health; as much about the actions of international stock exchanges, the marketing of the food, drugs and drinks industries as it is about people's diets and lifestyles. The WHO's torchlight on the economic dimensions of healthcare has, therefore, highlighted the responsibility of the richer nations for the healthcare and economic development of the poorer ones; not just in preventing global pandemics and the spread of disease but equally in promoting the global economy and with it, global security. The global economy is now so integrated that, as COVID-19 has amply illustrated, ill health in one part of the world can threaten not only the health of nations across the globe but also their economic well-being too. It is somewhat ironic, therefore, that the developing nations of South East Asia seem to have learnt the lessons of past global pandemics far better than their apparently more developed western counterparts.

The national challenge

In stark contrast to the radical ideas above, while the UK's National Health Service has struggled heroically to cope with the coronavirus pandemic, it has been close to collapsing and its underlying weaknesses and severe underfunding have been openly exposed. Its current model of operation is recognised as no longer fit for purpose and even before the COVID-19 pandemic, the BMJ study in Nov. 2019 found that compared to other leading OECD countries in 2017, the UK had a one of the lowest healthcare spends per person and the fewest doctors, nurses and hospital beds per 1000 population with some survival rates from cancer amongst the lowest in Europe, utilisation lower than average and quality slipping as a result of "constrained funding". According to the IFS report in Nov. 2019, at that time we spent around £156 billion on healthcare in the UK, equivalent to 7.2% of national income. At nearly 18% of all government spending in 2018/19, healthcare was by far the largest single item of government expenditure. Yet, compared to healthcare spending in other developed nations, the UK healthcare system was dramatically underfunded after nine years of austerity and annual increases of barely 1.3%. Just prior to the coronavirus outbreak, England alone apparently needed an extra 64,000 hospital doctors and 171,000 extra nurses whilst social care was projected to need 500,000 more staff by 2033/34 just to cope with the UK's ageing population. Against this level of underfunding and understaffing, it is not surprising that the NHS was underprepared and under such strain from COVID-19 and that the UK has one of the highest COVID-related death rates in the world.

The "healthcare challenge" in the UK, however, is not just a financial one. It is equally a social and a political one; as much about the distribution of health as the distribution of wealth. Health inequalities in the UK tend to follow wealth inequalities; where and how you live in the UK tends to have a dramatic effect on the quality of your healthcare as well as on your life and the length of it. As was starkly illustrated in Chapter 3, Britain is a highly unequal and highly divided society with significant "health gaps" between the North and the South and between Scotland and Northern Ireland compared to England and Wales; gaps that COVID has not only exposed but amplified. In its 2014 Report on Inequality in Healthy Life Expectancy, for example, the ONS calculated that: "Males in the most advantaged areas can expect to live **19.3 years** longer in 'Good' health than those in the least advantaged areas as measured by the slope index of inequality. For females this (difference) is **20.1 years**". These figures are astonishing, if not scandalous, in a country as wealthy and apparently caring as Great Britain. A 20-year difference in healthy life expectancy between the richest and the poorest in British society is something of a moral as well as a social indictment of the basic principles of the welfare state. It represents a massive waste of human life, a profound class-divide and it should provoke "political outrage"; but it doesn't. It barely raises a media headline or a question in Parliament;

possibly because personal and class lifestyles seem to play such a significant part in ill health today, with smoking still a key cause of cancer and obesity earning the UK the reputation of being "the fat man of Europe".

So, clearly a radical new approach and a new culture of care has long been needed to restore the UK healthcare system to the world-class standards that it aspires. Back in 2014, the Barker Report declared that "the 1948 settlement for health and social is no longer fit for purpose" and the subsequent Health and Social Care Act in 2014 went some way towards the Commission's plea for integrating health and social care and for devolving responsibility for the delivery of public health from the NHS down to Local Health and Wellbeing Boards; boards that carry out Joint Strategic Needs Assessments (JSNA) and set up Clinical Commissioning Groups (CCGs), made up of GPs from local general practices, to commission the health services required in each locality. This strategic shift in power and responsibility for healthcare from central to local government is based on the premise that local authorities know their local populations and health needs best and so will be better able to target resources efficiently and effectively, will be more responsive to changes in need and more willing and able to innovate. However, although this shift in responsibilities was a step in the right direction, it was effectively an incremental change rather than the radical shift that the Barker Commission had called for; while the austerity cuts of that era, alongside the lengthy Brexit debate, left the NHS and social care severely weakened with little capacity for innovation and reform. The 2019 Queen's speech promised a multi-year funding settlement involving a £33.9 billion increase in cash by 2023/24, the merger of NHS England and NHS Improvement into a single leadership body, a commitment to reform mental health provision in England and Wales and a promise to "fix" social care. The declared ambition was to accelerate the NHS Long-Term Plan, provide a fully integrated and coordinated healthcare service, strengthen its prevention services and reduce health inequalities, improve care quality, improve outcomes and provide a more personalised and differentiated healthcare service. In particular, there was a recognition that a life-course approach to healthy ageing is not only the key to any modern health service but the key to a productive economy and a healthy workforce. The UK healthcare system was now to be linked to the UK Industrial strategy and the Centre for Ageing Better was charged with instigating a £98 million competitive healthy ageing challenge framework to attract businesses and social enterprises keen to innovate in the ageing market and develop new initiatives in such fields as sustainable physical activity, creating healthy workplaces and designing age-friendly homes.

Great promises, but then came the 2020 coronavirus pandemic which ruthlessly exposed how overstretched the UK's health service already was and how underprepared the UK's NHS was for such an unprecedented health epidemic. The UK's initial response and pandemic strategy was criticised as inept, ill-coordinated and under-responsive with care homes left exposed and under-protected and Britain's COVID-19 death rates the worst in Europe and amongst the worst in the world. And all this amid the threat of a second and third wave as new variants from South Africa, Brazil, the UK and now India mutated and spread with devastating speed and impact. On the other side of this tragedy, COVID-19 has forced innovation to the forefront of healthcare today, stimulated the miracle of new vaccines in record time and brought the need for drastic and dramatic reform to the head of all political agendas. The Deloitte Centre for Healthy Solutions (Nov. 2020), for example, believes that Covid-19 might accelerate the future of health "by at least ten years" by dramatically raising public awareness about healthy living, encouraging much healthier behaviours, exposing systemic weaknesses in public health systems that have to be urgently addressed and high-lighting the crucial relationship between ill-health and an unhealthy economy "We believe that the pandemic has been a watershed moment in creating the social and political will to raise the profile and priority given to public health".

The Health Foundation Briefing in Nov. 2020, in turn, advocated three key principles for strengthening the UK's public health system:

- Strengthening its strategy for levelling up health, enabling everyone to live five more years in good health and closing the gap between the richest and poorest communities.
- Strengthening its structures for delivering and integrating health and social care including the creation of an independent body (like the OBR) to report independently on the state of the nation's health alongside a national lead to oversee it and stronger regional and local health systems to deliver it.
- Strengthening its resources and long term investment so that "England could emerge from the pandemic with a system that is better at keeping people healthy and reducing health inequalities".

As the Kings Fund reported in Nov. 2020, government spending on COVID-19 was "truly eye-watering" with over £50 billion spent in 2020/21 on COVID-related care alone within a total Dept. of Health & Social Care spend for 2020/21 of "a colossal £201.7 billion" If government could spend such sums during a crisis, wouldn't it have been far better to have invested such sums beforehand as other nations did in say "track and trace" systems with far lower consequences to public health and the national economy. The contrast in death toll and economic loss with most other nations including the poorest and weakest is profound. If countries as diverse as Australia, South Korea, Cambodia and Venezuela as well as most of Scandinavia can keep their total CV-19 death toll to-date well below 10,000, then why can't a country as rich as the UK; a country with a Covid-related death rate of over 135,000 people as of September 21st 2021?

Social care

And if COVID-19 has shown the NHS to be in crisis, it has shown the social care sector in England to be approaching meltdown, if not total collapse. "Older people in care homes were abandoned to die amid government failures during the Covid-19 pandemic" claimed the 2020 NAO Parliamentary report; failures that included a lack of PPE or COVID-testing and the decision "to discharge thousands of untested hospital patients into care homes and the imposition of blanket DNARs resulting in over 28,000 excess deaths between March 2nd and June 12th 2020. As the Care Quality Commission report for 2019/2020 concluded, "The Social care's longstanding need for reform, investment and workforce planning has been thrown into sharp relief by the pandemic…and needs to be tackled now-not at some point in the future".

The Health Foundation Report in Aug. 2019 summed up the challenges currently facing the UK's Social Care service as follows:

- The cost of social care in England in 2017/18 was £18 billion, £22.7 billion for the whole of the UK or 1.1% of GDP. Compare that to the £153 billion or 7.1% allocated to health spending overall. Simply stabilising and improving the current social care system would cost an estimated additional £12.5 billion by 2023/24.
- Social care funding is only available currently to "those with the highest needs and lowest means". A total of 400,000 older people on lower incomes did not receive publically funded care as a result of cuts in funding between 2009/10 and 2015/16. The ASC funding per person in England at that time was £346, well below Scotland (£446) and Wales (£424). Similarly, the amount local authorities are able to pay towards somebody's care in care homes has increasingly been less than it costs to provide it. Small wonder that so many social care providers are handing back their contracts or going bankrupt.
- Social care faces a staffing crisis with 110,000 staff vacancies currently – 1 in 10 social workers, 1 in 11 care workers and with staff turnover exceptionally high, yet demand is growing at about 3.6% per year requiring an additional £2.7 billion by 2023/24.
- Comprehensive social care insurance is impossible unless government intervenes and pools risk. A universal and comprehensive social care system in England alone would cost between £6 billion and £11 billion, a Scottish-style system covering free personal care would cost £4.4 billion rising to £5 billion by 2023/4.

As the report concluded, "if it chooses, the government can afford to provide more generous care, support and security for vulnerable people in society. If it doesn't, it will be choosing to prolong one of the biggest public policy and political failures of our generation".

The State in the UK provides very little care directly. Rather, it commissions or purchases care at home or in residential homes from private and third-sector organisations but at such low prices that the care market is in a constant state of "churn" and increasingly dysfunctional. The number of care homes going out of business is increasing annually with all the disruption that entails to residents, clients, families and councils themselves while low pay, inadequate training and limited professional opportunities are generating a social care workforce turnover that was estimated at 30.7% in 2017/18 and that now, with Brexit and COVID, is inevitably escalating even further. According to the Care Quality Commission (CQC) in 2016, the sustainability of the adult care market is approaching a "tipping point" and with care home costs for self-funders now nearly £44,000 a year, soon only the wealthiest pensioners will be able to afford such provision. As the government's own Care Homes Market Report (Nov. 2017) has identified, local authorities will need "an extra £1 to £2 billion a year funding by 2025" just to cope and a dramatic improvement in their planning and commissioning strategies to build the supply of care homes up to the level needed. And if the strain on care staff is immense, the strain on informal care and families is probably approaching breaking point. The ONS (2019) estimated that nearly three in five carers in England and Wales are aged 50 years and over and that 20% of those aged 50–69 are informal carers; an informal adult care service that the ONS valued at £59.5 billion in 2016. One in four older female workers and one in eight older male workers apparently have caring responsibilities mainly for their own elderly parents and usually alongside part-time employment and possibly, childcare duties. Truly an intense and quite stressful "juggling act". The Chief Executive of Care England in 2017 described the current social care system as a "house of cards" ready to topple over at any moment and the National Audit Office in 2018 described it as the Cinderella service, the "ugly sister" to the beauty queen that is the NHS.

At the heart of the Social Care Crisis in the UK is the fault-line in the structure and philosophy of the NHS. When the British National Healthcare Service was conceived, it was based on two separate and distinct systems of cost and need. Whilst the NHS is available free according to need, paid for out of the public purse, social care is not free. It has to be paid for by the individual and therefore is subject to means-testing and depends on people's level of income. The costs involved in long-term residential care are immense; currently some £40,000 a year and rising, depending on where you live. There have been 12 green and white papers alongside five independent commissions since 1998 attempting to review and rethink the funding of social care ranging from the Dilnot Commission recommendation in 2011 that the personal cost be capped at £75,000, through to Theresa Mays proposal in the 2017 General Election campaign that a ceiling be set at £100,000 including the value of the pensioner's property; a proposal that nearly cost her the election and substantially reduced her majority. *Who Pays for Long-term Care (LTC)* therefore remains a major political and social dilemma for any ageing society. Few people seem aware of the immense costs involved, fewer still are actively preparing to bear it and according to the 2017 report by the actuarial consultancy Hyman-Robertson, only 3% of baby boomers and generation X expect to go into residential care in old age, over half of baby boomers (54%) and nearly half of generation X (43%) are adamant that they will never save for long-term care and both generations sadly and badly under-estimate the costs involved. What few families seem to have realised, though, is that this care nightmare will fall on them if the State cannot provide and here lies one of the most profound and disturbing of intergenerational debates at a time when it is not yet even a national conversation. The need for government leadership in raising public awareness and in encouraging the insurance market to create cost-effective packages for this eventuality is obvious, but as Theresa May found in 2017, social care is a potential minefield for any politician.

Proposed solutions to the UK Care Dilemma have been numerous and quite radical:

- Many, such as the Centre for Policy Studies (2019) and the Policy Exchange (2019) Report have recommended that, like the NHS, complex long-term social care in England should be available on the basis of need and largely free at the point of delivery, funded through public taxation. In addition, the Policy Exchange report recommended that the present income and capital means test for complex social care should be abolished and replaced with a means-tested co-payment system of the order of £5000 per person per year starting at approximately £27,000 and excluding any additional private payments for extra services. This would, in its view, be both a fairer system and convert care residents from being simply recipients of care to becoming consumers of care with the personal budgets to demand choice and quality. It also recommended far greater investment in the potential of new technology, notably AI and robotics in improving the delivery and quality of care as in Japan and Norway alongside the development of a "My Social Care" app to inform and support patients and families access to information about care options. The 2019 House of Lords Economic Affairs Committee Report similarly recommended that social care should be funded largely from general taxation and specifically highlighted the "post-code lottery" by which social care is available in some areas but not others; a lottery that according to the Which magazine in March 2021 can vary by almost £16,000 a year in the UK depending on where you live and how supportive your local authority is.
- The All-Party Parliamentary Committee Group on Social Care in 2019 recommended the establishment of a new national care body with equal status and affiliation with the NHS to professionalise social care and develop an appropriate training, qualification, pay and employment conditions and career framework to offset current low pay, low status image of caring as a profession and so address the current staffing crisis in recruitment and retention of quality and qualified staff.
- Finally, the 2018 Grant Thornton Report on the UK's Care Home Market highlighted the chaotic and unfair nature of a sector where the ten largest for-profit providers represent about a quarter of the market, a further 38% are small to medium organisations and the rest comprises operators owning one or two homes providing either nursing (4,053) or residential care (7,103).

Worse, whilst just under half of care home residents (47.5%) have their fees fully or partially paid by local authorities, these fees are on average 10% less than the true cost of care leaving self-funders not only paying the full cost of their own care but also inadvertently subsidising non-payers. Worse still, at the very time that demand for care home places threatens to accelerate as the age 85 plus population is projected to increase by some 62.6% or 1 million over the next 13 years, long-term care accommodation has declined by some 4.4% between 2001 and 2016 as a result of the underfunding above. A supply and demand crisis in social care is fast emerging and can only get worse; much worse unless solutions such as more differentiated offer of services, more varied room types within a home and new types of accommodation for both rent and sale are developed as in Australia and New Zealand.

At the start of his administration, Boris Johnson promised "to fix the crisis in social care once and for all, giving every older person the dignity and security they deserve". Unfortunately, alongside Brexit, the 2020/21 coronavirus crisis has intervened, swept all the 2019 election promises off the political table and relentlessly exposed not only how underprepared the UK's NHS was for such an unprecedented global invasion but also how unprotected its care homes are. It has left a trail already of well over 160, 000, mainly older people, dead and the worst COVID-related death rate in Europe. While virtually all care home residents have now been vaccinated against coronavirus, the UK's social care crisis remains a national scandal that is only now beginning to be addressed.

   Long-term care (LTC), however, is a major challenge for all ageing countries and their responses vary enormously depending, according to the OECD (2017), on each nation's welfare philosophy and funding regime; a spectrum of social care provision that ranges from:

- The universal & tax-funded systems providing comprehensive LTC as in most Nordic nations.
- The dedicated social insurance schemes which provide comprehensive coverage such as those in the Netherlands and Japan or provide partial coverage of costs as Korea and Germany.
- The cash benefit systems as in Austria, Italy and the Czech Republic.
- And finally, the means-tested, safety net systems which fully protect the poor but leave the rest to fund themselves as in UK and USA.

Whilst many European countries such as the Netherlands and Germany offer models of good practice, the Japanese LTC system, according to the WEF (June 2018) stands out as "one of the most comprehensive social care systems in the world". Its Long-term care insurance scheme was introduced in 2000 as a radical shift from the traditional family care system. It established a mandatory, public and universal system separate from its health insurance system covering both home and institutional care and 50% funded by general tax and 50% by mandatory LTC insurance premiums paid from age 40 onwards based on income with a means-tested co-payment of up to 10% of care costs capped at £75 per month for low earners. Income levels and informal care/family support is not taken into consideration and there are no cash benefits. It is based on the principles of equality and fairness and it is a "needs-based system providing care to all regardless of wealth or income" with residential care home places capped at 3% of the over-65 population. One of its key features is the role and position of a care manager, usually with a case-load of some 30 clients, to assess and advise on need based on 74 criteria and to help arrange provision for public, not-for-profit and private organisations that are generally small and embedded in the local community. This LTC scheme is popular, well-respected and widely used with little stigma attached to it. It has resulted in a very active, competitive market mixing not-for-profit and profit-making providers with light regulation designed to ensure minimum standards rather than quality improvement. Japan's *Healthy Japan 21* policy seeks to encourage healthy ageing while mobilising new technology to support the elderly at home and in institutions as family support especially amongst the young withers. Equally, as Japan's ageing population over 65 grows from 23% in 2010 towards 40% by 2050, the government has had to raise premiums and reduce entitlements and provision whilst increasing specialist support as the 85 plus age group swells in numbers and need. Private LTC is available but expensive.

The Nuffield Trust Study report in May 2018 concluded that whilst "the (social care) system as it is currently configured (in the UK) is unfit for purpose, inequitable and unsustainable, the Japanese system appears to be a model of clarity and simplicity" due to its needs-based principles, a breadth of provision that includes the promotion of wellness and active life as well as good quality care and the central and critical role of the Care Manager in leading families through and in providing personalised and ongoing support. All this, conclude the report authors, offers a "whole-system approach" and a clear vision of care in an ageing society, a strong preventative strategy and in-built mechanisms for estimating and adapting to future demand. The focus on prevention and on building communities of support to offset isolation and to engage and activate older people came through strongly while carers, both formal and informal, paid and voluntary, are considered by the Japanese a critical part of this network and in providing meaningful and engaging activities. The weakest point in the Japanese system seems to be its staffing strategy particularly given Japan's cultural reluctance to import foreigners, though in typical Japanese style, solutions are being developed here too. All this contrasts starkly with the fragmented and often dysfunctional system currently operating across the UK.

Ironically, the shake-up in social care that the UK desperately needs may not come from politicians fearful of the complexity of its challenge and the electoral legacy any reform may bring but from the Old themselves; the New Old baby boomers demanding far better quality and choice in later-life care – and prepared to pay for it. As the ILO/OECD report in 2019 highlighted, this whole market is changing dramatically as some 2.3 billion people worldwide flood onto the care market and both regenerate and rejuvenate one of the major growth sectors for future employment. With new technology and age-friendly robots working alongside human carers, the care home of the future is likely to be light years away from the traditional image today and companies such as Panasonic are already gearing up for this global market in care. However, as this report predicts, there is likely to be a global shortage of LTC workers of some 13.6 million notably in Asia and the Pacific and while today LTC work is overwhelmingly low paid, lowly qualified, part-time and female with limited training and career opportunities, countries across the world are going to have to offer better pay and more professional career prospects to attract the young at home or carers from abroad. The whole care sector is going to have to shake off its *Cinderella* image and become one of the professions of the future in an ageing world in which demand is likely to outstrip supply. Such a transformation will require government leadership and courage, social dialogue and political consensus as to the level and type of care available; who provides it – market or state – and who pays – taxpayer or consumer – and in what proportions in light of economic growth, social inequality and society's attitude towards the elderly. With populations across the world ageing fast and the old multiplying daily, then maybe the Old themselves as voters and as consumers might now have the final say.

The healthcare revolution

Healthcare and social care in the UK, however, are only examples of a healthcare revolution that is taking place across the world and that, ironically, COVID-19 has turbo-charged; a paradigm change summarised by the Economist 2012 report on "Megachange: The World in 2050", as a shift from:

- **A sickness service** designed essentially to provide treatment for ill health, to a health service that proactively offers prevention as well as cure, support in the "management of lifelong health as well as treatment for chronic disease".
- **A medical model** based on the directives of those in authority – the consultant, the doctor and the nurse – to one in which the patient has more of a voice, more power and control, more rights and can more effectively call the health authorities to account.
- **A state-run healthcare system** organised and controlled by government to one in which the consumer and market forces are increasing prominent, if not dominant.
- **A segregated healthcare system** that has separate health and social service; sectors separately organised and separately funded with distinctly different ways of working and differential status; to one that is a fully integrated service, supporting patients throughout their "medical journey" from consultation through to diagnosis, treatment and ultimately on to recovery.

- **A hospital-based model** of delivery through to one in which community care and home treatment are more prominent features as a way of both relieving cost and improving the patient experience and sense of control as active participants rather than passive victims of processes and procedures they barely comprehend.

Healthcare internationally is about to enter a new era and to be transformed in three critical ways, according to the Economist report:

Firstly, in the way that it is delivered through new technology as medical technology becomes simpler, more portable and easy to use "in the field" and at home, thus reducing the need for hospitals and expensive medical expertise and technology at the centre, increasing the capacity for home visits by paramedics and nurses and for home monitoring and self-diagnosis by enlightened patients. Telemedicine and e-therapy will enable doctors and specialists to counsel patients at home and enable patients to monitor and test themselves for minor ailments and even chronic disabilities under online supervision and support. Hospitals, currently the costliest form of medical treatment, will become hubs for community care – *the port of last resort* rather than the *first port of call* as so often at present. AI and machine-learning robots will enter hospital theatres and become resident companions in care homes. Wearable technology ,such as smartphones, will monitor individual health and 3D printers will provide specialist medical equipment and personalised patient limbs, tissues or organs whilst virtual or augmented reality will help with both medical training and complex body or brain surgery. Robotic nurses could be the future of hospital healthcare with doc-bots as the new generation of GPs in primary care, all controlled and integrated by AI within one fully integrated national health and care system not only treating illness and disease but predicting and preventing ill health and promoting good health across the community. As Deloitte (2020) has argued Connected Health seems to be the future, with technology-enabled care (TEC) integrating health technology, digital media and mobile devices in supporting patients as well as professional carers and healthcare workers in determining the best and most appropriate ways to prevent ill-health as well as to treat it.

Secondly, developments in genomics and biotechnology are already revolutionising our understanding of disease and our capacity to treat it effectively even to the point of literally being able now to transport drugs to specific target areas in the body, create artificial limbs or new organs and personalise drug treatments that match individual needs – "a pill for every ill delivered to your body part". McKinsey identified ten particularly promising healthcare innovations in July 2020 that might help reduce the burden of global disease by some 6% to 10% ranging from molecular technologies such as CRISPR in curing malaria to next-generation pharmaceuticals such as Senolytics to reduce or eliminate ageing cells and implantable microchips to mitigate chronic pain. "The pace of innovation may be breath-taking" but demand may escalate out of control – and out of funding – as the public increasingly expect the latest and smartest new innovation; a tension not only between supply and demand in healthcare systems already over-stretched and under-resourced but between those most in need – and those most able to pay. Whilst the coronavirus pandemic has shown just how fast the scientific community can move to treat disease when the political will and public funding is behind them, lurking on the global horizon are epidemics in existing diseases left untreated because of COVID-19 such as cancer and heart-disease; and in particular, the "elephant in every country's healthcare room" – dementia; a deadly disease that will soon swamp all ageing societies and devastate their older age groups just as ruthlessly as coronavirus. According to the Alzheimer's society, the UK alone has 850,000 people with dementia today, projected to rise to 1.6 million by 2040 at a cost by then of some £94 billion.

Thirdly, the healthcare industry is globalising like every other sector and in so doing, it is giving patients access to treatments and patient care right across the world. Global health is now big business – very big business. According to the 2019 Deloitte Outlook report, it is projected to be worth over $10 trillion by 2022, rising by over 5% a year as chronic diseases like diabetes increase from 415 million today to 642 million by 2040 and dementia doubles every 20 years from its 50 million today, with governments across the world struggling to contain both ever-rising demand for new wonder treatments and ever-rising costs. Large conglomerates are transforming traditional healthcare provision and the big tech companies are entering this market with ambitions to disrupt and transform it in the same way that they have businesses elsewhere. The hospital of the future is on the horizon – a SMART digital or augmented hospital offering highly individualised patient treatment and healthcare rather than, as today, a mass production system operating in a limited number of physical, centralised buildings. Multinational companies such as GlaxoSmithKline and AstraZeneca are integrating and expanding, and the healthcare workforce is going global with western nations recruiting some 70% of their doctors and nurses from developing countries; a *medical brain-drain* that may reverse back east in the near future, with huge consequences for the developed world. "Medical tourism" has become a boom industry as the rich – and even the not so rich – travel to South America, India or Asia for treatments unavailable or too costly at home. Outsourcing to call centres or hospital laboratories on faraway continents is now well-established. "The 21st century heralds the era of doctors and patients without borders. The internet, combined with advances in digital technology and affordable international travel, has severed the geographic links between healthcare providers and consumers, offering new options to receive and deliver healthcare services, information and products that were previously unavailable. The result is a burgeoning global health care system shaped by personal need, economic opportunity and technological innovation", European Observatory Report (2013) – but one that, as yet, lacks both regulation and political control.

Finally, as in every other sector and industry, the digital revolution in IT and in data management is having a profound and fundamental effect on the way that healthcare services are delivered, funded and managed. It opens up radical new approaches ranging from online diagnosis and prescription to the employment of drones and robots in delivering patient care. IT and data management is at the heart of the new NHS 10-Year plan and even the humblest and most personal technology – the ubiquitous smartphone – now has a critical role to play in tracking disease, targeting treatment and preventing its spread on one hand whilst nudging all of us into heathier life styles and more exercise on the other. Deloitte 2020 estimated the health technology sector alone to be worth $280.25 billion by 2021 as the tech giants move in with Apple's Gorilla diagnostic system, Google's API and Verily systems for lifestyle health monitoring, Amazon's acquisition of the US Pillpack pharmacy chain and insurance and Phillip's Connected Care Solutions for linking patient data with hospitals. Healthcare is big-big business and increasingly cross-national led by corporations such as the Singapore's Luye Medical Group and Malaysia's IHH Healthcare Berhad while improving employee healthcare has led corporations such as JP Morgan Chase and Anthem, the US insurance giant, to link up with providers such as Apple and Amazon respectively. Countries around the world are investing in digital-data systems from Australia's My Health Record to the UK's Digital Innovation Hubs all dramatically aiding personalised healthcare as well as raising immense questions regarding the recruitment and skill-set of future staff as well as the threats to patient privacy from cybercrime and identity theft.

Futurologists such as Michio Kaku (2012) have even gone on to predict that by 2070 gene therapy will be standard practice targeted initially against single mutations but gradually capable of tackling the multiple mutations that cause diabetes, Alzheimer's, Parkinson's and heart disease. The power of quantum computing promises to turn scientific investigation from a matter of years into a matter of moments. Molecular medicine and the Human Genome Project hold the promise of being able to reveal the very "secrets of life" and in this new era everyone will soon have access to his or her own genome profile, a sort of owner's manual to your body and your health with such predictions opening up the prospect of a longer life, of eternal youth and even of immortality. According to

Nobel Laureate, Richard Feynman; "By 2100, it might be possible to reverse the effects of aging by accelerating cell repair mechanisms to live well beyond that". If correct, then we are truly entering **the inner sanctum** of nature; and as the secrets of ageing are being unravelled at speed, so a new unified theory of ageing may emerge that will not only explain but also plot and treat any genetic or cellular errors in your DNA whilst nano cars or bodily drones use smart-bombs to destroy cancer cells, suffocate tumours or kill off viruses. Your body will become a biological "battlefield" and genomic medicine will become the "hottest" field in medical research and medical engineering; a new applied science for renovating and rebuilding the human body. The ethical issues involved will be immense – and, given past experience, they are likely to be swept away in the "gold rush" for eternal life; issues involving the ethics of "creating" designer children along with critical debates about cloning, brain transplants and cryonics and the freezing of human bodies for life "in the future" (a facility already provided by the *Alcor Life Extension Foundation* in Arizona, USA). The longevity and life science industries are expanding rapidly, new anti-ageing, companies such as Juvenescence, AgeX and Rejuvenate Bio are attracting millions in investment funding and even age-reversing treatments are increasingly everyday news as researchers such as David Sinclair explore the possibility of the 150-Year Life. Aubrey de Grey of Cambridge University has even been so bold as to declare that the first person to reach 1000 years old has already been born and that "a world free of age-related disease is (now) possible". So, the miracles of modern medicine are potentially leading us from the ageing societies of today towards the ageless societies, predicted by many radical researchers, for tomorrow; societies where age is no longer a social determinant of the main stages in life's journey and you can live as long as you want and be as young – or old – as you want; so long as you can pay for it. According to David Kekich of the Maximum Life Foundation, "We will be able to transform eighty-year-olds into twenty-something's visually and biologically", while, Ian Pearson, the futurologist, believes that by 2050 we will be able to upload our entire brain onto a flash drive saving our personalities forever. We appear to be moving from a debate about ageing and the *quantity* of life onto one about agelessness, the *quality* of life and mans' capacity to play God. Outside of such futuristic *fantasies,* about everlasting life and immortality, the reality of ever-increasing life is increasingly real. The Human Genome Project and its unravelling of our inner construct, DNA, is likely to generate a Genetic Revolution and accelerate human Longevity even further into the future and there are already scientists working on the creation of Cyberbodies – half human/half robot.

From healthcare to self-care

The healthcare revolution, however, is not only about new medical miracles but also about the liberation of the Individual from *passive* patient to *active* manager of his or her health, with the capability of self-diagnosis and self-treatment being counterbalanced by healthy living, by regulation and lifestyles that outlaw the ill health often promoted or induced by the food industry and the over medication prescribed by doctors and promoted by the drugs companies. Such a transformation in medical relationships and in consumer behaviour would represent a power shift away from the current monopoly power of the medical profession over health prescription and provision back to ordinary people and the local community with the patient taking on the role of consumer and so gaining far more control of their own health and the factors behind it as a result of their circumstances, lifestyle and psychological well-being as well as their genetic and biological make-up. Wellness has become a new self-care mantra as well as a global industry in its own right sitting alongside the exponential growth in personal fitness, mindfulness, healthier foods and veganism as self-health meets climate change and searches for deeper human happiness, spiritual as well as physical. The doctor today is no longer "God" nor are his words of wisdom accepted without question. Rather, the whole Western medical model of health and illness is under question as we in the affluent West – and increasingly the developing East – seem to be "killing ourselves" through our indulgent lifestyles, poor diet and lack of positive personal health planning.

And the baby boomer generation is the epitome of the ageing patient of the future given their dedication to active life and youthful living. This is the generation that will first benefit from the "break-through" discoveries above and the transformation in delivery promised by the new technologies. They are equally the most educated and (overall) most affluent post-war generation, the most demanding and the most ambitious, the most prepared to use their considerable powers in the political and commercial marketplace; and the least likely to be seduced or swayed by professional "techno-speak" or commercial promotions be it by the medical or care professions, the drugs or the food industries. However, as the Chief Medical Officer for England highlighted in her 2015/16 Report, the New Old, the baby boomer generation, themselves face particular healthcare challenges; challenges that include the likelihood that many older couples will now live into old age together rather than as widows or widowers as in the past and that while they may need later-life care themselves, they are equally likely to be caring for ageing parents on one side and dependent – or even adult – children on the other. They are also likely to be over-weight or even obese consuming unhealthy amounts of alcohol and many still smoking. Longevity maybe encouraging boomers to be more health-conscious than their predecessors, more physically and even sexually active as health plans, fitness centres and treatments for sexual dysfunction become more widespread. But lurking in the ageing background are the next epidemics and while dementia may now be recognised as possibly the biggest threat to family and community life in the future, less visible but just as damaging are the age-related "social diseases" of malnutrition (estimated at 1.3 million over 65s), mental health (estimated at 2 million people aged 65+ in England) and loneliness (estimated at 775,000 older people or 7% of the over 65s in the UK); social diseases that will overwhelm us very soon if the politicians fail to take a lead or generate the *Health Debate* that Britain so desperately needs.

This surge in patient power, this growth in self-care strategies, these populist challenges to the medical profession and to the food and drinks industries, however, all come with a wealth care warning that while they may well improve the health and welfare of the articulate middle-classes, will they do the same for the less well-off and, if not, will they exacerbate even further existing health inequalities of age and generation as well as social class and geography? As Richard Wilkinson and Kate Pickett so vividly illustrated in 2009, only a dramatic reduction in inequalities in wealth and income can seriously close the health gap in the UK; only a government committed to the NHS ideals of healthcare equality and prepared to institute radical changes in tax and financial controls as well as in healthcare spending can seriously impact on the current unequal and unhealthy distribution of healthcare expectancies and provision. The NHS remains the nation's "darling institution" and the recent coronavirus epidemic not only cemented this unique relationship but also brought to our TV screens the intense pressures hospital staff face daily and the dedication and devotion of their "Cinderella sisters" in care homes. The hope for health and especially social care in the future in the UK is that these profound and life-saving lessons are learned and built upon; the fear is that post-COVID-19 nothing changes until the next pandemic. As the King's Fund Report back in 2014 concluded, the true gift of longevity is the "**health legacy,** a 'win-win' situation for all generations: If we can get health and care systems and services right for our older population" – those with the most complex needs – then "we should get it right for other service users. The twin challenges of funding and demography demand no less".

So, for Laura, this voyage into the future was, on one hand, quite breathtaking and salutary and on the other, quite poignant and quite personal. This walk through the medical literature had opened up a whole new world; a bold and very brave new world, that on one hand had lifted her spirits as well as opened up her horizons about what a forward-looking healthcare strategy might look like and what it could do for her generation as well as the elderly; but on the other hand, it had highlighted real dangers for the weak, poor and the lonely and raised immense ethical and political dilemmas that were not readily apparent beneath all the magic and mystery of everlasting life and instant repair. Most especially, living through a global pandemic and losing her uncle had brought home how vulnerable we all are and how critical good health is for the individual as well as for society at large. Most especially, it brought home the lesson that living longer is not a "natural right" or an inevitability; it has to be earned. It is not a responsibility for government alone but one that literally rests in our own hands and on the diets and health styles that we all adopt. A Timely Warning for All of US – Young and Old – as COVID-19 has dramatically and ruthlessly exposed not just how vulnerable we are as a nation but how vulnerable we are as individuals.

4.5 THE HOUSING CHALLENGE AND THE INTERGENERATIONAL HOUSING CHAIN

Coronavirus has not only brought home to every household the importance of good health but also the importance of a good home. Lockdowns, working from home and home-learning have dramatically brought families together and stress-tested many to the limit. Lockdown in warm summer months was possibly bearable; lockdown in cold winter months has tested everyone and isolated the only and lonely to a degree rarely experienced before. It has equally turbo-charged home improvements, home hobbies and a daily scrutiny of home space in and out-of-doors as all ages seek to work, live and exercise side-by-side often in very confined spaces; and generated a frenzy of house-buying in early 2021 when stamp duty was temporarily released. Working at home has revolutionised working and learning practices and the use of new technology as most people during lockdown, apart from key workers, stopped commuting to work or travelling to school. As a university student, Laura had got caught up in this whirlpool of accommodation, going back to university in the first lockdown but then being locked-in before being sent home to study – and socialise – at a distance alongside parents also working from home. Lockdown has also stimulated intense discussions about the adequacy of housing in the UK and whether it is fit for purpose in an ageing world where the older generations are likely to be living alone and where the younger generations are desperate to leave home. Like most of her age group, Laura aspired to a place of her own; like most of *Generation Rent,* Laura saw buying your own home as the key to a better life in the future. She didn't want to be left behind, yet right now with student debt after her degree likely to be £40,000–50,000 and with house prices so high especially where she was studying in London, then buying her own home was a distant dream at best; a lost cause at worse. What a contrast, she reflected, with her parents and grandparents. How had they managed to buy their comfortable homes in Eastern England or live, like Uncle Donald, in both London and Marbella when prices in both were now in the millions at a time when she couldn't even save a deposit?

The housing challenges facing ageing Britain

Whilst pensions and healthcare have been at the forefront of the ageing debate, housing has tended to be the *Cinderella of the Silver Revolution*, relegated by public costs and lower priority to an afterthought. Yet, to pensioners in particular, home is the *centre of their universe*, "their castle and their keep" in the remaining years ahead and fundamental to their independence and sense of self-control. Moving home, moving into residential care is seen by many as the final rite of passage from independence to dependency and departure. The importance of housing therefore is often underestimated in debates about ageing and its value – symbolic as well as financial – to the individual is often overlooked in discussions about down-sizing, equity release and legacy-planning. As the housing charity Shelter highlighted in its 2019 Reports "Today, we live in a country that is feeling the effects of 40 years of failure in housing policy". But it is not only a failure to build enough new houses for the young but also a failure to provide a choice of housing for the retired, both those wishing to downsize ownership and those wishing to rent irrespective of their income; a severe and intergenerational indictment of both government planning and private provision just at the time that Britain's ageing population is about to surge.

> **Firstly,** there appears to be a massive shortage of housing for all ages. The shortage of housing for the young, first-time buyer is well known and well publicised; the shortage of housing for late-lifers is not. In 2016/17, for example, whilst only 184,000 new houses were apparently built, only 3% of new housing was granted planning permission specifically for elderly or sheltered housing. Add to this shortage is the fact that much of the older housing that does exist is inadequate and in need of substantial renovation. An estimated 8.4 million people in England live in an unaffordable, insecure or unsuitable home according to the 2019 National Housing Federation report while the July 2019 APPG report on rented housing for older people declared current provision to be "woefully inadequate" and much of it insecure and unfit for purpose. It estimated that more than 1 million low cost rented homes will be needed for the older age groups by the late 2040s. "We urgently need a national strategy for renting in later life".
>
> **Secondly,** whilst the size of the first-time market is relatively well-understood, the size and the wealth of the market for last-time buyers is seriously underestimated. The Savills Retirement Living Consultancy 2017 estimated that the over-65s own almost £1.7 trillion worth of property; older people today, aged 55 and above, constitute nearly a third of all households and according to the ONS, nearly two-thirds of the projected increase in the number of households from 2008 to 2033 will be headed by someone aged 65 or over. Whilst most older people are owner-occupiers and have already paid off their mortgages, many may soon wish or need to move. Either way, they are likely to create in their wake a perfect housing storm by either staying in houses beyond their needs so "blocking up" the housing chain or "downsizing" to smaller properties for rent or to buy, so intensifying pressure and raising prices on the very housing that younger people are aspiring to. Millions of older people are currently locked into their existing homes, desperate to get out with housing equity all round them estimated to be worth some £1.2 trillion in 2020. As the Smith Institute report in 2015 illustrated, the number of over-65 households is increasing by nearly 110,000 a year and the number of over-75 households by 66,000 a year, yet the supply of developers and builders for the older markets

remains remarkably small. Moreover, while many older homeowners are "asset rich", they are "income poor"; they have a valuable house but are now living on a small pension whilst their counterparts in more deprived regions of the UK, tend to rely on the rented sector, and so are likely to face rising rents as well as tenure insecurity. As the National Housing Federation concluded in 2017, "*there is a growing divide in housing wealth both across generations but crucially within generations*" and most of the increases in housing wealth in recent years "*have been captured by the top 20% owners of housing wealth, regardless of age*"

Thirdly, there is an even more urgent need for social housing not only for younger families but also for pensioners living primarily on state pensions and needing significant support with their health and mobility. Shelter estimated in 2019 that some 3 million new social homes alone are needed in the next 20 years, yet, as the 2015 Smith Institute Report concluded, Housing Associations are no better prepared for the Ageing Population than the private sector: "The scale of population change has massive implications for social landlords, especially as their current middle aged and elderly population are disproportionately vulnerable to poor health, economic insecurity and social isolation".

As the Ageing of the UK escalates, with one in three people projected to be over 55 by 2030 and with 7.3 million or more older households with only couples or single pensioners – usually female – living in them, ageing is increasingly generating **intergenerational tension.** Older couples "rattling around" in larger houses appear to be blocking the need of younger couples with growing families for larger accommodation to move up the Housing Ladder and in turn release smaller houses or flats for the next generation of first-time buyers; a tension that, according to the Intergenerational Foundation (2021) has dramatically increased during the coronavirus lockdown, creating "two housing nations" with the older generations well-housed, well-off and with space to work and self-isolate in, while the younger generations often live in cramped flats or shared homes with little or no outside space. Add to this generational log-jam the rise and size of the *baby boomer generation* as it hits retirement and explodes across the whole of the UK housing market, then inevitably this tension is likely to get worse and intergenerational inequality to widen. The baby boomer generation today is a wealthier and more dynamic generation than ever before with the resources and know-how to demand choice, quality and style that reflects their self-image and social status and eager, in many cases, to invest not only in new homes but also in second homes in the UK or abroad and even invest in buy-to-let schemes, potentially becoming landlords to their own children's generation. They are disrupting an already chaotic market place and in turn generating a whole new housing dynamic that is likely to wash right through the UK housing market and potentially turn it on its head as their size and wealth gradually redirects developers and government attention. Baby boomers are homeowners personified.

They grew up as homeowners and according to Savills, the estate agency, those aged 65 and over control 46% of housing wealth in Britain today. They created the post-war housing market; they now sit on top of the housing ladder that their children are trying to get on and they are now, once again, seeking to transform the housing market in their own image and according to their own style. They are still fit and energetic, looking for fun and adventure as well as fixtures and fittings. They are not going to downsize to some dreary bedsit, bungalow or "granny stacker". They expect and will demand elegance and style, Wi-Fi and new technology and spare rooms for themselves and their grandchildren. They are the "new boys and girls on the housing block"; they are a whole new, multifaceted generation of homeowners ranging from the *Homillionaires*, of London and the South-East whose property values have now soared to £1 million plus as a result of the explosion in house prices around the capital; the *Grandlords* who have gone into the buy-to-let market in a big way as an investment and to supplement their pensions through interest only mortgages and the *Smarties* (Senior Retirement Town Retirees), who are retiring to the smart market, cathedral or university towns of Winchester, Dorchester and Banbury in search of lively, suburban life in contrast to the traditional sleepy coastal retreats favoured by their parents.

Intergenerational inequality and potentially intergenerational conflict over housing is therefore emerging as a significant issue in ageing Britain. The young are increasingly becoming *Generation Rent* and the Institute for Public Policy Research (IPPR) predicts that by 2020 the total number of young people owning their own properties will fall by approximately 1.1 million, the number living with their parents in their 30s will grow by 500,000 and an additional 1.5 million 18–30-year-olds will live in the private rented sector; a generational housing divide that was neatly summed up by the Intergenerational Commission in 2016 when its researches showed that while 66.5% of baby boomers owned their own homes when they were 25–34 years old, only 36% of young people in this age group, do so today. This age-related housing divide is, in turn, becoming something of a geographical divide. According to the Resolution Foundation (2019), the retirement towns and villages along Britain's "silver coasts" in counties such as Norfolk, Suffolk, Devon and Dorset, are now being joined by Silver Cities such as Blackpool and Bournemouth as many boomer retirees go in search of the thrill and excitement of theatres and restaurants rather than the peace and quiet of suburbia or the coast; a trend that according to the Future of London Report in 2018 is likely to impact on London too by 2035 and an age boom that according to the 2018 Grosvenor Report, is already hitting cities, such as Tokyo and Madrid. London, for example, is predicted to see its over-65 population increase by 48% to 2 million and its over-80 population to grow by 70% by 2035; an explosion in elderly that is likely to put immense pressure on London's housing stock and its distribution and on its city planning in terms of transport, localised facilities, health and social care provision. London may soon have to follow in Manchester's footsteps and be registered by the WHO as an age-friendly city. Meanwhile, older people in rural areas face increasing isolation and ever-declining services and support as banks, shops and even health services shrink and withdraw – a process that COVID-19 has tragically accelerated.

Housing solutions

As the housing charity, Shelter set it out long ago in its 2012 Report the Housing Challenge for Ageing Britain is fairly simple: "England's population is ageing, and fast. By 2030 one in three people are projected to be aged 55 and over. Older people will be a diverse group, ranging from economically powerful 'baby boomers' to over-85s with high care and support needs. How will the housing market respond to this demographic change? Do we have the right kinds of accommodation for older people, in the right places"? As Shelter equally recognised, the solutions unfortunately are anything but simple and made worse, far worse, by a lack of government foresight, planning and investment despite years of government promises, three more general elections and the advent of a new conservative administration under Boris Johnson committed to "levelling-up" Great Britain and "Building Back Better". Solutions, however, are vital and extremely urgent, if Britain is to unlock this housing log-jam and build a sustainable platform for a healthy and harmonious ageing society in the years ahead; solutions that to date include:

• **The single chain solution:** This was a solution proposed by the think-tank Demos in their submission to the All-Party Committee on Housing in 2014. It was based on the view that instead of the housing for young and old being viewed separately, they should be viewed as a **single chain**; a sort of circular housing escalator in perpetual motion with the young first-time buyer climbing on at the bottom, the second/third-time buyers stepping off on the middle floors and the last-time buyer on the top floor stepping down from their larger 4-bed detached properties into bungalows, apartments or retirement villages. Release the *last-time buyer*, argued the Demos researchers, and you set the whole housing chain in motion and radically realign housing supply and demand. Open up the *later-life market* through, for example, more liberal planning permission rules or through more innovative or trustworthy later-life financial products and you immediately unblock the top end of the housing chain and generate a chain reaction down below, releasing larger properties for growing families who, in turn, release smaller properties for first-time buyers. Moreover, argued the Demos researchers, the funding for such a revolution is already there, locked up in the trillion pounds worth of assets owned by the older generation across the country. And so too, is the demand; it simply needs releasing. Demos estimated that if just half of the over 60s interested in moving from their survey were able to do so, this would release around £356 billion worth of (mainly family-sized) property. Unleashing the "housing chain" in this way would additionally help enhance older people's health and wellbeing, rejuvenate young people's aspirations and housing needs and in the process providing a major boost to the building industry and associated trades. *Generation Rent* may then be able to move out of rented accommodation – and the family home – reduce their costs and get on with their lives; apparently a perfect solution to a "perfect storm"; a "win-win" solution that would – and should – grace any political manifesto, particularly with the grey vote so critical to any election to come. However, while the Demos proposal won over the 2014 All-Party Committee on Housing, it has not yet persuaded conservative administrations then or since; administrations that remain fixated with first-time buyers and although the 2020 reductions in stamp duty and the 5% mortgage deposit helped provide a brief "jump-start" to the housing market, they are not the real long-term solution to the UK's housing crisis that is so desperately needed.

• **Ageing-in-place:** This is the alternative and for many older people, the preferred, solution to later-life living than moving. Adapting, improving and enhancing your existing house allows older couples to feel more at home, more safe, secure and comfortable in their local environment, and still connected to their friends, community and to their families. Ageing-in-place, therefore, has to be a key feature in any housing strategy in an ageing society not least with the advent of new technology that is already dramatically transforming family communication and home security alongside with the promises of age-friendly Alexas and intelligent home-robots currently being trialled and personalised in Japan and Korea. Ageing-in-place, however, needs a much broader and deeper vision that just new tech toys. It needs an integrated housing and community vision and supporting strategy. As Age UK argued in its 2015 Report, housing for later life involves health and social care provision integrated with pensioner housing that on one hand actively promotes independence and accessibility through the age-friendly redesign of older homes and on the other hand provides easy access to local shops and facilities through inexpensive and integrated local transport; all backed up by high-quality and trustworthy financial products and advice that will provide regular income and protect the elderly from fraud and scams. Ageing in place may even hold the key to the grey hurricane of dementia that is gathering force on Britain's horizons today. The pioneering work of the British Research Establishment (BRE) and Loughborough University (2019) in seeking to design dementia-friendly homes is clearly a step in this direction; homes that include clear lines of sight throughout, user-friendly technology to control heat and light, familiar features from the past such as colour-coded taps and the potential to adapt the house to one floor living as memories fade and confusion sets in.

• **Multigenerational and cooperative living:** Many countries are now experimenting extensively with multi-generational living. In Alicante in Spain younger people under 35 years of age and on a low income are offered housing units at low rent in return for providing services and support to the older community living there. Homeshare schemes, widespread in Europe, are slowly emerging across the UK whereby young people become housemates and companions to elderly people as well as paying them rent. Co-housing schemes, like that of the grand ladies of the Older Women's Co-Housing Group (OWCH) in North London and widespread in Holland and Europe, are slowly emerging too whilst Silver Co-operatives, designed, owned and run by the residents, are also gaining ground but largely without government incentives or commercial support.

- **Housing finance:** Whilst huge attention has been given by government and mortgage companies to the financial needs of the first-time buyer, little time or attention has been given to the financial needs of older or last-time buyers seeking to "downsize" to a smaller property, up-size to a larger, possibly multi-generational one or simply age-in-place. Mortgages, the traditional vehicle for purchasing property in the UK, are still very much directed at the young and first-time buyer. They usually have tight age restrictions on them, and often require some form of secure income stream to finance them other than a pension or interest on savings. Such age limits, how-ever, now look increasingly outdated and unnecessary given that retirees today live much longer and many enjoy generous pensions guaranteed for the rest of their life. Retirees are often far more secure borrowers than many younger buyers facing todays' turbulent and insecure job market but few mortgage companies or mortgage products seem to recognise this funda-mental shift and its potential benefit in unlocking and lubricating the inter-generational housing chain. Moreover, the financial needs of the emerging silver housing market today are much more diverse and wide-ranging. Some older households are asset-rich and income-poor; some are asset-rich and aspiration-high, looking to fund holiday homes abroad as well as luxury apartments at home and others are simply poor with few savings and simply a state pension for daily living. Clearly, these are quite distinct and separate housing markets with very different dynamics – the market demand of the better-off compared to the community need of those in poverty. Moreover, many older couples do not necessarily want to move as such but need to release some capital to fund daily life. Some still have mortgages – including interest-only mortgages; some wish to move or buy abroad; some wish to support their children's first-time house with a deposit or loan. The UK's housing finance market clearly needs the sort of dramatic shakeup that the annuity market got in 2014 and a fundamental redesign based on the indi-vidual or couple's capacity to pay, not on an arbitrary age limit drawn up when average life expectancy was much lower. Initiatives such as the Barclays Springboard Mortgage allowing older generations to help the young get on the housing ladder while still protecting and rewarding their savings, and shared ownership schemes for older couples such as that of Platinum Skies Retirement Living offering half-rent alongside half-deposit may well be the way forward.

- **Innovation and redesign:** But housing in an ageing society isn't just about more houses, and worse, more of the same. It is a huge opportunity to rethink housing and later life living for the future in a radically different way. The commercial opportunities are immense and the market size exponential as the baby boomer generation retires and begins to bring "bankloads" of equity to the housing table. As the 2018 Policy Exchange Report concluded with only 8.4% of the current 10.3 million households aged 55 and over moving home each year, government policy needs to generate "a societal change in attitude towards downsizing-and for it to be seen as a natural (and positive) progression in someone's life". Just imagine, for example, older and younger people's attitude to retiring in the UK if they had anything like the huge and immensely attractive choice of senior living on offer in the USA, whether it be the sunshine in Florida or the mountains of Nevada. The gated community of Laguna Woods Village in California, for example, has a beach coastline, seven clubhouses, five swimming pools, a performing arts theatre and an equestrian centre. In the USA, retirement is a pathway to paradise – at least for those that can afford it; in the UK, retirement is often seen as the first step into the grave. In the USA, senior living is a mass market and very big business; in the UK, retirement communities are still a niche market restricted to the better-off. In the UK, only 1.7% of older people live in tailor-made specialist housing compared to 15% of over 60s in USA and 13% in Australia and NZ. The purpose-built retirement market in the UK is dominated by a limited number of developers such as McCarthy and Stone, Churchill and Pegasus Life and aimed primarily at the mid- to high-end markets; yet, as Knight-Frank estate agency estimated in 2016, the private retirement living sector is worth some £29 billion, twice that of the care home sector, while older people at large, are sitting on some £1 trillion of housing equity and over half are living in houses larger than necessary. The APPG Report: Housing and Care for Older People in July 2019, called for a National Drive to build more purpose-built rented accommodation for older people at affordable rents with a yearly target of 38,000 units amounting to 1.1 million homes by 2040. Such housing could range from shared ownership and co-ownership to extra-care; from garden villages, urban extensions, intergenerational housing and other innovations offering community and all-age living and ensuring security of tenure by abolishing section 21 of the 1988 Housing Act on "no fault" evictions.
- Meanwhile, building innovators such as Joseph Daniel and his Project Etopia are not only looking to reverse Britain's obsession with brick-built housing and encourage the shift to the sort of factory built, modular timber-framed designs found abroad but they are looking as well to incorporate new technology and solar panels as part of a strategy "to reverse climate change through housing". The partnership of the housing association, *Your Housing Group*, in 2016 in a £2.5 billion joint-venture with a Chinese construction company for the building of some 25,000 factory-built modular homes in 2016 is just such a leap-forward particularly as SMART technology offers

the means to transform many older people's homes and save the NHS billions each year. Such projects offer high-quality and eco-friendly solutions to Britain's housing crisis not only for homeowners of all ages but also for landlords and employers such as the NHS seeking long-term investment and employer-built communities in the tradition of such 19th-century pioneers as Rowntree and Cadbury. Urban planners in the UK might equally look abroad for innovation and inspiration in creating the ageing communities of the future; and, in particular, explore the options for ageing in cities rather than living in isolation outside them. The Arup Foresight Series (Cities Alive: Designing for Ageing Communities: June 2019), for example, offers a *flowerbed* of new ideas ranging from:

★ Walkable environments such as Toyama Compact City strategy, Viborg Denmark's accessibility design strategy, Richmond Council's Community Toilet Scheme, Lyon France's Metro and tram Optiguide service for older and disabled travellers, Australia's Whole Journey Guidelines, Denmark's FlexDanmark service for door-to-door public transport.

★ Toyama's Comprehensive Care Centres, London's Quietways to guide cyclists and pedestrians away from traffic, Berlin's Preussen Park's Outdoor Exercise machines and Beijing's outdoor gyms, Portland's Memory Park for Alzheimer patients, the Hogeweyk dementia village in Weesp Holland and the BRE Inovation Park in Watford England which includes a demonstration dementia home.

★ Vancouver's Making Room Housing program, Singapore's Silver Housing bonus to encourage "rightsizing" and its Silver Zones designated residential areas for older people including safety measures to forewarn traffic, Portugal's Pedestrian Accessibility Plan, New York's Safe Streets for Seniors programme. If schemes like these were the future, then many more older people might be attracted away from the coast and country back into city life.

As the 2017 LGA report concluded, England desperately needs a *Residential Revolution* comparable to that in the USA or Australia and the 2018 Report of the Communities and Local Government. Committee offered a detailed framework for a National Strategy on Housing for Older People that included:

• A national planning policy framework that emphasised the housing needs of older people and set a new standard – an age-proofed sub category of C2 planning classification – for specialist retirement housing and for providing social care alongside home and residential care.

• A local planning requirement that councils integrate house planning more with health and social care; and that they specifically identify how they intend to meet the housing needs of older people in their local plans with specific targets for such housing and for suitable sites.

- Legislation to promote consumer's and lender's confidence in financing specialist housing.
- A funded and revitalised first-stop advice service to provide user-friendly and holistic housing advice to older people and signposts to local services.
- Support for ageing-at-home such as a local handyman service under a Trustmark accreditation scheme; and support for moving – for *rightsizing* – including mortgage, sheltered-renting, co-housing and shared ownership advice as well as the practicalities of actually moving house to another area.

Conclusions

So, housing in the UK is at a generational crossroads. It is in crisis, not only for the young but also for the old too. As the government's own *Foresight Report* predicted back in 2016 a "perfect storm" is brewing, one that may not only fuel a massive boom in house prices – and so potentially rents – but also price the young and the less affluent pensioners out of the housing market altogether. Or it may generate a mass movement *Back Home*; back home at age 20, 30 or even 40; or even at 70 and 80 as older people seek too to live with their sons and daughters, children and grandchildren in some form of 3G or 4G living. What all these statistics and all these studies showed Laura, however, was that the housing crisis in the UK is not just about building houses; it is about building an ageing society where longevity is reshaping demography, where longer and longer lifespans are creating new needs, new lifestyles, new intergenerational relationships that the current stock and type of housing in the UK cannot meet. The chances of conflict, of escalating inequality and even of social alienation and isolation are rising daily. An *Age War* over housing becomes a serious possibility as does a dramatic rise in pensioner poverty, ill health and early death through inappropriate housing and social isolation. "Unsuitable housing has a direct and proven linkages with ill-health, including pneumonia, asthma, mental health, and falls and hip fractures; for example falls amongst older people, it is estimated, cost the state well in excess of $1 billion per year and the 'winter excess' of around 30,000 pensioner deaths has been linked to the thermally inefficient, ageing housing stock" (ILC-UK: 2016). In contrast, new homes offer new life, healthier life, particularly if fitted with smart technology, reducing healthcare costs in the process as well as helping to alleviate the social illnesses of isolation and loneliness that are fast spreading across ageing Britain. Yet, all this could be avoided, or at least moderated, by a radical rethink of how housing market could be liberated, of how the *housing chain* could be integrated and set in motion; and of how far greater innovation and imagination could be brought into designing and building homes and houses for the ageing, multigenerational, multi-market society ahead. The need is for the integration, not separation of services, and for the adaptation and transfer of housing as ageing needs change, and as generations of homeowners and tenants move up and down the "housing ladder", to and from the city and the town to the coast and the countryside – and possibly back again. Britain needs a better image of retirement housing; an attractive and active image more akin to the American Dream than to the *British Bungalow*; more in keeping with the "Building Better, Building Beautiful" Commission Report (Feb. 2020) that beauty be put at the forefront of future planning and that towns and cities should be "regreened" with 2 million street trees and a fruit tree for every new home and that ugliness be banned from the UK's housing scene.

So, as Laura's discussions with her grandmother, Polly increasingly brought home, housing in the UK can no longer be considered in isolation. It could – and should – be the centre-piece of any integrated and inclusive strategy for the ageing society for tomorrow; part of a Holy Trinity alongside pensions and healthcare that might transform ageing Britain and form the foundation of any new intergenerational social contract to come. And, finally, as Professor Mayhew warned in 2020, the young need not despair completely. Even baby boomers won't live forever and by the late 2020s, they will start to die out and begin to pass on their homes and a "wall of wealth" to their children and grandchildren. A sobering thought for British baby boomers; a possible bright light at the end of the housing tunnel for generations X, Y and Z so long as they don't mind waiting.

4.6 FAMILY, MARRIAGE AND THE MULTI-GENERATIONAL BEANPOLE

The British Royal Family – depicted in Figure 4.2 – or even that living today, may not be your "average" British Family, thought Laura, but it is certainly a classic example of an ageing one with the present Queen Elizabeth in her late 90s, Prince Phillip "passing" just before his 100th birthday and their children and grandchildren extending four generations into the future in a multigenerational, multi-national family history that dates back to the 19th century and possibly stretches ahead into the 22nd. What an extended family and what a future, thought Laura as she began sketching out her own family tree and wondering how it would spread in the century ahead. Just imagine getting all your family together for a full extended family photo of all of you today and then again say in 2030 or 2050; just imagine the changes; just imagine how much older everyone would look; just imagine the sheer variety and diversity of a family that may now or in the future be multigenerational, multicultural, even multinational, related across the country, possibly across continents by remarriage and cohabitation as much as by blood. Laura used to love family get-togethers when Uncle Wilfred's "northern army" came down south to her see her great nan Christina at Christmas or occasionally for a "party in the park" in Southwold where her grandparents Polly and David lived. She loved meeting up with her aunts and uncles and her cousins Edward and Molly, exchanging gossip, rumour and reflecting where they all stood in a family chain that not only stretched from North to South in the UK but across the globe now from Uncle

FIGURE 4.2 Image of the British Royal Family

Sam and his Mexican wife Sunita in New Orleans and to cousin Tony living in Australia with his Japanese wife Aoi and their two sons, Tim and Tom. And that was only what the family currently knew. Aunt Wilhelmina had just begun her new genealogy course and was already digging up fresh new family history as well as a family skeleton or two! *Family* really was Laura's type of sociology and she dived into it "head first" and this is what she found.

The world family

The modern family is clearly changing dramatically. After the so-called "extended family" of the 19th century and the "nuclear family" of the post-war 20th century, we now seem to be entering the 21st-century era of the "**Ageing Family in the Age Chain**" – longer in length, *beanpole* in shape, multigenerational in character, multiethnic in composition, multinational, even global in range and multifamily in structure as divorce and remarriage generate "step families" that add immensely to the diversity and complexity of family life in the early 21st century. The family of the 21st century is both diverse and organic adapting to both the global forces that now impact on family life such as multinational immigration, escalating divorce rates and the fast changing roles of men and women. Cohabitation seems to have replaced marriage in many Western societies as the primary form of personal and familial relationship for the young – and increasingly the old – while single-parent families and reconstituted "stepfamilies" have grown dramatically in recent years. As Professor Sarah Harper explained back in 2006 "Reconstituted or recombinant step-families, single parent families and cohabiting couples now comprise around 25% of Western European families, for example, together with a growing number of ethnic minority families, whose kinship roles and relationships differ from the majority white population". Traditional family trees and family networks are being redrawn and reshaped by remarriage and less formal forms of relationship. New forms of "extended" family are being created by global migration, multiethnicity and by extended longer life. "Whilst marriage rates still remain high over a person's lifetime.... more marriages in the Western world now end in divorce than ever before. This has led to a bipolar situation. On the one hand, the length of many marriages are similar to those of earlier centuries"...but instead of death, twenty-first-century marriages are likely to be cut short by divorce....The chances of an individual being never married or widowed are, therefore, falling. The chances of being, or having been, in a marital or cohabiting relationship, are increasing". And such changes are not confined solely to the West. China's single-child policy created the phenomenon of the 4-2-1 family, provoked the mass migration from the countryside into the burgeoning cities and shattered the traditional extended family networks of rural Asia as a result. Meanwhile, fertility rates across the developed and developing worlds are now falling as rapidly as longevity rates are rising. Whilst fertility rates in the Americas and Oceania remain close to or slightly below the replacement level of 2.1, fertility rates in Europe – with the exception of Ireland – remain well below this replacement level with Germany and Italy as low as 1.4, the UK at 1.7 and France at 2.0. The big fall, however, has been in Asia with no country in East Asia having a fertility rate above 1.6 – the implications of which have yet to be seen. China's abandonment of its one-child policy shows just how seriously the largest country in the world is taking this demographic revolution and yet even the mighty Chinese State cannot turn back the tides of ageing.

Add to this downfall in fertility, the increasing global mobility of the young and no country can plan with confidence its future population size and profile. The exodus of young people from developing countries across to the West for better opportunities and of the young *within* developing countries from the countryside to the city is *hollowing out* traditional family hierarchies. Add to such economic and urban migration the romantic opportunities offered by international dating through the Internet and with it the emergence of the **multinational family** as young people from the West marry spouses from countries as far afield as Argentina and Thailand, then inevitably family life and with it all the ages and stages of childhood, adulthood and retirement are undergoing fundamental and global transformation. Even that most basic "rite of passage" of leaving the family home is being transformed with the *arrival* – or at least non-departure – of "Boomerang children" in the USA, Europe and even Asia; adult children who are leaving home much later or returning home in their early 20s under the pressures of high house prices and rentals and the devastating rise of youth unemployment that has followed the 2008 crash and now coronavirus. Moreover, young women today appear to be delaying marriage as they seek to establish themselves in careers rather than in part-time jobs and this in turn is leading to a delay in childbirth – or none at all! Hence the fall in fertility rates across both the developed and the developing world. Hence too, the delay in the transitions and rites of passage of the traditional life course as children leave home, marry and start families later, retire later; and now through longer life expectancy start "second lives" enjoy second marriages and some even start second families and second parenting.

So, the **world family** is being transformed both vertically and horizontally. The **beanpole** family, the **rainbow** family is fast emerging as significant features of the multigenerational family chain that is being created by the extended life span of the 21st century. As the world family map summed it up in 2015, the whole world – *developed and developing* – is undergoing a social transformation in its familial structures and functioning as ageing progresses; the implications of which are only now beginning to emerge:

- **Two-parent** families are becoming less common in many parts of the world, though they still constitute a majority of families around the globe, especially in Asia and the Middle East.
- **Extended families** (which include parent(s) and kin from outside the nuclear family) also appear to be common in Asia, the Middle East, Central/ South America and sub-Saharan Africa, but not in other regions of the world.
- **Marriage rates** are declining in many regions. Adults are most likely to be married in Asia and the Middle East, least likely to be married in Central/South America, with Africa, Europe North America and Oceania falling in-between. Co-habitation is more common among couples in Europe, North America, Oceania and – especially – in Central/South America.
- **Childbearing rates** are declining worldwide with the highest fertility rates are in sub-Saharan Africa (6.1), moderate in the Middle East, at replacement level (2.1) in the Americas and Oceania and below replacement level in East Asia and Europe. Childbearing outside of marriage is high in Central/South America and Western Europe, moderate in North America, Oceania, and Eastern Europe and lowest in Asia and the Middle East.

"Marriage is becoming more of an **option** for adults, rather than a **necessity** for the survival of adults and children. Cohabitation has emerged as an important precursor or alternative to marriage in many countries (as) adults look for more flexibility or freedom in their relationships, or they may feel that they do not have sufficient financial or emotional resources to marry, or they may perceive marriage as a risky undertaking, or simply unnecessary once they are cohabitating". Ironically, this is likely to mean that the numbers of older people needing care will be rising just as the numbers of children and adults available to care for them will be falling; the implications of which could be socially devastating.

The British Family is equally experiencing a radical shift in its family structure in this age of ageing and a new form of "ageing family" is emerging in the UK of the 21st century. As the ONS illustrated in 2021:

- There are approximately 19 million families in the UK. Of these nearly 13 million consisted of a married couple or civil partnership with or without children.
- The number of cohabiting couple families has increased significantly, from 1.5 million in 1996 to 3.5 million in 2019, with the number of dependent children in such households rising from 1.4 million to 1.9 million over the same period.
- There were 2.9 million lone parents with dependent children in 2019, up some 200,000 on 2003.
- There were 27.8 million households in the UK in 2019, of which 28% consisted of only one person and 20% consisted of four or more people.
- The *fastest* growing household type was multifamily households containing two or more families, an increase of 75% from 170,000 in 1999 to 297,000 in 2019. However, such multifamily households still only represent 1.1% of all households.
- The UK fertility rate has fallen to 1.65 children per childbearing woman – well below the natural replacement level of 2.1 children and raising the serious possibility of half of all families having only one child within the next decade.

So, the British Family too is undergoing a radical reshaping, becoming more *beanpole* at its core but more extended in terms of its branches and offshoots so fundamentally changing family relationships. As the think-tank Civitas (2018) concluded: "We are now a society in which more than 4 in 10 children are born out of wedlock, and in which a teenager has less chance of being raised by both biological parents than any other country…and our nuclear families now share the stage with an assortment of stepfamilies and kin networks with potentially dramatic effects on traditional family obligations". As Andrew Cherlin (1992) has summed it up, "Over the course of our lives we're accumulating more and more kin to whom we owe less and less". Add to this dramatic reshaping of the British family, the waves of ethnic change in Britain since World War Two, and the increasingly global nature of working and family life today as young – and older – British men and women marry foreign spouses, then the multiracial, multinational character and shape of the modern British family becomes increasingly evident. Despite Brexit, the UK is increasingly a member of the global family network that is stretching from the western world to the far east and like many children elsewhere, British children face what Professor Harper (2006) poignantly described as "a voyage into the unknown": "An individual born now or late last century has the expectation of a variety of family and household formations. He or she may be born into a consensual union, which then becomes a marital union, which ends in divorce, resulting in a single parent-probably female-led-household. This then becomes a reconstituted family with cohabiting adults, then married adults with a combination of step-siblings within one household".

Two of the driving forces in reshaping and pruning the British Family Tree are divorce and single-parenthood. Certainly, family break-up of some form or other now seems almost inevitable. According to the Marriage Foundation (2017), marriage appears to be increasingly the preserve of the affluent and educated; co-habitation and single-parenthood that of the less well-off with about one-third of children in lone-parent families never seeing their father after three years of separation. While nearly 90% of couples in the most prosperous areas of the UK such as Harrow and Surrey are married, only 30% of parents with dependent children in the poorer 20 council areas such as Liverpool and Knowsley are. This is an astonishing and dramatic disparity in marital relations between the poor and better-off and potentially a major factor in explaining the gulf in both equality and social mobility that lies beneath the surface of modern Britain. Moreover, the Foundation's conclusion that "A child born in 2017 has only a 50% chance of living with both parents by the time they reach 15" is not only a devastating indictment of family life today but also a sociological dilemma that fundamentally undermines one of the central planks of government policy; its assumption that the traditional family has two parents at its core and they will take responsibility for the upbringing of its children. "Fatherless" families are becoming a feature of modern Britain and the UK is today "a world leader in family break-up" according to Ian Duncan Smith (Sunday Times: February 2017); a breakup that he claimed is costing the Exchequer some £48 billion. The 2019 CSJ report "Why Family Matters" spelt out the huge impacts of family breakdown in terms of homelessness, crime, educational underachievement, alcoholism, teen pregnancy and mental health issues. "Family breakdown is a root cause of poverty and a social injustice that demands attention and actions of those who walk the corridors of power" concluded this report and it recommended the creation of a cabinet-level office for family policy to reform child-benefit and target it at low-income families and create local family-hubs or one-stop shops to provide families in need help and support. In addition, the dramatic changes in Britain's ethnic composition are also having a profound effect not only on the structure and diversity of family life in the UK but also on inter-racial relationships – be they marriage or cohabitation – and on child-rearing. Given the global nature of working life and family life today, an increasing number of young – and older – British men and women are marrying foreign spouses, creating extended family networks that are international and multinational in nature and scope and leaving grandparents with grandchildren at home and abroad.

So, the modern British family appears to be going through an immense and intense reshaping; a reshaping verging in places on break-up, with children as primary victims of both a social transformation and the severe cutbacks in public spending since 2009/10; cutbacks that have particularly impacted on poorer families. The 2020 CRAG Report calculated child poverty in the UK in 2018–19 at

4.2 million children particularly amongst one-parent families and families with three or more children; and estimated that 45% of black and minority ethnic families in the UK live in poverty compared to 26% of white British families. As the 2020 Buttle UK report highlighted, coronavirus has inevitably escalated existing inequalities in educational access and digital provision, generated rising mental ill-health and family tensions and forced many more families to use food-banks and welfare assistance "for many children and young people, the pandemic has only amplified the difficulties that already existed in their lives, increasing their isolation and forcing them to spend many hours in homes that lack the bare essentials most other children take for granted".

Such stresses and strains have led commentators like John Harris of the Guardian (12 January 2020) to ask whether the British family is still fully functional whilst David Brooks (2020) in America, has gone as far as to claim that "The Nuclear Family was a Mistake"; a freakish historical moment as people now marry less and later, have fewer children and divorce, live apart and alone; a familial structure that has insulated and isolated the better-off and so helped create a chasm of inequality between two "entirely different family regimes" in America; between the better-educated, mainly white and healthier, affluent families and the vulnerable, dysfunctional family structures of the less well-off, unmarried and mainly ethnic communities where state or external family support is limited. Certainly, coronavirus aside, tensions in British family life have been increasing and, according to the C'M'S 2019 Report will get even worse by 2041 as the baby boomer generation moves into their 70s and 80s, gen-X nears retirement and younger working families find themselves sandwiched between having to care for their ageing parents – and grandparents – while also providing for their own families and futures and attempting to save for their own retirement in an era of shrinking pensions and government cutbacks in the aftermath of COVID and the current economic recession. This is likely to put an immense strain on future intergenerational relations and on the UK's traditional social contract unless the government adopts a far more strategic and constructive role in supporting the modern British family by, for example, investing in a far better childcare system and one that supports all parents and not just the better-off. As the 2019 Coram Family Childcare Survey showed, childcare in Britain today is not fit for purpose. It is a postcode lottery of highly variable provision with persistent gaps in virtually all regions, prices often eye-wateringly high and some parents worse off in work than out of it once they have paid for childcare services, particularly those with large families or those with young children.

Meanwhile, older people with their children gone, with 20 to 30 years of healthy life ahead of them, appear to be embarking on new lifestyle, new relationships, new challenges. Silver divorce, cohabitation, late-life dating and single-life living are all emerging as new lifestyles after 50 and whilst older men may well be enjoying new romances and new freedoms, it is older women who are often enjoying and driving this new women's liberation; the liberation of older age. They are choosing to remain single, choosing cohabitation rather than the security – or the "servitude" – of second marriages, choosing to enjoy grandchildren and family life or choosing to seek new horizons and new adventures abroad. "Intimacy at a distance" seems to have become the baby boomer *relationship of choice* for this generation of older women and with the financial independence of their own pensions or supportive divorce settlements, they are out to explore and exploit their new freedoms and enjoy life to the full, free from the dictates and demands of husbands and children, free to be themselves – at last!

However, the joy of being "alone at last" may diminish once late-life illness, disability and loneliness "kick in", and, as in ageing Japan, "silver suicide" rates begin to rise. And families in the future may not only face the horrendous possibilities of Elderly Parent Responsibility Stress Syndrome (EPRSS); of trying to cope with divorcing grandparents, elderly parents living apart and both needing care and support at the same time just at the point that when they too thought that they were free at last to pursue their own lives; a toxic intergenerational mix that may well *eat* into family life as the millennial generations inherit eldercare and themselves become the "squeezed" or "sandwich generation", trying to juggle family, work and ageing parents without support or respite.

Longevity, however, is also generating a major new source of family support: the grandparent. And not just a grandmother, as in the past, but a grandfather too as older men also begin to enjoy longer, healthier later lives. This *demographic boom* in grandparents, ironically, appears to be happening at the very same time that there appears to be a demographic *bust in babies*. The world now has more grandparents than grandchildren and by 2050 this ratio could be 2:1 if the current fall in fertility continues. The engagement of grandparents in family life, however, varies enormously across societies depending on tradition, culture, government support and state of the economy - and the role of women. In North European countries such as Sweden, Denmark and to a lesser extent France, for example, parents are expected to work full-time and formal childcare is widely available with generous maternity pay and support for mothers who stay at home. In these countries, grandparent support is fairly limited, less intensive and more occasional. In South European, Mediterranean countries such as Portugal, Spain, Italy and Romania, however, the reverse is true with welfare support much more limited and grandparental childcare much more extensive and regular. In Germany and the Netherlands, public support for families is more varied again and less universal; childcare a mixture of private and state with women more likely to work part-time than full-time and grandparental support occasional rather than regular; more "a reserve army of care" called on in emergencies, school holidays and to "bridge" gaps in provision.

In the UK, this new generation of grandparents is gradually moving from the periphery of family life to the heart of it, acting as the family godparents and "family bank of last resort" providing both free childcare, calculated by the Government's Foresight Report in 2016 at £7.3 billion, and financial help with mortgages and housing not only for their children but increasingly for their grandchildren as they face student fees and burgeoning house prices. A new form of "inheritance skipping" is emerging as grandparents pass on their wealth to their grandchildren while they are still alive; wealth currently estimated at £4 billion a year; a Grandparental Generosity that according to the ILC-UK (2013) might "have undesired consequences for the financial well-being of grandparents (facing uncertain future costs such as long-term care) and that may perpetuate class divisions across generations"; a conclusion reflected strongly in the Grandparents Plus study "The Poor Relation" in 2009: "Grandparents from higher socio-economic groups tend to become parents at a later age, with their children adopting the same delaying behaviour. This is not generally true of grandparents from lower socio-economic groups; both generations being more likely to have children at a younger age. Therefore, generally we find that middle class families tend to follow the 'bean-pole' pattern, with families getting longer and thinner, with large age-gaps between the generations and less children per generation, while working class families are becoming increasingly 'compact', spreading across four (even five) generations. These separate trends each have their own implications in terms of grandparents' financial well-being". Working-class grandparents are therefore more likely than middle-class grandparents to belong to four-generation families and also more likely to be poor with higher levels of great-grandchildren poverty. Working-class women are four times more likely to become a grandparent before their 50th birthday and more than twice as likely before their 60th birthday than their middle class counterparts. As a consequence, "working age grandmothers on low incomes are the ones providing the highest levels of childcare. They are also more likely to report that they have given up or reduced work in order to do so and are under the greatest pressure to combine work and care". In contrast, grandparents from higher socio-economic groups are more likely to enjoy higher incomes, generous final salary pensions and be part of a dual income household living with a spouse who also had a professional career, a good income and a substantive occupational pension. Such affluent grandparents can afford to provide financial support and pay for childcare in a way low-income grandparents simply cannot. Moreover, research at Essex and Manchester universities in 2019 has identified a "grandparent effect" as better-off grandparents use their influence, contacts and finances to help ensure that their grandchildren not only do not slip down the social hierarchy but also enjoy a "helping hand" up the social or occupational scale. So the "poverty cycle" of family deprivation and inequality, long recognised and researched by sociologists, is now becoming an intergenerational cycle of advantage and disadvantage in Britain; a cycle that is somewhat distinct from the rest of Western Europe where generally pensions are significantly more generous and social mobility more fluid.

Grandfathers, too, are increasingly becoming part of modern family life now older men live almost as long as older women. As Anna Tarrant illustrated in her 2012 study, "Grand-parenting in the 21st Century", grandfathers in the past did not live long into retirement nor engage extensively in the lives of their grandchildren. They were more peripheral or distant figures remembered more in family photos or family mythology than in real life. The grandfather of today and tomorrow, however, is much more visible, engaged and active; enjoying a "second fatherhood" but without all the trials and tribulations that possibly came with the first one. A new generation of grandfather is emerging, a boomer generation determined and more willing to be involved in childcare, more involved in extended family life, keen to relive a second parenthood – particularly if the demands of a full-time career restricted the quality of parenthood they practised the first time round. They are likely to be more determined to make a mark, to leave a legacy and to "steer" the family through the "jungle" of today's intergenerational relationships, step parenting and multiethnic traditions – with, of course, his wife or partner's advice and guidance! The role of family counsellor, family coach, and family banker – even head of the family – plays to older male skills and offers them a critical and fulfilling sense of purpose post-retirement. And as Baby Boomers, they likely not only impose their own image on grand-parenting today but also create a whole new identity and a whole new way of fulfilling this role, often engaging in child-rearing to a far greater extent than they did – or could – when they were young fathers themselves.

So, the grandparents of today and tomorrow are therefore likely to be both *active and ageless*: a whole new generation of grandparent, the like of which the world has not seen before. They are not an "extended" version of grandparents in the past – nor of any of the stereotypical images that traditionally come with that title. They are still living life to the full, often as healthy and socially active as their adult children and free now to travel the world. They are likely to live not only through their grandchildren's childhood but possibly into their early and mid-adulthood too. Mick Jagger may not be everyone's ideal grandparent, but he is already a great-grandfather with the potential in 20 years' time of becoming a great-great-grandparent, over 90 years *young*. Yet, amid all this longevity bonus for enjoying extended family life, grandparents face the paradox of trying to balance out family demands and opportunities with their own ambitions and dreams for retirement, free of work, childcare and housework. Which ambition takes priority in the small number of years left is increasingly becoming a key question?

Conclusions

So, Longevity is having a dramatic and profound impact on family life in the 21st century. It is lengthening the "chain of family life" and creating "serial living", serial marriages and even serial or second lives as longer, healthier life creates the opportunity to enjoy extended family life or a new stage of independent living. Family life in ageing societies is no longer linear and longitudinal, predictable and predetermined. Rather, multigenerational families and multistage living is becoming the "norm" whilst the "beanpole" may be becoming the "daisy-chain" as globalisation and international migration encourage the emergence of multinational, multiethnic global families. The lengthening of the lifespan is likely to lead to the delaying of the traditional stages of life and certainly the grandchildren of the 21st century are likely to experience a much more varied and diverse journey through life and "marriage" than their counterparts in the 20th century: "Most will experience old age, most will marry at least once, most will have children, most will have a married child by the time they are in their 50s, and most will have a grandchild before they are 60". As Richard Jackson summed it up in a Leading Edge interview back in 2011, whilst on one hand the traditional family structures seem to be disappearing, to be "withering on the vine", a new more organic species of family life seems to be emerging in the 21st century, a multigenerational model better adapted to face the challenges to family life and relationships in the fluid and unpredictable future ahead.

Laura was dumbfounded by such dramatic and profound changes in the one social structure that she thought was relatively stable and strong. Maybe because she had enjoyed such a warm and loving upbringing, she had been sheltered from the familial storms that were clearly raging within other families within her own age group and in her own country, let alone abroad. And while she was well aware of the shattering effect of divorce on the lives of many of her school friends, she had only vaguely been aware of the way the family acts as one of the most powerful forms of transmitting, perpetuating and even promoting both social inequality and social problems right across society. Her cosy and romantic image of the modern family had been shattered, and she was all too aware now how fragile family life in Great Britain is likely to be in the future and how many people might be well be living alone for a long time as a result. For her, the one great shaft of sunlight that appeared to be illuminating the horizon of ageing Britain, as well as her own life, was the emergence of the Grandparent, the great grandparent and especially the grandfather as significant figures in future family life. They may well turn out to be the *Silver Saviours* holding up the pre-carious beanpole that is the modern family at the very time when globalisation, urbanisation, new technology– and now even global pandemics – seemed to be tearing it apart geographically and socially. Grandparents are in an increasingly unique position to support the younger generations coming through. They are in a unique position to contribute to the quality of life and the well-being of their grandchildren and so possibly help the UK improve its lowly position in the UNICEF League of Child Well-being in Rich countries which ranks the UK 27th out of 41 wealthy countries; well-behind most of Europe and only just below Romania and Slovakia; one that warns of a "looming children's crisis and an urgent need for UK to take action to improve lives of children". If, however, society wants even more from the grandparents of today and tomorrow, then, as Professor Ann Buchanan (2018) has argued, the government may need to for-malise and incentivise such support or watch the modern British family wither even more on its precarious vine.

One final thought though occurred to Laura, namely, how far this *boom* in elders is being driven by a *bust* in babies and whether her generation, led possibly by the Royals, might take on the challenge of rebalancing Britain's demography. Countries facing "demographic implosion", such as Hungary, are now offering tax incentives to women having four or more children and many countries are beginning to fundamentally rethink their attitude to immigration if they are to attract new *young blood* from outside and avoid super-ageing in the future. Ultimately, though, can any country control its own *demographic destiny* in an era when global forces are so powerful? Will Brexit or any other attempt to close or control national borders ultimately fail and possibly accelerate ageing? If mighty China with its one-child policy could not control its demographic future, who can? Laura had expected the sociology of the modern family to be a fascinating subject in itself and a key part of her dissertation. She had not expected that it might change her own philosophy of life nor potentially the number of children that she might have in the future. Nor had she expected a global pandemic to throw the British or world family into such turmoil; locking them down, locking their grandparents up, tearing them apart as family members contract the virus or worse get hospitalised and die; forcing every family everywhere to rethink their priorities and their relationships. The scars from coronavirus and the effects of lockdown on family life across the world are likely to be immense and long-lasting, not least for the most deprived and exposed leaving them even further behind economically, educationally and socially – and even more in need of a new social contract and much stronger government support.

4.7 SEX, SEXUALITY AND LATER-LIFE RELATIONSHIPS

Sex at 60 – or worse 70 and 80 – was not something that a young woman in her early 20s like Laura had ever thought about; nor wished to think about. Like many others her age, she assumed that sex was no longer part of life much beyond 40; although through family gossip, she knew that Uncle Rupert was something of a 'ladies' man' and that Aunt Alwyn had had a series of affairs after leaving her husband Ivan. However, beyond such racy stories, Laura preferred not to even imagine oldies having sex, let alone leading an active sex life. That was until, in one quiet and intimate moment, she confided in her nan and subsequently delved deeper revealing not so much the saucy side of sex in later life but its importance to healthy and happy later life living and its potential as a mass market of the future now that the baby boomers of the 60s and 70s are entering older age. The Age of Aquarius – of "Hair", Woodstock, of hippy communes, of sexual liberation and free love – may have given way to the Age of Viagra, Silver "Splitting" and Internet Dating; many of the New Old may have given up on sex and settled for a cuddle and a kiss rather than an orgasmic climax but a new style of sex life, a new type of sex life does seem to be coming to the surface in later life just as powerful but a lot more subtle and sensual than that earlier on. As the ILC-UK Report on Sex and Intimacy in Later Life in the UK *(2017)* concluded "positive sexuality and intimacy throughout the life-course is linked to higher levels of happiness and well-being-irrespective of age".

Moreover, it appears that older people are not only still having sex but apparently, they are still having quite a lot of it. Numerous national surveys such as the National Survey of Sexual Attitudes and Lifestyles in the UK (2013), the English Longitudinal Study of Ageing (2015) and The Independent Age survey in 2018 have revealed not only that many 70-year-olds are still sexually active but so too are a quarter of men over aged 85 and over, and one in ten women (Manchester University study: 2017). The sex lives of the older ages has even become the subject of journalistic or academic investigations such as Esther Perel's State of Affairs (2017) and Stephanie Theobald's Sex Drive (2018) while websites such as *Ann Summers* in the UK or *Pleasure Boutique* and *Good for Her* in the States now cater as much for older women as the young and middle-aged. Writers in their 60s and 70s such as Jilly Cooper still turn out raunchy romances and ageing beauties such as Kim Basinger still make cameo appearances in such erotic films as "Fifty Shades Darker". So, leading the way, once again, are women; women in their 60s and 70s, free now from the menopause, free from childrearing, free to enjoy their own sexuality to the full with either their existing partner or through *singles sites* or LAT ("living alone together") relationships. As Deirdre Fishel and Diana Holzberg discovered in 2008, women over 60 are not only "still doing it" but they are doing more of "*it*" and as Margaret Manning, editor of the website "Sixty and Me" has argued, "forget the stereotypes, if you ask the 43,000 members of our Sixty and Me community, you will find that they are adventurous, curious, and passionate about living a life that is healthy, wealthy and independent".

However, while the sex industry may well be tapping into the "sexual re-awakening" of the older age groups, academia is still some way behind in analysing and explaining this social and cultural revolution. In one of the relatively few academic studies in this area, Dr Merryn Gott (2005) identified the healthier life styles – and healthier bodies – of older people today along with the rise of the Internet, the advent of Viagra and most especially Baby Boomers apparent determination to "stay young forever" and their rejection, as in their youth, of traditional mores. Later-life divorce and re-marriage rates are escalating, there is a growing trend of intimate but non-cohabiting relationships among older people and older lesbians and gay men are now more open about their sexuality. A whole new industry is being built up around providing dating services for older people and new images or stereotypes seem to be emerging for both older men and older women. The *Sexy Oldie* is not only a label of description or even admiration but, argues Gott, it is fast becoming the new expectation, as older women are encouraged, even expected to stay sexy, active and attractive as part of active ageing, even anti-ageing revolution against the traditional "grey" or "blue-rinse" image of older women in the past. Women are under pressure to have sex as a means of remaining young and beautiful and expected to keep their ageing at bay if they still wish to feel or be valued as glamorous or attractive; a situation, the feminist writer, Germaine Greer (1991) summed up in her usual strident way, arguing that the middle-aged woman today has a duty to go on being attractive no matter how fed up she is with the whole business. She is not allowed to let herself go: "letting herself go is a capital offence". Looking "young and sexy" is at the heart of the health and beauty industry today and inevitably the food, fashion, media and beauty industries have latched onto the "older" market using the images, styles and even the "icons" of the 1960s – Twiggy, Cher and even Jane Fonda (now over 80) – as the faces of the new glamorous 60s.

Sexy at 60 is therefore being redefined but not necessarily by older women themselves but by the *young* men and women of the media, fashion and pharmaceutical industries seeking to create whole new markets. The Helen Mirren's and the Susan Sarandon's of this world are not "typical" 60/70-year-old women. Rather, they are admired precisely because they are exceptions and seem to have outwitted nature. Inspiring though Judi Dench might be at age 79, and 'hot' as Madonna might still picture herself at age 60, many women today would be much happier ageing as they wish, plodding into old age at their own pace and style rather than slavishly following stars from the 60s and 70s, however, inspiring and image changing they might be. As India Knight (2014) has argued, older women are not in decline but in their prime; on a journey from *Nymph to Nana*. After a rich and hopefully rewarding lifetime, older women need to liberate themselves from the stereotypes of the sixties and design an image for the 2020s; a new more mature and imaginative version of the women they are now and the women they aspire to be in the future. Older women, in her view, must reject the traditional assumption that the only way to look and feel sexy, is to look young. Instead they should celebrate the fact that "Older women have it all… wisdom, knowledge and dramatically better sex lives than we did at 20. We're not invisible, and there are millions of us, and we look great. Who needs a youth bus when you can have an ageing Bentley"? A *plea* beautifully conveyed by mature models such as Pamela Lucas (65) in her advertisements for M&S, Maye Musk (68) – the mother of Elon Musk, the PayPal billionaire – modelling for Revlon and Virgin and by the host of glamorous women and men, now in their 60s and 70s and still setting new standards of glamour for all ages. One marketing campaign that really did try to put real women of all ages at the forefront of their advertising was that by the *Dove* range of beauty products a few years ago. It was an overnight sensation, attracted intense media attention and went viral on social media. It offered a new direction for the health and beauty industry and inspired many older women to feel glamorous and confident even when posing in the nude.

Older men in contrast have traditionally been allowed to "grow old gracefully" – and been admired for it. The *silver haired*, mature male conveys an image of control and authority at the peak of manhood. He can now retreat quietly into retirement – into the study, onto the golf course or off on the cruise ship to far-away places to reminisce about and revisit old conquests or youthful liaisons. However, with the advent of Viagra, spread of fitness centres and the growing demands of Boomer women for more active and intimate relationships, Boomer men, too, are under pressure to perform against a new standard of mature but "active" masculinity; to keep pace with and emulate the likes of George Clooney and Alex Baldwin. Some older men respond to such expectations with resig-nation and retreat from sex altogether. Others go hell for leather to prove their prowess, proudly displaying symbols of their older manhood – the sleek-nosed sports car or the sleek and sexy yacht.

So, modern masculinity too is no longer safe at 60. Mature men too still have to perform in and out of bedroom, and an active sex life is now considered part of a healthy and happy relationship in older age. Yet, as other studies have argued, a high level of sexual performance is not a "statutory requirement". For many older men, with the onset of ageing limbs and diminished testosterone, retirement is the opportunity to relax and enjoy a "kiss and a cuddle" as much as an orgasm and an orgy. As Arlene Heyman (2016) described it so very vividly in her book *Scary Old Sex*, sex at 70 can be challenging and require as much fore-planning as foreplay. It is like a military campaign "with plans drawn up, equip-ment in tip top condition and troops deployed and coordinated meticulously" as the couple prepare for engagement according to a strict timetable and a ready supply of Vagifem and Viagra beforehand and a nap afterwards to recuperate. As she explains, sexual spontaneity at this age is often difficult, not least when, for example, one participant suffers from acid reflux and has to sit upright; and the other needs clomipramine, an anti-depressant to retard ejaculation. Alternatively, as the French psychologist, Marie de Hennezel (2011) has argued, perhaps sex in later life should be more loving than lusty, more emotional intimacy than genital gymnastics – a gentle, more sensual approach to orgasm that may lead to more satisfying and fulfilling relationships for some but lack the physical engagement and adrenalin for others. She cites the Taoist *art of love* as an approach that many older couples may find more sensual and less stressful given its core principles of controlled ejaculation (coitus reservatus) and the separation for male satisfaction from ejaculation alone. Its strong focus on female orgasm and sexual pleasuring is almost the reverse of the traditional western model and one born of the belief that men over 50 will gain far greater sexual satisfaction – and live longer – if they ejaculate less and make love more. Under this philosophy, love-making moves from an individual or solo spasm into a whole body one; a more shared experience that proponents claim is a far more relaxing, erotic and even spiritual experience all round; a new level of love-making designed for a new age-and a new stage-in life; a deeper and more enduring experience beyond the brief phys-ical pleasure that ejaculation alone can bring.

Sex after Sixty, however, is still something of a taboo subject, rarely discussed and openly shared. Terms such as "dirty old man" or MILF still represent very powerful social stigmas that no respectable older person would wish to bear, par-ticularly in front of their family or children. Yet, as Dr Borz of Stanford Medical School argues, "People that have sex, live longer. Married people live longer. People need people. The more intimate the connection, the more powerful the effects." And in an era where loneliness is increasingly one of the greatest threats to older people's health and wellbeing, then social stigmas that condemn or inhibit sexual relationships in later life become counter-productive as the cost of elder isolation increasingly falls on society at large and on younger families faced by ageing parents living on their own. The joint study by Salerno University in Italy and Imperial College London in summer 2019 even concluded that regular sex can potentially delay Parkinson's disease and generate a better quality of life as well as reduce stress, lower blood pressure and boost the immune system. Sex may not burn off the same calories as an intensive power-walk but, according to research from Wilkes University, orgasms release hormones that boost your immune system, relieve pain, lower risk of prostate cancer in men, boost self-esteem and strengthen relationships through oxytocin, the "love hormone" and happy hormones such as testosterone. A positive and healthy society would seek to accept if not actually applaud, active sex after 60 in the same way and for similar reasons as it promotes it for the young. The health industry would seek to support and enable active and safe sex to help relieve the burden of an ageing population on the NHS whilst sex would seem to be a prime target for the Silver Economy if addressed in a supportive not patronising manner. Perhaps now is the time for a post-60s Kinsey Report to challenge and shatter current sexual stigmas and for sex shops such as Ann Summers to extend its range of lingerie and sex aids specifically for the amorous oldie – male and female – and possibly introduce a new range of sex furniture to support and re-energise ageing limbs. Certainly, the baby boomer will not tolerate sexual ageism and probably quite enjoy embarking on a second sexual revolution shattering all the traditional sexual conventions in their wake aided and abetted as before by new treatments to combat physical decline or revive sexual appetites.

Finally, if mature 60 year olds are still struggling to redefine their sexuality, what of the health practitioner faced by a whole new generation of demanding baby boomers determined to prove themselves again, determined to restore their prowess to that of their youth, anxious to enliven their marriages and to regain the "joy of sex" that everyone else seems to be raving about. Healthcare policy and practice is still well behind any silver revolution in sexual attitudes and behaviours. GPs apparently still find sexual health a difficult area of consultation and nurse training is only now beginning to catch up with this new phenomenon. Should doctors and nurses promote and prescribe ways of improving sexual activity amongst older patients in the same way as they promote dieting and medication? Or is this still an area outside their responsibility and beyond their professional "comfort zone"? This dilemma is at its peak for care workers working in residual homes where the traditional boundaries between public and private space are less evident and less easy to man. The CQC report "Promoting Sexual Safety Through Empowerment" in Feb. 2020 argued for leaders across adult social care to create a culture of openness to enable patients in care homes to enjoy sexual relations in safety, with complaints about sexual abuse taken seriously. Too often sex is a taboo subject with staff training and awareness limited or non-existent leading to significant under-reporting and failure to properly address such incidents and so effectively protect residents, especially older women. In response to this challenge, the Royal College of Nursing issued guidance for staff in 2011 and again in 2018 that affirms the importance of sexuality in later life, its potential contribution to health, wellbeing and positive relationships as well as to patient dignity and sense of independence "Sexuality remains a fundamental aspect of who we are as individuals throughout our lives. It influences identity, self-image, self-concept and self-worth. It also affects mental health, social relationships and quality of life". So, sex in the care home is a dilemma and likely to be an urgent one as numbers grow and sexually active residents increasingly become the norm. The resulting image of residential homes as "hotbeds" of sexual activity may initially seem amusing but this is a serious issue of residential management and even human rights and it is especially difficult and often quite distressing when dealing with older people with dementia at a time when an individual's very *person-hood* is at stake and their consciousness is disappearing. This "last taboo" as the ILC-UK has called it, may be one of the few remnants of individuality still remaining.

Inevitably, new technology is getting in on the act and the advent of the Sexbot is likely to add a whole new dimension to human sex lives and relationships. Sexbots – or humanoid robots programmed to be sexually active – are apparently already freely available and futurologists such as David Levy (2009) believe that soon "Love with robots will be as normal as love with humans". Sexbot brothels already exist in cities such as Dortmund in Germany, a home service is on offer in Barcelona and in Japan these artificial *Passion Dolls* are apparently known as "Dutch Wives". All very convenient, and apparently mutually beneficial, particularly for an ageing population, ageing couples and especially the disabled or isolated. Equally, all very challenging for a culture built on monogamous human relationships and based on personal intimacy, belonging and such emotional bonds as love, loyalty and longing. The whole architecture of that most intimate of human relationships seems to be under threat and inevitably a strong and passionate Campaign Against Sex Robots (CASR) has been launched by those fearing such an "invasion of intimacy" – not least as this robot invasion seems to threaten women more than men whether in attractiveness or availability. In her study, Sex Robots: The End of Love (2019), Kathleen Richardson, the founder of CASR, sees Sexbots as a new form of male corporate power designed to marginalise women and even replace them in the lives of men and society at large. In contrast, Helen Driscoll (2015) has argued that sex robots could significantly enhance – or complement – couple's sexual relationships making affairs a thing of the past and prostitution obsolete; a view supported by Danaher and McArthur (2017) who see Sexbots more as sexual companions offering novelty and variety rather than replacement and rejection, mitigating any disparities in desire and so enhancing not threatening long-term relationships. Ultimately, though, as Bryan Appleby has argued (2017), Sexbots are not just another technological intrusion into human life but an existential challenge to the very notion of what it is to be human, what it is to have sex. Just as Alexa is already making friends with our families and beginning to run our households on behalf of Amazon, so *Selexa the Sexbot* is likely to both share our bedroom and transform the very nature and dynamic of this most intimate and personal of human acts; even more so if David Levy is correct in claiming that within a century Sexbots may be able to give birth to children. Sexbots may, however, equally herald another phase in women's liberation if, as Janet-Street Porter has refreshingly put it, they could be trained to do the ironing, cooking and cleaning and "The sooner inventors manage to devise a decent robo-man, women everywhere will be reaching for their credit cards".

Finally, contrast this "sexual revolution in later life" with the picture portrayed by the British Pregnancy Advisory Service in 2018 that teenagers today prefer a quiet life at home in front of a computer screen texting, sexting and sending romantic or even erotic messages to secret or unknown lovers rather than venturing out into the reality of an actual date or intimate liaison. Such virtual dating is apparently easier, less physically dangerous and a lot less embarrassing than a fumble in the dark or personal rejection. Despite the widely advertised dangers of internet dating and sexting, *Generation Sensible* seems to be living safer and more responsible life than previous generations. They drink less, smoke less and are less likely to have unwanted pregnancies. Sexting allows them to enjoy online flirting and even phone sex without commitment or physical effort as a form on extended foreplay before trying the "real thing". Some, however, feel exposed and inadequate on social media and seem to find normal relationships hard to establish or sustain. Some young people, according to the *Next Steps Project* (2018) are even reverting to celibacy, intimidated or appalled by today's culture of hypersexuality and pressure for sexual perfection; a stark contrast apparently to the wild and outgoing teenage years claimed by their parents.

At first, Laura was taken aback, even shocked by sex even being part of her thesis on ageing today. The thought of including *Sex at Sixty or Seventy* in her seminars initially made her squirm but on reflection, she started to recognise that sex and relationships had as much importance to older people as to the young; that a healthy sex life in later life could well be a major contributor to living longer, healthier and happier lives so reducing the possible burden on both the family and the State. From this perspective, sex and personal relationships are not a peripheral issue in any ageing strategy but potentially quite central to it, not only from a health and financial point of view but also as a critical factor in any housing policy, or care-home provision. If the current rate of "silver-splitting" persists, for example, more and more boomers will be seeking single housing, even if their partner now lives next door or down the street. Moreover, good sex and ongoing personal relationships are likely to be a significant source of self-esteem and independence in later life particularly for older women who are not only likely to live longer alone but who may increasingly prone to feelings of no longer being attractive, wanted or needed. Later-life intimacy and sex, internet dating and sexbots may be outside the normal sociological agenda but with so many people living longer and healthier lives, and determined to live them to the full, Laura was at least now alert to the issues and potential implications both personally and politically. Moreover, the idea that she as a young woman today might still enjoy a very pleasurable and fulfilling sex life in later life as well as when young, was such an inspiring "light-bulb" moment that she couldn't stop thinking about it all day or contain herself when chatting to her girlfriends later that night. If healthy happy sex is still on the agenda in later life, than longevity truly is delivering one of its ultimate promises.

4.8 DEATH, DYING AND THE GOOD DEATH

Death and dying may not be standard topics in any traditional Sociology text-book; nor at the forefront of any young student's mind. For most young people, death and dying are things that happen elsewhere in the world, be it in war-torn or disaster-hit areas such as Syria or Yemen or when they happen to other people in the news caught up in knife crimes or terrorist attacks elsewhere in the UK or Europe. Certainly death is not one of the top ten topics on young people's agendas or part of any "cool" conversations to be found on Facebook or Twitter, except perhaps as a young person's cry for help or a terrorist's declaration of war. Death and dying, however, have come to the forefront of every person's thinking today as COVID-19, in its numerous variants, strikes without warning and leaves a trail of older people in its wake without the time or opportunity to say goodbye to their loved ones. Death and dying are, therefore, central to any textbook about ageing where the end of life for most of the older people looms larger and larger on their everyday horizons and increasingly informs many of their decisions about life remaining. This is particularly so, for a baby boomer generation that swore to die before it got old and among whom, few, even now, have yet prepared for their final Woodstock, planned their own funeral or last will & testament. Nevertheless, with the death toll from coronavirus escalating daily and with public debate now much more open and unrestricted, even this most taboo of subjects is now entering public debate with a fear and a force that is unlikely to abate. According to the 2000 Millennium Debate of the Age, ideally, most people, especially baby boomers, would have hoped:

- To know when death is coming and understand what can be expected.
- To retain control of what happens.
- To be afforded dignity and privacy in death.
- To have control over who is present and who shares the end.
- To have time to say goodbye.

Coronavirus has shattered such dreams and forced families across the world to face up to the realities of death and dying and left millions of families across the world mourning their loved – often without the opportunity of ever seeing them again. With death and dying now an everyday discussion, adverts like the Marie Curie hospice *Symmetry* one in 2016, explicitly and deliberately contrasting the indignity of death today with the joyful celebration that greets every new baby, would no longer be quite so shocking after scenes of COVID-related dying in our hospitals have been beamed daily onto our living rooms. Discussions about dying and about the "good death" no longer seem beyond the pale and Joan Bakewell, the Age Ambassador and journalist, now in her 80s, has long campaigned for the need to plan ahead and not just leave dying to the doctors and the hustle and bustle of a hospital ward where saying good-bye to loved ones can be a disturbing and badly disrupted event (2016). Moreover, with new legislation in Spain, Switzerland, Canada and now Scotland offering the opportunity for those with terminal or degenerative diseases to seek the *Right to Die,* so the right to assisted suicide has rapidly risen in recent years with the campaigns of such public figures as Chris Woodhead, Terry Pratchett and Ian Banks. Baroness Meacher's private members bill to legalise assisted dying in England & Wales is gaining increasing support while new technology such as the "suicide machine" (SARCO) developed by Dr Philip Nitschke in the Netherlands and activated simply through the blink of an eye, means that no one else need be involved-or prosecuted.

Even before coronavirus, **Deathcare** in the UK was far less rosy and cosy than many people believed. For many people today, death is a highly impersonal, conveyor-like process over which the dying and their families have little if any control. Modern medicine has lengthened life dramatically in the UK, but it has also lengthened death, taken it out of the home and placed it in a hospital environment there is little time for ceremony or care; simply a professional decision and then a procedure to be followed as the next body is wheeled in. Given the warmth of emotion and compassion expressed when life begins at birth, consultants such as Kathleen Mannix (2017) have been aghast at the coldness of departure at death, and she has campaigned tirelessly for everyone to have an Emergency Healthcare Plan that in discussion with the family, decides whether we die in hospital or at home. Consultant Atul Gawande (2014) has been even more scathing in his indictment of the way modern medicine treats the old and the dying, putting medical considerations first and patient needs, comfort and control last, subjecting terminal patients, in his view, to "barbaric" procedures solely to keep them alive with little consideration of their quality of life in these last stages. As Henry Marsh (2018) aptly summed it up "Although scientific medicine has brought great and wonderful blessings, it has also brought a curse-dying, for many of us, has become an unpleasantly prolonged and institutionalised experience". Whilst 50% of people in the UK currently die in hospital, this is far higher than many other many other European countries and several NHS Trusts such as those in East Anglia are now working to give patients far greater control over their End of Life Care; a control that COVID-19 brutally took away.

The "death" business in the UK, meanwhile, is booming, not just because of COVID-19, but with thousands of baby boomers now on their *Stairway to Heaven* as this generation begins to die out. The UK may therefore be facing a "funeral time-bomb" according to the ILC-UK (2014) with baby boomer deaths alone projected to soar from just under 30,000 in 2019 to well over 100,000 by 2044. Meanwhile, the average cost of dying according to the Sunlife Survey in 2020 is also soaring from below £2000 in 2004 to £9,493 today once professional fees etc. are added in. A potential and catastrophic funeral debt, calculated to be as high as quarter of a billion in less than 20 years' time, is piling up unless families plan ahead and government raises its funeral payments significantly.

According to the IPR/Bath University study in 2017:

- Death in modern Britain is overwhelmingly now in old age
- Most people – almost half – die in hospital and care homes provide the location and care for almost a quarter of all deaths across the UK.
- Nearly two-thirds of the UK population have no will in place and so potentially leave serious chaos and complexity for their relatives to sort out. Equally, family conversations about death and dying rarely take place until serious illness or dementia set in.
- Funerals and burial arrangements are something of a local and national lottery, so intensifying and extending the bereavement and recovery experience for all those remaining.
- The Funeral Business is still highly uncompetitive with the market dominated by just a few key players such as Dignity and the Co-Op Funeralcare. It is surprisingly unregulated and generally under-inspected so increasing the potential for exploitation and over-charging at a time when those involved-particularly the remaining spouse-are most vulnerable and least able to control the situation and make rational decisions.

The death sector in the UK currently operates in something of a policy and planning vacuum that will soon be unsustainable as the baby boomer generation *passes on* over the next 50 years. Even a grave for tomorrow may need booking today given the shortages of places currently available and some councils have even begun to adopt new forms of cremation as a way of solving the shortage and environmental issues of traditional graveyards. West Midlands council, for example, has apparently experimented with water cremation, liquefying human corpses and then "flushing them down the drain", out to sea and back to nature. Alternatively, as Laura's boyfriend, Clive discovered from a local radio phone-in, you might want to organise your own funeral yourself. The idea of a D.I.Y funeral might initially sound like "black humour", but according to the Natural Death Society, it is all perfectly legal – provided that you don't leave the deceased corpse "on the side of the public highway" or contravene any health and safety regulations. It can all be done quite cheaply with online companies providing coffins made to order, a civil service conducted by a voluntary vicar, and a burial on private ground or even in your own back garden so long as two policemen are in attendance as witnesses for land registry purposes.

Debates about death, especially about how to plan a good death, have increasingly inspired celebrities such as Ian McKellen to compose their own funeral oration and Billy Connolly to write a final poem. Funeral websites and electronic graves have begun to appear on Facebook and funeral directors have reported a rise in celebratory funerals with milk floats and even racing cars replacing the traditional hearse whilst the *Ideal Death Show* in Bournemouth in 2018 included designer coffins, a Viking death ship, ash-scattering rockets, a Death Café and a series of Good Funeral Awards – or *Death Oscars* – for the gravediggers and coffin-makers of the year (see Katy Butler: 2019). The 2019 Global Wellness report on "Dying Well", in turn, identified the rise of the *positive death movement* with death doulas and death coaches to help the transition to another world while death tourism is apparently helping clients view death sites abroad. Finally, while most western funerals seem to be shrouded in grief, many other cultures and religions seek to celebrate this passage into the after-life and the paradise beyond. In New Orleans, for example, local people don't only give their dearly departed a raucous party and a lively musical send-off, but they have created family mausoleums to store generations of the same family together in one resting place; an idea that appealed to Laura and her grandparents but not, apparently, to the rest of her family.

Everlasting life

Finally, given Boomers appetite for life and their determination not to leave it, there are some in this ever-young, ever-optimistic, generation, who see continued living as an article of faith and that they have the *right to live forever*. And with new technology advancing at such a rapid rate, their wishes may be granted – if they can afford to pay. As outlined earlier, academics such as Dr Aubrey de Grey at Cambridge University believe that living forever, or at least to 1000 years is a serious possibility and companies such as the Alcor Life Extension Foundation in Arizona, USA has been "freezing" willing subjects since 1967 using cryoprotective substances to preserve their bodies for perpetuity. David Kekich of the Maximum Life Foundation has designed "a scientific roadmap to reverse ageing" using gene restructuring techniques and artificial intelligence to extend youth into pensionable age and so "transform 80-year-olds into 20-somethings again, visually and biologically". While such claims at present, may seem far-fetched and more *scientific fiction* than scientific fact, the rate and depth of scientific advance in biological, genetic and medical science is at least raising the very real possibility of even longer and healthier life for generations to come. Limbs can be replaced even now, and the blind can see again through stem cell advances, so why not life extended further – or even forever? Certainly, the Big Boys of the New Technology World see this as a future market with Google are now investing in companies like Calico to develop anti-ageing agents, capable of extending the health-span rather than, at this stage, the lifespan. Leading members of the Silicon Valley are offering prizes of $1 million for anyone who can "hack the code of life" and the transhumanism movement is growing in wealth and ambition as it expands amongst the rich and powerful in Silicon Valley. Elon Musk, co-founder of PayPal and pioneer of electric cars, is apparently investing in the "pursuit of immortality" with the Neuralink project to connect human brains with computers capable of downloading and uploading human thoughts, while Jesse Karmazin, Chief Executive of Ambrosia, is seeking to rejuvenate older patients with transfusions of teenage blood as a way of countering dementia and other diseases of ageing; truly an intergenerational exchange of young life for old despite its vampirish image while members of the Alcor project have signed up for "heads-only" preservation on the basis that they will be given a new body later on; a sort of anthropoid robot in the distant future. Ray Kurzweil, the *high priest* at Google believes mankind is approaching a new singularity that will transcend biology and elevate mankind into a partnership with artificial intelligence (see Mark O'Connell: 2017 for a fascinating tour of this Brave New World). But as Professor Kaku gently warned in 2012, always be clear what you are asking for "I once read a story about a genie who offered to grant a man any wish he wanted. He promptly asked to live for 1000 years. The genie granted his wish and turned him into a tree".

Conclusions

Death and dying are not standard topics in any sociology textbook, yet increasingly they are key features of any debate about ageing and the Ageing or Ageless society ahead; features that COVID-19 has thrust to the fore. Much as the baby boomer generation loathes the idea of death and even promised to die before it gets old, it is here now and it's daily news as leading figures from the 1960s and 1970s begin to pass away and the government starts warning people to plan ahead and ensure that their wills and executive authorities are all in place. Death and dying in an era of mass ageing is equally generating a public debate about the good death and the individual's right to die in their own chosen way. And if there is one generation with the power and personality to effect and demand such change, it is likely to be the baby boomer generation who may loathe death but who will loathe a bad death even more. For many young people like Laura, death has been a rare experience; a taboo subject rarely discussed. Until, that is, COVID-19 arrived and made it the topic of daily government briefings and the everyday topic of family discussion especially if it affected a family member or close relative as, for example, when Laura's Uncle Alfie passed away. The previously hidden world of death and dying is now much more exposed to public scrutiny with daily media insights into intensive care units and care homes struggling to cope and fearful of further outbreaks. The pandemic, equally, struck a highly emotional and intergenerational cord for Laura as she now began to think about the implications for her generation of a mass exodus of a generation of grandparents and older people, many of whom are still very active and engaged. Very salutary thoughts for any age person; very sad and soulful ones for a young student devoted to her elders. Initially, it was not intended to be part of her thesis, but on reflection, it is a pretty crucial theme in the ageing world ahead.

Epilogue

So, this is the current state of ageing in Great Britain; a state of demographic ageing and social inequality that as the Centre of Ageing Better (2020) commented, COVID-19 has truly laid bare. "We are on the path to a future of ageing badly". Without action "pensioner poverty could return" and old age for younger generations already "facing less secure work, smaller pension pots and much less housing wealth" could be even worse. "These trends are the result of deep and complex structural inequalities in our society but they are not great immovable truths, never to be shifted". What is needed is bold leadership and inspiring innovations "to ensure that the next and future generations of older people are able to reap the benefits of longer, healthier and happier lives". As set out in Chapter 3, the present government may have a grand vision for healthy ageing, may have a plan for reforming social care but it is a long way from the National Plan for Ageing Britain that numerous Parliamentary reports have repeatedly called for. That now became part of Laura's thesis and part of her grandmother's election campaign but first Laura needed to be clearer who the New Old – and New Young – are, if her ideas of Generation, and especially Intergeneration, are to have any sociological validity as agencies of social change.

Bibliography

4.1 The retirement revolution and longer, later life

Aviva: *The Future of Retirement* (2019)
Bolton, Clive: Aviva Real Retirement Report (2013)
Centre for Social Justice (CSJ): *Ageing Confidently-Supporting an ageing workforce* (2020)
Demos Publications: *Next Steps: Life Transitions in the 21ˢᵗ Century* (2015)
Global Retirement Index: Natixis Investment Managers (2020)
'Golden era' of retirement according to the Institute for Fiscal Studies (IFS) Reports on Dynamics of Ageing? Savings after Retirement (2016)
ILC-UK Fact-Pack: *When I'm 64* (2017)
ILC-UK: *The Future of Ageing* Conference & Report (2020)
OECD: *Society at a Glance* (2014)
Royal London Policy Paper: *The Death of Retirement* (2016)
SIRC/Friends Provident Report: *Freetirement Generation* (2007)
The Aegon Center for Longevity and Retirement & Associates: *A New Social Contract for Retirement for the 21st Century* (2018 and follow-up reports 2019–2021)
The Aegon Retirement Readiness Survey (2013)
The Great British Retirement Survey (GBRS) (2020)
World Economic Forum (WEF): *Global Pensions Timebomb* (May 2017)

4.2 The future of work and the multi-generational workforce

Bains Macro Trends: *Labor in 2030: The Collision of Demographics, Automation and Inequality* (2018)
Business, Energy and Industrial Strategy Parliamentary Committee (2019)
Cass Business School Report: *Talentocalpse* (2013)

Centre for Better Ageing: *A Silver Lining for the UK Economy* (Feb. 2018)

Centre for Social Justice (CSJ): *Ageing Confidently-Supporting an Ageing Workforce* (2020)

Franklin, D; Andrews, J: *Megachange: The World in 2050*: Economist/Profile Books (2012)

House of Commons Library: Report on *The Future of Work* (Nov. 2020)

ILC-UK: *Maximising the Longevity Dividend* (2019)

International Delphi Forum: *2050 The Future of Work* (2018)

McKinsey & Company: *The Future of Work after COVID-19* (Feb.18 2021)

McKinsey Global Institute (MGI): *The Promise and the Challenge of the Age of Artificial Intelligence* (2018)

Meister, Jeanne C and Willyard, Karie: *The 2020 Workplace*: Harper Collins (2010)

Mercer Workforce Monitor Report: *The Impact of Brexit, Migration and Ageing on the UK Workforce* (March 2018)

PWC: *Megatrends: 5 Global Shifts Changing the Way We Live and Do Business* (2020)

Technopolis Group: *A Mapping of Smart Ageing Activity in Ireland and an Assessment of the Potential Smart Ageing Opportunity Areas*: (April 2015)

UKCES Report on *the Future of Work, Jobs & Skills in 2030* (2020)

WEF Report: *The Future of Jobs* (Oct. 2020)

WEF: *The Longevity Economy* (2019)

4.3 The Pensions Revolution and financing longer, later life

Esping-Andersen Gosta: *The Three Worlds of Welfare Capitalism*: Princeton University Press (1990)

Financial Conduct Authority (FCA): *Ageing Population and Financial Services* (Sept. 2018)

ILC-UK Study on *Linking the State Pension Age to Longevity-Tackling the Fairness Challenge* (2014)

ILC-UK: *Universal basic income (UBI) have again risen to the fore as solutions for post pandemic-Britain* (2020)

Johnson, Michael: *Why We Should Scrap State Pensions for the Rich*: Money Marketing (April 2017)

Johnson, Paul (IFS): *Golden era* of retirement quote at ILC-UK Conference (2016)

McPhail, Tom (Hargreaves Lansdown): Telegraph (June 2013)

Melbourne Mercer *Global Pension Index* (2017)

Mercer CFA Institute: *Global Pension Index* (2020)

National Audit Office Report (2013)

New Economic Foundation: *Nothing Personal* (2019)

New Economics Foundation: *Scrap Personal Allowance and Replace with a New Weekly Cash Payment* (March 2019)

OECD: *Pensions at a Glance* (2014)

OECD: *Society at a Glance* (2014)

OECD: *Fiscal Challenges and Inclusive Growth in Ageing Societies Report* (2019)

OECD: *Pensions at a Glance* (2019)

OECD: *Pensions at a Glance* (Table 8.5) (2019)

Office for Budget Responsibility (OBR): *Fiscal Sustainability Report* (July 2019)

Pensions Advisory Service: Annual Report (2014)

Royal Society of Arts (RSA): *Collective Defined Contribution Pensions* (2018)

Scottish Widows: *Retirement Report* (2019)

Scottish Widows: *Retirement Survey* (2020)

Standard & Poor: *Global Ageing: An Irreversible Truth* (2010)

World Economic Forum (WEF): *Global Pensions Timebomb* (May 2017)

4.4 The healthcare challenge and eldercare in later life

All-Party Parliamentary Group (APPG): *Adult Social Care* (June 2019)

Alzheimer's Society Report on UK (November 2019)

Barker Commission/Commission on the Future of Health and Social Care in England: Final Report: The King's Fund (2014)

BMJ: *Performance of UK National Health Service Compared with Other High Income Countries* (Nov. 2019)

Care Quality Commission (CQC): *The State of Health Care and Adult Social Care in England* (2017/18)

Care Quality Commission (CQC): *State of Care Report* (2019/2020)

Centre for Policy Studies (CPS): *Fixing the Care Crisis* (2019)

Chan, Margaret, Director-General of the World Health Organization (WHO): *Global Population Ageing: Peril or Promise*: WEF (2012)

CMA: *Care Homes Market Study* (November 2017)

Daniels, N et al.: *Setting Limits Fairly*: Oxford (2002)

Deloitte Centre for Health Solutions: *Connected Health* (2020)

Deloitte Centre for Healthy Solutions: *Covid-19 as a Catalyst* (November 2020)

Deloitte PLC: *Global Healthcare Outlook: Shaping the Future* (2019)

European Observatory Report on Health Systems and Policies (2013)

Feynman, Richard: Quotes: Today in Science History (2011)

Franklin, D; Andrews, J (eds.): *Megachange: The World in 2050*: Economist/Profile Books (2012)

Grant Thornton: *Care Homes: Where Are We Now?* (August 2018)

Harper, Sarah: *Ageing Societies*: Hodder/Arnold (2006)

Health Foundation: *What Should be Done to Fix the Crisis in Social Care?* (August 2019)

Health Foundation Briefing: *Improving the Nation's Health* (November 2020)

House of Lords Economic Affairs Committee Report: *Social Care Funding: Time to End a National Scandal* (July 2019)

Hyman-Robertson: *Report on Residential Care* (2017)

ILO/OECD: *New Job Opportunities in an Ageing Society* (2019)

Institute for Fiscal Studies (IFS): *UK Health Spending* (November 2019)

Kaku, Michio: *Physics of the Future: The Inventions That Will Transform Our Lives*: Penguin Books (2012)

Kekich, David: *Maximum Life Foundation* (December 2015)

Kings Fund: *What Does the Autumn 2020 Spending Review Mean for Health and Care?* (November 2020)

King's Fund Report: *Time to Think Differently* (2014)

McKinsey Global Institute: *The Obesity Crisis* (July 2015)

McKinsey Global Institute: *Ten Innovations That Can Improve Global Health* (July 2020)

National Audit Office (NAO): *Adult Social Care at a Glance* (July 2018)

National Audit Office (NAO): *Readying the NHS and Adult Social Care in England for Covid-19 Peak* (June 2020)

Nuffield Trust: *What Can England Learn from the Long-term Care System in Japan?* (May 2018)

OECD: *Long-term Care Workforce* (2017)

Office for National Statistics (ONS): *Living Longer: Caring in Later Working Life* (March 2019)

Policy Exchange: *21st Century Care* (May 2019)

WEF: *Nearly a Third of the World's Population Is Now Overweight* (June 2017)

WEF: *What the World Can Learn about Japan's Social Care System* (June 2018)

Which magazine: *Paying for Care in Later Life* (March 2021)

WHO: *Active Ageing: A Policy Framework*: Madrid International Plan of Action on Ageing (MIPAA) (2002)
WHO: *Decade of Healthy Ageing 2020-2030* (2019)
WHO Declaration of Alma Ata (1978)
WHO Report on *Ageing and Health* (2015)
WHO's Follow-up Document *'Implementing a Health 2020 Vision'* (2019)
Wilkinson, Richard; Pickett, Kate: *The Spirit Level: Why More Equal Societies Always Do Better*. Penguin Books (2009)

4.5 The housing challenge and the intergenerational housing chain

Age UK: *Housing for Later Life* (2015)
All-Party Parliamentary Group (APPG) Report on Rented Housing (July 2019)
APPG Report: *Housing and Care for Older People* (July 2019)
Arup Foresight Series: *Cities Alive: Designing for Ageing Communities* (June 2019)
British Research Establishment (BRE): *Design for Dementia* (March 2019)
Building Better, Building Beautiful Commission: *Living with Beauty* (February 2020)
Demos: *The Top of the Ladder*. Submission to the All-Party Committee on Housing (2014)
Future of London Report: *Are We Ready for the Boom? Housing Older Londoners* (2018)
Grosvenor Report: *Silver Cities; Planning for an Ageing Population* (2018)
House of Commons Communities and Local Govt Committee: *Housing for Older People Report* (February 2018)
ILC-UK: *The State of the Nation's Housing* (2016)
Institute for Public Policy Research (IPPR): *Generation Rent: No Place to Call Home* (2012)
Intergenerational Commission: *Home Affront: Housing across the Generations* (2017)
Intergenerational Foundation (IF): *Stockpiling Space: How the Pandemic Has Increased Inequalities between Older and Younger Generations* (April 2021)
Local Government Association (LGA) Report (2017)
Loughborough University News: *Loughborough Researchers Develop Dementia-friendly Home* (Aug. 2019)
Mayhew, Les: *Too Little, Too Late? Housing for an Ageing Population*: Cass Business School (2020)
National Housing Federation: 1 in 7 People in England Directly Hit by the Housing Crisis (September 2019)
Policy Exchange: *Building for the Baby Boomers* (December 2018)
Resolution Foundation: *Ageing Fast, Ageing Slow* (October 2019)
Savills: *Retirement Living* (2017/2018); *Housing Solutions for an Ageing Society* (July 2020); *Retirement Living* (June 2020)
Shelter: *A Better Fit? Creating Housing Choices for an Ageing Population* (2012)
Shelter: *This is England: A Picture of Homelessness in 2019; A Vision for Social Housing* (2019)
Smith Institute: *Are Housing Associations Ready for an Ageing Population?* (2015)
The National Housing Federation: *Housing and Intergenerational Inequality* (2017)

4.6 Family, marriage and the multi-generational beanpole

Brooks, David: *The Nuclear Family Was a Mistake*: Atlantic Magazine (March 2020)
Buchanan A; Rotich A (eds.): *Twenty-first Century Grandparents*: OUP (2018)
Buttle UK: *The State of Child Poverty* (2020)
Centre for Social Justice (CJS): *Why Family Matters* (2019)

Cherlin, Andrew J: *Marriage, Divorce, Remarriage*: HUP (1992)

Child Poverty Action Group (CRAG) Report (2020)

Civitas: *Family Factsheets* (2018–2020)

CMS Report: *Our Future Financial Lives* (August 2019)

Coram Family Childcare Survey (2019)

Government Office for Science: *Future of an Ageing Population* (2016)

Grandparents Plus: *The Poor Relation* (2009)

Harper, Sarah: *Ageing Societies*: Hodder Arnold/OUP (2006)

Harris, John: *The Guardian* (January 12, 2020)

Ian Duncan Smith Quoted in Sunday Times (February 2017)

ILC-UK: *Grandparental Generosity* (2013)

Jackson, Richard: Leading Edge Interview (2011)

Marriage Foundation: *Annual Family Breakdown in the UK* (March 2017)

ONS: *UK Family Statistics* (2021)

Tarrant, Anna in Arbers, Timonen T: *Contemporary Grand-parenting*: Policy Press (2012)

UNICEF Report Card 16: *Worlds of Influence: Understanding What Shapes a Child Well-being in Rich Countries* (2020)

World Family Map: *Mapping Family Change and Child Well-Being Outcomes*: Child Trends (2015)

Zhang M; Yaojun L: The Persisting Grandparents' Effects in Contemporary British Society: *Social Science Research*, Volume, 77, pp 179–192 (2019).

4.7 Sex, sexuality and later-life relationships

Appleby Bryan: *Sunday Times* (October 22, 2017)

Borz, WM: *The Roadmap to 100*: Palgrave McMillan (2010)

British Pregnancy Advisory Service: *Social Media, SRE and Sensible Drinking Report* (2018)

Centre for Longitudinal Studies/UCL Institute of Education: *Next Steps Project: Learning from your Generation* (2018)

CQC report 'Promoting Sexual Safety through Empowerment* (Feb. 2020)

Danaher, John; McArthur, Neil (eds.): *Robot Sex*: MIT press (2017)

De Hennezel, Marie: *The Warmth of the Heart Prevents Your Body from Rusting*: Pan McMillan (2011)

Driscoll, Helen: *Sex with Robots*: Independent (August 4, 2015)

English Longitudinal Study of Ageing (2015)

Fishel, Deirdre; Holzberg, Diana: *Still Doing It*: Penguin (2008)

Greer, Germaine: *The Change: Women, Ageing and the Menopause*: Hamish Hamilton (1991)

Gott, Merryn: *Sexuality, Sex Health and Ageing*: OUP (2005)

Heyman, Arlene: *Scary Old Sex*: Bloomsbury (2017)

ILC-UK: *The Last Taboo* (2011)

ILC-UK: *How Long Wil I Love You? Sex and Intimacy in Later Life in the UK* (2017)

Knight, India: *In Your Prime*: Penguin (2014)

Levy, David: *Love and Sex with Robots*: Gerald Duckworth & Co: (2009)

Manchester Institute of Collaborative Research on Ageing (MICRA): *The Golden Generation* (June 2017)

Manning, Margaret et al.: '*Sixty and Me*' Website (2014)

Perel, Ester: *The State of Affairs*: Yellow Kite (2017)

Richardson, Kathleen: *Sex Robots: The End of Love*: Polity Press (2019)

Royal College of Nursing: *Older People in Care Homes: Sex, Sexuality and Intimate Relationships* (2011/2018)
Salerno/ICL Study: *Times* (July 7 2019)
The Independent Age: *(Sex) Survey* (February 2018)
The Lancet, UK: *National Survey of Sexual Attitudes and Lifestyles* (November 25, 2013)
Theobald, Stephanie: *Sex Drive*: Unbound (2018)

4.8 Death, dying and the good death

Bakewell, Joan: *Sunday Times* (December 11, 2016)
BBC News: *2000 'Millennium Debate of the Age'* (July 15, 1999)
Butler, Katy: *The Art of Dying Well*: Simon & Schuster (2019)
Gawande, Atul: *Being Mortal: Illness, Medicine and What Matters in the End*: Profile Books (2014)
Global Wellness Institute: *Dying Well Initiative* (2020)
ILC-UK: *'I Can't Afford to Die: Addressing Funeral Poverty* (2014)
Institute of Policy Research (IPR)/Bath University: *Death, Dying and Devolution*: (September 2017)
Kaku, Michio: *Physics of the Future*: Penguin (2012)
Kekich, David: Maximum Life Foundation (December 2015)
Mannix, Kathleen: *With the End in Mind*: William Collins (2017)
Marsh, Henry: *A Time to Die*: St (July 1, 2018)
O'Connell, Mark: *To Be a Machine*: Doubleday Books (2017)
Sunlife: *Cost of Dying Report* (2020)
The Centre for Ageing: *The Experience of People Approaching Later Life in Lockdown* (July 2020)

PART III

The New Old, the New Young and the forces for change

FIGURE III.1 Image of baby boomers

FIGURE III.2 Image of intergenerational family

5

THE NEW OLD AND THE NEW YOUNG

Baby boomers & generations X, Y & Z and intergenerational relations today

Introduction

Laura's grand tour of ageing Britain had highlighted the huge challenges facing ageing Britain socially, economically and politically. What this tour hadn't really revealed though was who the New Old are, how they see ageing in the future and how they might respond to longer life, a second life and life in a multigenerational society. Their behaviour, their involvement in creating a New-Age Britain was central to her thesis and to life ahead for her generation as well.

But who exactly is this mythical and mysterious generation that older people and the media talk so nostalgically or disparagingly about? What powers do they have for changing the future and how – or why – might they use them? More important to Laura's thesis, will they as a generation assert themselves again as the agents of social change? Will they give Karl Mannheim's concept of generation a new lease of life and will they, in collaboration with the New Young, create a new social contract, an intergenerational social contract fit for the 21st century and fit to be this generation's final legacy?

The New Old

As you can imagine, when Laura first presented the first draft of her degree thesis to her study group, it was shouted down and derided as ridiculous:

> **The idea of** *Ageing as a Global Force for Change* ranking alongside globalisation, new technology and urbanisation as one of the global forces of the 21st Century contradicts every known notion of social and political change. Ageing is normally perceived as a slow process of social decline

DOI: 10.4324/9781003029373-9

and decay. Only the most progressive countries have yet perceived ageing as a positive force for change; as a potential demographic dividend
in the way that the UN/WHO and EU have advocated.

The idea of the Old as *a new revolutionary force*, is even more absurd. The
Old are usually perceived as a "drag" and a drain on economic and social
progress, a reactionary force looking to back to the past rather than
looking forward to the future. The idea that Grey Power, Granny-or
even Grandad-Power might be a radical, even revolutionary, force for
the future flies in the face of common sense and all previous theories of
people power and social change.

However, as Laura argued in response:

The New Old, in both the western and the eastern world, in the
21st century, are no longer a minority population living for a short period
of time in small numbers. They are a mass population living in large
numbers for nearly ninety years or more. They are a New Generation
of Old; a generation born into a century of dramatic changes economically, politically and socially brought on by two World Wars, a Cold
War, a post-industrial transformation in the world economy and an era
of affluence way beyond the incomes and lifestyles of their parents and
grandparents-the Silent Generations. The New Old are not the Old
Old. They bring with them a new dynamic, a new determination NOT
to retire, not to withdraw from society at large but to be part-possibly a
leading part-in shaping the world ahead not only for their own sake but
for their children and grandchildren.

The New Old are the advance guard for the *Grey Wave* of Ageing that is
now sweeping the planet; but they are still something of an unknown
quantity. They have no manifesto of their own, no leadership with a
public profile and no collective consciousness to build a political or
social movement on. Brexit and the election of Donald Trump may
have been examples of Grey Power but their potential impact on the
world economy and world balance of power is still little understood.
The power of the New Old is, at this time, potential power, not as yet
actual power. They have yet to use it in common cause. Whether they
will, only time will tell.

So, this was the heart of Laura's thesis, the central theme of this reader and
the conclusion of such internationally renowned consultancies as the McKinsey
Global Institute and World Economic Forum. It is not, however, the conclusion
or central theme of most traditional sociological theories nor of most introductory textbooks in the social sciences. However, once you look at the emerging
power of ageing as it sweeps across the globe; once you look more closely at
this new generation of Old, once you look at the other great forces for change

sweeping the world ahead – and their speed and impact – then all past assumptions about social structure and social change disappear and the potential for a new sociological paradigm, for a new set of sociological theories and a new perspective on change in the 21st century begins to become a serious possibility.

So, asked Laura's study group, who exactly are the baby boomers and what makes them different from previous generations of older people? Laura's answer was to cite Wikipedia – the encyclopedia used by most of her study group. Wikipedia described the post-war baby boomer as "a person who was born during the post war baby boom between the years 1946 and 1964, who, according to the U.S. Census Bureau, as a group 'were the wealthiest, most active, and most physically fit generation, and amongst the first to grow up genuinely expecting the world to improve with time. … One feature of the Boomers was that they tended to think of themselves as a special generation, very different from those that had come before … This rhetoric had an important impact on the self-perceptions of the boomers, as well as their tendency to define the world in terms of generations, which was a relatively new phenomenon". Baby boomers created and generated a social and cultural revolution that lives on even today. They were the first generation to grow up with television; the first generation really to be defined by their music, fashion and distinct lifestyles; the first generation to think of themselves and act as a generation with a distinct identity – the "My Generation" proudly proclaimed by the British pop group The Who, and one that consciously sought to culturally and socially separate itself from generations and traditions before, creating the so-called "generation gap" that lives on even today. As Richard Croker, author of The Boomer Century: 1946–2046 (2007) explains, "The 1960s was the decade that defined the boomers. The music, events, and social changes left a permanent imprint…The Sixties were turbulent, owing to the unrest of civil rights marches, 'free love', rock music, drug experimentation, long hair and dishevelled clothes, and the winds of war in Indochina". As he goes on to explain: "The needs and desires of our massive generation became the primary concern of business as well as unstoppable force shaping popular culture. We didn't just eat food, (We) spawned the fast-food industry.…We didn't just wear clothes. We transformed the fashion industry… We didn't just date and marry. We transformed sex roles and practices, broke taboos of divorce, and transformed the traditional models of the nuclear family". Baby boomers grew up amid the Cold War, the Cuban Crisis, the Berlin Wall, the Assassination of President JFK and his brother Bobby. They grew up in what Daniel Coleman (in Croker: 2007) has called the paradoxical environment of a world of affluence and a world MAD(ness); the paradox of a world of plenty and a world threatening *mutually assured destruction* that could end it all in seconds. And, in recognition of its distinct contribution, the baby boomer generation was named *The Person of the Year* by Time magazine in 1966.

The notion that baby boomers had a worldwide impact is generally beyond dispute; the notion that constitute a distinct and self-conscious generation, however, is wide open to debate. The term baby boomer is much stronger and more widely used in the United States than in Europe and the United Kingdom. Baby boomers are loud, proud and big business in America but relatively low-key in Britain and abroad, more a newspaper headline than a flag on the front lawn. Even the boom in births that gave this generation their name is subject to debate with different countries identifying very different "baby-boom" periods. Some countries in Europe and Australasia had more of a "baby blip" than a baby boom; others like the United States and United Kingdom not only had a post-war demographic surge but a second baby boom or "demographic after-shock"; one that generated two distinct sub-generations of baby boomer with distinctly different attitudes to life as both lived through the era of tumultuous change that was the late 1960s and early 1970s. Early or leading-edge boomers "tend to be optimistic, strongly individualistic and who seek a life that is personally fulfilling but believe that it is up to them to create that life". Whilst late boomers "tend to be less idealistic and optimistic, more practical, pragmatic and realistic" (Wikipedia). However, as Dr Zeitz (Croker: 2007) has commented, even in the United States not every baby boomer was radical or "revolting". "One of the great myths is that everyone was marching and protesting for a cause and that these causes were all on the Left. In fact...at best 20% of college students in the 1960s participated in one or two marches, and only 2%or 3% identified themselves as 'activists'....which is to say that at least 80% of the population was probably apolitical and managed to stay on the side-lines in the 1960s".

However, even today as we move into the 2020s and 2030s, the size and power of baby boomers as they move "like a pig through the python" appears to grow with age rather than decline. Year 2020 was declared as the beginning of "the decade of the old" with 134 million 65–74-year olds across all rich countries – the most numerous, healthy and wealthy generation ever. As the Cushman and Wakefield 2020 Report declared, the world economy is soon to experience a series of seismic demographic shifts as 693 million boomers move out of work over the next ten years and 1.3 billion Gen Z workers move in. "Ageing societies are set to be one of the most transformative changes of the twenty-first century" (Ipsos Mori/Centre for Ageing Better: 2019).

So, replied Laura's classmates, while we might agree that a generation called the baby boomers actually lived and apparently lived quite lively and exotic lives in the 1960s and 1970s, does this age group actually represent a distinct generation? Do they genuinely feel a "generational allegiance", a generational consciousness powerful enough to motivate them to take some form of collective action above and beyond their own self-interest? Or is all of this myth and mirrors, media hype and historical "nostalgia" dreamt up and dressed up by those who, having lived in the post-war era, are still alive and "young" enough to remember it – and to celebrate it – aided by a generation of rock stars, politicians and film stars who still seem determined to take centre-stage even now? Laura's initial response was simple. Go and look at your own grandparents and those born and brought up in the period 1946–1964. Go and look at what active lives they are now still living and what they looked like when they were our age. Have a look at these pictures of my Grandma Polly – now a politician in her 60s – when she was our age dressed in hotpants and miniskirt while my Uncle Donald – now a prosperous businessman was a typical "rocker" in his youth with his leathers, winklepickers and brylcremed hair. These images quickly had her study group in fits of laughter and scouring their iPhones for comparable pictures of their own ageing relatives; images that brought this academic debate about ageing hippies to life and generated a much more real and much more personal discussion about what rich and active lives this baby boomer generation seems to have had. This insight also alerted Laura's classmates to the possibility that they too might be part of a generation in the making and that they too might have a place in history. Quite an eye-opener when you are only just 21 and only just becoming aware of your place in society and in the world ahead.

The British baby boomer, in contrast to his/her American, Canadian or Australian "cousin", the British boomer is a relatively reserved figure, reluctant to declare generational allegiances or seek media attention. There is no British boomer *magazine* as such, *no* Boomer spokesperson, *no* political lobby for the Boomer comparable to the membership and immense political clout of the AARP in America and the CARP in Canada. Whilst there are numerous organisations in the United Kingdom representing the elderly such as AGE UK, there are none with a specific "boomer" orientation, none with a strong political platform, none with the self-conscious "attitude" of boomers in America, Australia or even New Zealand. Nevertheless, British boomers are a force to be reckoned with:

- **They have the numbers** with some 600,000 boomers every year from now until 2030, creating a potential "older" population of some 16–17 million (nearly 22% of the British population), all of whom are now living on average some 20 years longer than their parents.
- **They have the wealth** with the 50–64 age group owning more than 80% of the nation's £12.8 trillion wealth, £1 trillion of the country's £2.6 trillion shares and savings, a third of the £1.8 trillion held in pension funds and 40% of the £2.5 trillion tied up in property … and one in five baby boomers owns a second home.
- **They have the power**; economic power through the "Silver Economy", political power through the "Grey Vote" and the "Grey Lobby" and technological power through the raft of new age-friendly technologies spreading slowly over from such tech giants as Panasonic and Samsung and their ageing markets in Japan and Korea.
- **They have the media presence** through a phalanx of ageing but still very glamorous and high-profile celebrities such as Paul McCartney, Elton John and Twiggy – "rock-stars" of the 1960s and 70s, many of whom are still performing today.

As Harkin and Huber described them back in 2004, British baby boomers remain **"Eternal Youths"**. They have a generational identity and they are still keen to engage in, even "colonise" popular culture, particularly "the youth culture" that they helped create and adapt it to their own self-image whether it be through fashion, beauty products or even motorbikes. Personal fulfilment is a priority for this age group and the overriding ambition of British boomers apparently is to "have their time again", to travel to places they couldn't previously afford and to make up time with their grandchildren that might have been lost on their own children through the demands of their working careers and outgoing lifestyles. They are as "youthful" as their American cousins and they have no intention of growing old gracefully. "Baby boomers refuse to pass on the baton of youth culture which they believe is (still) rightfully theirs". However, on the downside of such "boomer" optimism and youthful ambition, Harkin and Huber also found a fear and a loathing of old age, a hatred of being patronised, a distrust of authority and a demand that all forms of service – public or private – meet their expectations: a dread of loss of independence in old age and a desire to control their own death, although few of them seem to have had the foresight to plan ahead and fewer still seem to have appreciated living later life alone. These researchers, however, found little evidence of generational solidarity or appreciation of the *two classes* of pensioner now emerging in later life – the affluent oldie with their own home, investments and secure pension compared to the pauper pensioner living in social or rented housing and existing on a state pension alone.

In a later study, Rebecca Leach and her colleagues (2013) made a distinction between early and later baby boomers; between the *first wave* of Boomers (1945–1954) who *broke the* "mould" and "set out a new and distinct course through adult life....one marked by change, challenge and transformation" and a *second wave* (1955–1964) who enjoyed a more settled upbringing and moved into adult life in the 1970s and 1980s after the 1960s rebellions of their older brothers and sisters and prior to the economic and political upheavals of the Thatcher era. These two "waves", each in their own way, created what the Keele researchers called a *generational bridge* with the past as well as a breakthrough into the future; an attachment to continuity and identification with their parental values, as well as identification with younger generations in the realms of technology, fashion and social life; a modified materialism and a bridge between the strict and stringent values of their parents about the value of things during the austerity of the post-war years and their own experience of affluence and relative prosperity in the 1960s and thereafter. The baby boomer code of consumption therefore puts high value on quality, durability and value for money and deplores cheap and nasty products that have limited lifespans. Nevertheless, whilst boomers still hark back to the values of the past, ultimately, they apparently see themselves as having more in common in the future with their children's values and lifestyles than with those of the past and their parent's; a millennial shift from *grey to silver* that was neatly captured in the title of the 2015 *Colour Report* sponsored by the retirement home developers McCarthy and Stone; a report that characterised modern-day baby boomers as:

- **Ageless** – determined to live life to the full and feeling younger – much younger – than they actually are with many in their 60s still feeling like 50-year olds and age 70 now referred to as "the new 60"; still very conscious of their looks and very fashion conscious with 14% of women shopping alongside their daughters in Topshop, Zara and H&M; and heavily into new technology with 95% having a mobile phone and 59% a tablet with Facebook, Skype and various "apps" widely used.
- **Relationship-conscious** – with family and friends as top priorities and new relationships a particular focus given the very high number living alone as a result of divorce or widowhood. More than 79% of 65–74-year olds remain sexually active and nearly one in five 75+ year olds is still having regular sex.
- **Active, ambitious and independent** – and determined to stay so with healthy living a priority, exercising a major activity and travel to new places and distant shores a life-fulfilling ambition.

Far from retiring from society, today's late-lifers are ahead of the young and full of ambition for the future – their future. Nearly 60% of respondents to this survey felt that their generation was more special and more radical than previous generations and all of them refused to be stereotyped. They are part of a bright new future for themselves and their families. They want to feel part of society; inside, not outside it and they certainly will not tolerate being excluded by any form of ageism. Moreover, as the 2015 Chief Medical Officer's Annual Report illustrated, this generation of older people is much more diverse than the past, more a generational rainbow than a simple shaft of silver light. According to this report:

- Baby boomers are overwhelmingly ethnically white, though 11% of the older age groups now are from ethnic minorities following the influx of "Windrush" immigrants from the Caribbean in 1948 and of Asian Ugandans expelled by Idi Amin in the 1970s.
- Divorce rates between the boomer generations are high but so too are remarriage rates and cohabitation.
- Baby boomers are more likely to be working after age 60 than previous generations with increasing numbers going part-time or self-employed.
- Baby boomers are apparently as eager to embrace new technology as younger ones with increasing numbers adopting social media too, although most boomers still have a predisposition towards traditional forms of mass media such as TV and newspapers than their children and are less likely to be found on Twitter or Instagram.

So, the New Old are clearly no longer the Old Old; they are *sixty shades of silver*, leading increasingly active and healthy lifestyles with later life as a sort of "lifestyle crossroads", a bonus life to be lived to the full. They are giving birth to super-boomers in their 70s, 80s and even 90s such as David Attenborough and Judy Dench, starring in new films, running new enterprises and even going into political life. However, on the "dark side", worrying numbers of this ageing generation are reverting back to the rebellious lifestyles of the past with rates of alcoholism, obesity, drug-taking and even sexually transmitted diseases amongst the over-60s appearing to be on the increase. So, while some members of this charmed generation are out to live life to the full, others unfortunately seem determined to throw away the very thing that has made this generation special and unique; the gift of extra life, the gift of longevity and with it the opportunity of a longer lifetime with their children and grandchildren.

The 2019 Ipsos-Mori Global Survey found that many of these boomer traits were international in nature and described baby boomers generally as Perennials, as "ever-blooming, relevant people of all ages who live in the present time, know what's happening in the world, stay current with technology, and have friends of all ages. We get involved, stay curious, mentor others, are passionate, compassionate, creative, confident, collaborative, global-minded, risk-takers who continue to push up against our growing edge and know how to hustle".

However, this survey also found that:

- Attitudes to ageing strongly reflect a county's stage of ageing. While people in ageing Japan and South Korea tended to be the most worried about ageing, those in youthful Indonesia and Egypt were far less so.
- A total of 60% of respondents felt that older people do not get the respect that they deserve leading some countries such as Japan to introduce National Respect the Aged Days or Grandparents Day as in the United States whilst adult children in Singapore and China are required by law to either visit their elderly parents regularly or help fund them.
- More than 60% of respondents would like to stay at home rather than go into care homes and receive care either from friends or family, trained carers or even home robots such as Pepper in Japan, the Care-o-bot in Germany, Dinsow in the United States and Alexa everywhere.
- Across all countries, older age groups tended to long nostalgically for the past; a nostalgia captured by Vince Cable's comment in 2016 that many older voters in Britain were driven to vote for Brexit by a "nostalgia for a world where passports were blue, faces white and the map was coloured imperial pink".

Generational theory

However, whatever their size, aspirations and potential power, do baby boomers generally, and in Great Britain in particular, seriously constitute a *self-conscious generation*; a generation with a common sense of identity and a common agenda for action? Do they fulfil the criteria set out by the German Sociologist, Karl

Mannheim in 1929 that the era in which a person was born affects, even determines, their collective consciousness and actions in the same way that social class, gender or ethnicity apparently do? Do baby boomers have a collective mentality that "mirrors a dominant view of the world, reflecting similar attitudes and values and providing a basis for shared action". Writers such as Graeme Codrington (2008/2017) believe that they do: "They (Baby Boomers) intend, in years to come, to morph into revered 'silver heads', who will lead their nations and industries through dangers to a better world beyond, as a result of their principled, optimistic outlook on life. Their 'defining' and guiding values include: Idealism; image; optimism; team orientation; personal growth; personal gratification; group togetherness by similarity of belief; self-expressive; media savvy; excellence; big talkers; youth; work; involvement; health/wellness; nostalgia". American sociologists, Howe and Strauss (*Generations*: 1991/The *Fourth Turning*: 1997) have gone further, arguing that **Generation** is a force for historical change and that generations breed generations in a sort of historical cycle of change and stabilization, "History creates generations, and generations create history. The cycle draws forward energy from each generation's need to redefine the social role of each new phase of life it enters. And it draws energy from each generation's tendency to fill perceived gaps and to correct (indeed overcorrect) the excesses of its elders"; a cycle illustrated in Figure 5.1 below.

Baby Boom Generation: Prophet (Idealist)*: 1st Turning: Post-War: American High (1946-1964)

Generation X (13th Generation): Nomad (Reactive)*: 2nd Turning Awakening: Consciousness Revolution: fourth Great Awakening (1964-1984)

Generation Y (Millennial Generation): Hero (Civic)*: 3rd Turning Unravelling: Neoliberalism/Culture Wars/Tech Bubble (1984-2007)

Generation Z (Homeland Generation): Artist (Adaptive)*: 4th Turning: Crisis: War on Terror; Great Recession: Covid-19 Pandemic/ Recession)

FIGURE 5.1 Howe and Strauss: Post–war historical chart: Millennial saeculum (75+ years)

Source: Sampled and adapted from Wikipedia (*Archetype)

Certainly, the concept of generation has risen up the public and academic agenda in recent years with publications such as The Pinch (2011), the creation of the Intergenerational Foundation (IF) in 2011 and the launch of the Intergenerational Commission in 2016 by the Resolution Foundation. Older voters were certainly perceived to be key figures in the 2016 Brexit Referendum and thereafter whilst Donald Trump's triumph in 2016 has been described as "a rebellion of the aged-a bygone generations last furious gasp against modernity". However, many boomers across the western world have remained true to their radical roots, actively campaigning in support of environmental as well as political and social issues and even taking once again to the streets in support of causes headlined by the young such as Extinction Rebellion and Black Lives Matter. Brexit may seem to have been a generationally divisive issue in the UK, but concerns about the young, about the future of their children and grandchildren may prove to be a much more enduring and life-lasting cause and one that brings the generations in the United Kingdom and elsewhere together rather than splitting them apart. As Harry R. Moody wrote back in 2001 (American Society on Aging), "aging boomers (need to) find a new story, one that not only makes sorrows (of the past) bearable, but also converts our experience into hope for future generations".

The New Young

So, if baby boomers were the *golden generation*, of the late 20th century, how will generations X, Y and Z be remembered? What distinguishes them from previous generations and those to come? A contrast in generational traits summarised in Figure 5.2 overleaf.

As Graeme Codrington and Sue Grant-Marshall argued in their study *Mind the Gap* in 2011, while generational idealism may still be a feature of the baby boomer generation, generational pragmatism is certainly a feature of younger ones. Generation Z, for example, is the digital or *iFacebook Generation personified*. Facebook, Twitter and WhatsApp "are their life", their social persona and their window on a world where connectivity is as crucial today as networking or class was in the past. While boomers were used to planning the future using the wisdoms of the past, the younger generations have grown up in an age where the future in the 21st century seems to bear little or no relationship to the past; it seems have a force all of its own, to be totally unpredictable and more in the hands of bright young whizz-kids and tech-giants outside of normal government control, unhampered by past practices or business models and now aiming quite literally for the moon and beyond. Google, Facebook and Amazon seem to rule the western world whilst Alibaba and Tencent control the east.

However, Generation Z, today's teenage generation and tomorrow's future parents and politicians, are not as happy and hopeful about the future as their baby boomer predecessors appear to have been. On one hand, the Ipsos-Mori Report in July 2018 found Britain's Gen Z to be more trusting, socially minded and less materialistic than millennials; and better behaved, smoking, drinking and drug-taking less, being less politically minded and closer to mum and dad. They relate to brands in terms of access rather than possession; to consumption as an expression of individual and ethical identity. A total of 76% say they are religious but with very liberal views including gender-fluidity and self-expression. They respect diverse thinking and ideas but are less confrontational in attitudes to change. They are self-learners who are more comfortable with online knowledge than traditional sources. They are keenly aware of job instability and fluidity, especially now, and so they tend to prioritise job security over high salaries. They are not a possessive generation preferring access to ownership, streaming music and online videos, renting or leasing cars or personal possessions to actually owning and possessing them. They are relatively comfortable with the gig-economy, trading insecurity for flexibility and they expect personalised

Baby Boomer (1946-1964): I am Ambitious and will Question Everything: Work Defines Me:

- I want to make a difference
- I am highly motivated and hard-working
- I believe in equality and expect respect
- I will challenge authority and take risks if need be.
- I am driven and experienced and like to see my achievements recognised.

Generation X (1965-1979): I am Self-Reliant but I like Structure and Direction: I am a Pragmatic Realist:

- I work to live and want a work-life balance.
- I work smarter but not harder; can multi-task.
- I don't like to be micro-managed.
- I like rewards and gratification
- I can innovate, am tech-savy and a problem solver.
- Family is important to me.
- I expect to live comfortably.

Generation Y (1990-1994): I Expect Support to Achieve: I Need a Sense of Purpose and Contribute to the Greater Good.

- I need nurturing, frequent recognition and feedback.
- I am career-motivated but not company loyal.
- A flexible work-life balance is crucial.
- I need to work with you, not for you.
- My friends are important to me and I want to be liked and have a sense of belonging.
- I earn to spend.

Generation Z (1995-2010): I am Self-Directed: Personal Freedom is Non-Negotiable.

- I don't fit into a traditional work environment.
- Connectivity is as important as breathing.
- I expect everything to be inter-connected.
- I expect to be kept informed and involved.
- I expect to be less well-off than my parents.
- I struggle with independent household management.

FIGURE 5.2 Generational traits chart

Source: Adapted from Health Education, England Report: Narrowing the Gap: 2017

products and service and value brands that are ethical, non-sexist, idealistic and take a public stand. They avoid companies involved in scandals but respect those that admit and rectify mistakes.

On the other hand, the Gen-erators Z Report in 2015 found today's 16–25-year olds to be haunted by fear of failure not only from their parents and families but also from their peers on social media. Worse, as the *Prince's Trust's Youth Index* found in 2018, many young people (16–25) in the United Kingdom today, now feel more gloomy about the future – and their futures – than any time in the previous eight years. A total of 25% do not feel in control of their lives, almost half do not feel that the traditional goals of a good job or owning their own house are realistic whilst the advent of Brexit and the election of Donald Trump, apparently, generated "a staggering deterioration in young people's confidence about the future". The Cigna Loneliness Index in 2020 found 79% of Gen Z and 71% of millennials reporting loneliness with social media exacerbating rather than mitigating their feelings of isolation and emotional distance. Such youthful pessimism today contrasts starkly with the boundless optimism that their parents and grandparents enjoyed as early or late baby boomers, and it raises huge concerns for a generation now feeling that their lives – and the world around them – are out of control at the very time that change in the 21st century is apparently going into warp – speed on one hand and facing the aftermath of a global pandemic on the other. Is that fear, asked Laura's tutor Jonathan, the common cause that might – just might – bring all generations together in the common cause of "taking back control" but this time for all future generations as well as for the future of the planet.

However, beneath all this debate on generational diversity and intergenerational relations, what is often lost and under-appreciated is the profound and enduring impact that longevity is having and will have on the future lifestyles and generational relationships in the United Kingdom or elsewhere. As Figure 5.3 below illustrates, successive generations in the United Kingdom have enjoyed successive increases in life expectancy that have undoubtedly had profound impact on the shape and outcomes of their future lives. While men born into the Silent generation

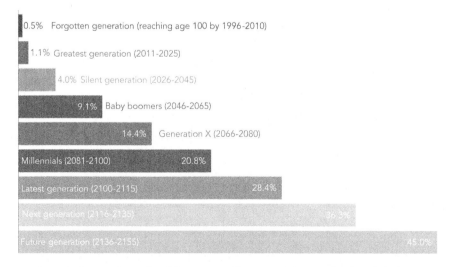

FIGURE 5.3 Proportion of each generation living to 100: England and Wales/UK, birth cohorts 1896–2055

Notes: Cohorts born prior to 1956 cover England and Wales only, cohorts born after cover the UK

Source: ONS, UK lifetables (2014-based) and ONS England and Wales (2014-based)

(1926–1945), for example, could expect to live on average, for some 52 years and women for 57 years, today only some hundred years later, Generation Z can expect to live to 89 and 93 years, respectively, and even more astoundingly, a third of babies born today are predicted to live over 100 years. Even more astonishingly, as people live into old age so their later-life, life expectancy rises according to their underlying health. At age 65, for example, baby boomers today can expect to live on average another 27 years for men and another 30 years for women – virtually twice the post-65 longevity of their parents.

Such dramatic increases in life expectancy may be rarely recognized, but they have been socially, politically and economically transformational. As illustrated in Figure 5.4, they have changed the shape of our lives, delayed the traditional staging posts in life of leaving school, getting married, starting a family and even entering retirement; all of which now seem to get later and later.

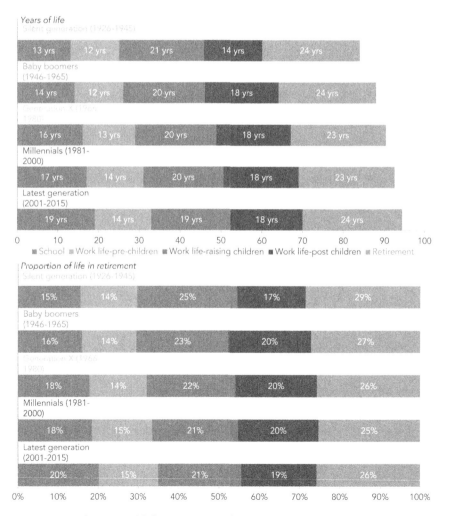

FIGURE 5.4 Lifetimes and life stages across the generations: UK: 1926–2015

Moreover, the intergenerational age-profile is now a pillar rather than a pyramid, the age-related dependency ratio of 3:1 or 4:1 as in the past appears to be approaching 1:1 by 2065 and by 2050 robots may well be everywhere in the workplace and at home. All generations are advancing into a "Brave New World". Whether they advance together will be one of the greatest intergenerational challenges of this century. Whether Covid-19 is having an enduring impact on generational attitudes and priorities is equally a fascinating sociological question; one that the Sunday Times/Britain Thinks survey in September 2021 sought to explore and one that revealed significant differences not only between 16–24 year olds and those over 65 but between today's youngsters and those over 25.

Intergenerational relations

Whilst intergenerational harmony may well be what the world at present desperately needs and most people want, intergenerational tensions, even conflicts, are as much a feature of intergenerational relations today as the so-called generation gap was back in the 1960s. Much of this debate can be traced back to the publication in 2011 of David Willetts book "The Pinch" and its provocative sub-title "How the baby boomers took their children's future – and why they should give it back". Willett's thesis was that those lucky enough to be born between 1945 and 1965 are the biggest and richest generation that Britain has ever known – and that they attained this position at the expense of their children; children who are finding it harder than ever to get on the housing ladder, find a secure job and settle down with a family. In Willett's view **the Social Contract** that should exist between the generations has been broken; or at least forgotten: "It is not that the baby boomer generation are 'bad'", argued Willetts later. It is simply that they appear to have failed "to attach any value to the interests of the younger generation. It is a profound break in the intergenerational contract from which Boomers themselves have gained so much… Boomers are enjoying a one-off offer which will not be available to their kids and grandkids as they grow older" (2019). Willett's book inspired a whole host of critiques of the baby boomer generation, all with withering titles and accusations of gross selfishness that ranged Francis Becket's "What did the baby boomers ever do for Us" (2010) to Howker and Maliks "The Jilted Generation: How Britain has bankrupted its Youth" (2010). Even such "senior" baby boomers as Jeremy Paxman expressed outrage at being "part of the most selfish generation in history" (Mail in Oct. 2011) while Thaddeus Best predicted an "Age War", and the London School of Economics went so far as to host a "public trial" in February 2014, accusing the baby boomer generation in the United Kingdom of violating "the human rights" of generations X and Y. The Intergenerational Foundation (IF) was set up in 2011 to fight on behalf of the young against generational injustices in such areas as housing, employment and benefits while politicians as old as Vince Cable, the leader of the Lib-Dems, accused older people who voted to leave the EU of

New Old and New Young

having "comprehensively shafted the young". A similar *Age War* has erupted in America with Bruce Gibney's (2017) describing post-war baby boomers as "A Generation of Sociopaths" who have betrayed America's young while Joseph C. Sternberg accused boomers of "The Theft of a Decade" (2019). Time Magazine even declared a **Youthquake** on its cover in January 2020 predicting a generational uprising and a step-shift in political priorities and direction once the millennial generation begins to replace the current boomer gerontocracy.

Responses to such generational accusations have been swift and vigorous. As Professor Alan Walker argued in the 2014 British Academy Debates, the vast majority of Boomers are not millionaires, or anything like it and far from baby boomers having stolen their children's future, they have given their children a standard of living and a start in life, far beyond any previous generation. They have contributed at least what they will receive in pensions, healthcare and other services, with 31% of over 65s providing financial support to younger members of their families and with older boomers now contributing some £40 billion annually to the UK economy. However, as the reports from the Intergenerational Commission (IGC) have shown, Millennials do seem to have fallen behind previous generations at this point in their lives becoming both a **Stagnation Generation** in falling terms of incomes and lifestyles and a **Generation Rent,** unable to get on the today's housing ladder without parental support. The traditional intergenerational expectation that each generation would enjoy greater prosperity and opportunity than its predecessor has apparently given way to a national pessimism that the youth of today might never catch up – until possibly the baby boomer generation eventually passes away and their adult children inherit a "Wall of Wealth"; an inheritance that the Commission feared in its final report in 2018 might severely exacerbate intragenerational inequality in future years as it would likely be the better-off millennials that inherit this wealth, rather than their poorer counterparts who need it most.

The Parliamentary Report on Intergenerational Fairness in 2019, however, put the blame firmly and squarely on "the action and inaction of successive governments"; inaction that has left "Many in younger generations struggling to find secure, well-paid jobs and secure, affordable housing, while many in the older generation risk not receiving the support they need because government after government has failed to plan for a long-term generational timescale". The Committee found no public support for the idea that older people are to blame for the woes of the younger generation but rather that while the "spirit of intergenerational support" is still willing, it is weakening and that if "the government takes no action, there could be a breakdown in the intergenerational compact". On that basis the committee recommended six key areas for reform ranging from the increased provision of secure and affordable housing through to the radical reform of an education and training system that at present is "ill-equipped for the needs of the rapidly changing labour market". Controversially, it also recommended some redistribution of intergenerational benefits including the phasing out of free TV licences over a certain age. However, the main thrust of this report was that government needed to adopt a life-course approach and not a generational approach to all these issues as youngsters today prepare for the 100-year life ahead. As Anna Dixon, CEO of the Centre for Ageing Better (Feb. 2020), has argued "We need to abandon the narrative of blame and instead demand bold, long-term policy change that ensures that everyone is able to enjoy later life now and in the future".

As Kate Alexander-Shaw summed it up in 2018, millennials across the western world have grown up in a period of exceptional economic uncertainty in which market forces have plunged the western world into economic chaos and uncertainty and left them facing "a blockage" in the traditional life cycle; an "adult purgatory" that has left them deeply frustrated by their inability to match their parents and grandparents' ascent into adulthood. This blockage has generated in turn an intense sense of generational unfairness that is evident across Europe and not just in the United Kingdom as this *age of ageing* has seen swathes of government spending directed to the needs of the older populations apparently at the expense – and taxes – of the young. Media images of baby boomers as a privileged and selfish generation only fuel the growing generational conflict that threatens to undermine the social solidarity of the post-war social contract and plunge ageing countries like the United Kingdom into an Age War where every generation – and every family – loses its sense of community and mutual support. Such stereotyping is, unfortunately, reinforced by the fact that increasingly, older and younger generations not only live in different social worlds but also live physically and geographically apart and so rarely interact with each other nor empathise with each other's needs or ambitions – a generational segregation that was possibly reflected in the 2016 UK Referendum. The recent and sharp rise in political mobilisation of the young and the shift towards greater age-based campaigning is likely to exacerbate, if not exaggerate, age-tensions and so contribute towards a self-fulfilling spiral in which British politics moves from its traditional class-based paradigm onto an age-based one, inciting young against old. As the Intergenerational Commission concluded in 2018, the British social contract hasn't yet collapsed but it certainly "looks at risk of fraying". The answer, it believes, is not in generational warfare but in generational harmony with "three big players" – the State, the Markets and the Family – taking the lead, renewing this contract and redesigning it for the century ahead. That is the mission that the Commission set itself and the reason that it produced its own Intergenerational Manifesto Recommendations in 2018, summarised in Chapter 7. And whilst the Resolution Foundation's Intergenerational Audit in 2019 identified some improvement in the living standards of young adults in their 20s in terms of pay, homeownership and savings, the scars of the 2008 recession continue to affect those in their 30s. And all this was before COVID-19 now threatens to put the younger generations back for years to come and has condemned many of them to perpetual underemployment, if not unemployment. Yet, despite all these inequities, despite the young and working age overwhelmingly bearing the brunt of the proposed tax increases to support health and social care, as Professor Bobby Duffy (2021) has recently argued,the younger generations "are not, in fact, up in arms and revolting against their elders." Quite the opposite. All ages still seem to be highly supportive of old age benefits; not least as at some time they will inherit them themselves. What is clear though, argues Professor Duffy is that despite all the stereotypes and myths, "understanding age-based and generational perspectives is vitally important" not only in explaining the yawning age-gap in party voting now evident in the UK but in analysing the deepening and dangerous gulf in social equality emerging in Britain today; a gulf that generational structures and attitudes are threatening to reinforce rather than break down; "the story of the next decades will be how the incredible increase in private wealth tumbles unevenly down the generations....as advantage and disadvantage is increasingly handed down between the generations in an incipient caste system." (Sunday Times: 12th Sept.2021).

So, this intergenerational debate has brought out into the public arena not only emerging intergenerational relations in Britain-and elsewhere- today but two underlying but less developed themes. Firstly, it has shown that beneath any apparent disparity in intergenerational equality in the United Kingdom or elsewhere lies the far deeper and darker national and global economic and social inequality described in Chapter 6; a level and depth of inequality that only concerted and committed government action can really tackle whether it be by the *levelling-up* strategy promised by Boris Johnson or by clamping down on tax avoidance, particularly by Big Tech, that governments across Europe, the United Kingdom and the United States now seem to be pursuing.

Secondly, whilst it has put a spotlight on intergenerational relations and inequality, it has tended to ignore **intragenerational** inequalities. From this perspective, the real generational debate may not be that ***between*** generations but ***within*** generations. As Craig Berry argued back in 2012, while baby boomers may well appear to be very supportive, if not selfless, in service to their own family, they seem quite indifferent to the plight of those in their own age group who are less fortunate than themselves; a fear echoed by Phillip Stephens (2012) in the same year; but this time with regard to the younger generations as the better-off young inherit their parent's wealth whilst the less well-off inherit their parents' poverty: "The fortunate among the new generation will pick up house deposits, and ultimately property from their parents. The rest will be locked out of a globalised labour market ever less tolerant of a lack of skills, and from a welfare state facing a fierce financial squeeze. The 'gap' that matters is not between fee-paying students and their parents, but between undergraduates and the undereducated young jobless".

Conclusions

So, Laura's research into generational relations brought home two critical strands for her emerging thesis. Firstly, as the Intergenerational Commission has shown, the concept of generation has the potential for effectively describing and analysing forces for change in the early 21st century; and secondly, that intergenerational and even intragenerational relations may well be a driving force not only in future British elections but in any attempt to redesign a new and fairer intergenerational social contract. This would be a titanic task but given the growing tensions and divisions within Great Britain post-Brexit, an essential one; and one that ironically, the coronavirus crisis may well have helped strengthen. Certainly, there has been an outpouring of intergenerational support and sympathy for the plight of elderly patients dying alone in hospital or care homes while intergenerational heroes of all ages from Captain Tom to Marcus Rashford have inspired the whole nation. Certainly, there is much greater public awareness now that while the older ages may have suffered overwhelmingly from the loss of lives from COVID-19, the younger ages are most likely to suffer most from the loss of jobs and fall in incomes arising from national lockdown. As David Willetts claimed in Feb. 2021, "The idea that young people today are getting a raw deal is now widely accepted"; as is the claim by the Intergenerational Foundation (IF) in Oct. 2020 that many young people have seen the "slow cancellation" of their futures. Think tanks such as the Social Market Foundation (April 2020) have gone further and proposed that the older generations ought to agree to giving up the current pension *triple-lock* as their contribution towards the escalating cost of COVID; a proposal that no longer creates an immediate outcry or is rejected out of hand but rather one that is currently, the subject of intense political debate within the British Cabinet over the fair funding of social care in the future. Whether any politician or party will fly the intergenerational flag and seize the moment offered by all this Intergenerational *Good Will* remains to be seen. Maybe, speculated Laura, it will fall instead to a non-political figure, young or old to inspire all ages in the same way that Greta Thunberg and David Attenborough seem to have been doing for Climate Change.

Bibliography

Alexander-Shaw, Kate: *Baby Boomers versus Millennials: Report for the Foundation for European Progressive Studies*: SPERI/Sheffield Political Economy Research Institute (January 2018)
Becket, Francis: *What Did the Baby Boomers Ever Do For Us?*: Biteback Publishing (2010)
Berry, Craig: *How the Growing Grey Vote Could Undermine British Democracy*: openDemocracyUK (April 2012)
Chief Medical Officer's Annual Report: *Baby Boomers-Fit for the Future* (December 2015)
Cigna *Loneliness Index* (2020)
Graeme Codrington: *Detailed Introduction to Generational Theory*: Tomorrow Today (August 2008)
Codrington, G; Grant-Marshall, S: *Mind the Gap*: Penguin (2011)
Croker, Richard (ed): *The Boomer Century 1946-2046*: Springboard Press/Hachette Books (2007)
Cushman & Wakefield: *Demographic Shifts: The World in 2030* (2020)

Dixon, Anna (CEO of the Centre for Ageing Better): *Covid-19 Has Shown that We Don't All Age Equally* (December 2020)

Duffy B: *Generations: Does When You Are Born Shape Who You Are*: Atlantic 2021

Gen-erators Z Report Commissioned by Lucozade Energy (2015)

Gibney, Bruce: *A Generation of Sociopaths*: Hachette (2017)

House of Lords Select Committee: *Tackling Intergenerational Fairness and Provision* (2019)

Howker, Ed; Malik, Shiv: *The Jilted Generation*: Icon Books (2010)

Huber, J: Skidmore, P: *The New Old*: Demos (2003)/Harkin, J; Huber J: *Eternal Youth*: Demos (2004)

Intergenerational Commission: *Live Long and Prosper?*: Resolution Foundation (2017)

Intergenerational Commission: *A New Generational Contract* (2018)

Intergenerational Foundation (IF) Blog: *The Pandemic: Testing Intergenerational Solidarity* (October 2020)

Ipsos-Mori/Centre for Ageing Better: *The Perennials: The Future of Ageing* (2019)

Ipsos-Mori Global Survey for the Centre for Ageing Better: *The Perennials-The Future of Ageing* (2019)

Ipsos-Mori National Citizen Service Report (2014): National Citizen Service: Youth Report: *Welcome to Our World as a Teen* (2017)

Ipsos-Mori Social Research Institute Report: *Beyond Binary-Communicating with Generation Z* (July 2018)

Kennedy Carole: *Baby Boomers: The Ultimate Boomer Generation Guide*: Lulu Press Inc. (2017)

Leach, Rebecca et al: Baby Boomers, consumption and social change: the bridging generation?: *International Review of Sociology*, 104–122 Volume 23, Issue 1 (March 2013)

Mannheim, Karl (1927/28): The Problem of Generations in Kecskemeti, Paul (ed): *Essays on the Sociology of Knowledge*: Routledge Kegan (1952)

McCarthy & Stone: *The Colour Report* (2015)

Moody, Harry R: *Aging: Concepts and Controversies*: Sage (2002)

Prince's Trust's: Macquarie Youth Index *Annual Report* (2018)

Resolution Foundation's *Intergenerational Audit*: (2019)

Social Market Foundation (SMF): *Intergenerational Fairness in the Coronavirus Economy* (April 2020)

Stephens Phillip: *Financial Times* (March 3, 2012)

Sternberg, J.C: *The Theft of a Decade*: Public Affairs (2019)

Strauss, William; Howe, Neil: *The Fourth Turning: An American Prophecy*: Bantam Books (1997): *Generations*: William Morrow (1991)

Sunday Times/ Britain Thinks Survey: Mind the generation Gap: 19 Sept. 2021

Sunday Times: Duffy B.: *Boomer V Broke: Why the Young should be more angry*: 12 Sept. 2021

Walker, Alan: *Ageing: The Best Years of Our Lives*: British Academy Debates (2014)

Wikipedia Encyclopedia: Baby Boomers

Willetts, David: *New Statesman* (February 10, 2021)

Willetts, David: *The Pinch*: Atlantic Books (2011); *Prospect Magazine* (October 2019)

6

THE NEW OLD AND THEIR POWERS FOR CHANGE

So, challenged Jonathan, Laura's tutor, even if the New Old have the character and tradition for radical change, do they have the power and appetite to actively lead or at least sponsor a fundamental shift in our social structure, culture and intergenerational relations in what sociologists might call a "paradigm change" and so generate a sociological shift to the more age-friendly, more ageless and more equitable society advocated by the UN/WHO and aspired to by the advocates of Generativity? Does *generational power* have sociological force?

In response, Laura identified and described four specific sources of generational power; each one powerful in its own right but collectively powerful enough to provoke, propel and sustain societal change:

- The Economic Power of the Grey Pound and the Silver Economy.
- The Political Power of the Grey Vote and the Silver Lobby.
- The Technological Power of New Technology and the Robot Revolution.
- The Judicial and Moral Power of Social Justice and Human Rights.

6.1 ECONOMIC POWER

For many analysts, the silver economy is the future. It is part of the future global economy as the world's silver markets mushroom and the world's older population doubles in the next 25 years to nearly 2 billion with a spending power of some $15 trillion. The WEF (2015) declared longevity to be the **Great Awakening of the 21st Century**; one where "humanity stands at the brink of a world with more old than young" and one where "the majority of the world's wealth is concentrated in the burgeoning 60+ segment of the population". And, now, one for which the OECD set out a series of *Principles on the Silver Economy*

DOI: 10.4324/9781003029373-10

and Active Ageing in 2015 to help guide its G20 members as countries across the world, such as those below, start to "Go Silver or Grey":

- Japan, as a super-ageing society, is leading the way, becoming the world laboratory for developing innovative products and services for older people ranging from talking dolls like Tamogochi to communicate with dementia patients, pets for care homes such as Pepper and elderly tracking systems such as Intelligent System's Parobarcodes. Fujitsu have developed the Raku Raku range of mobile phone for the elderly while supermarkets such as Aeon are developing consumer strategies specifically for older customers ranging from one-stop medical clinics in its stores to much improved store signage and access. The Japanese government has set out a series of General Principles Concerning Measures for the Aged Society to direct Japan in becoming an "age-free" society in which people over-65 will be encouraged to stay active, healthy, keep working and not automatically consider themselves or be considered senior citizens.
- The European Silver Economy was described by the Technopolis and Oxford Economics report in 2018 as "the third largest economy in the world, behind only USA and China". It will apparently be worth some 5.7 trillion euros by 2025 operating in such diverse fields as connected health, robotics and games, integrated care, smart homes, active and healthy lifestyles, silver tourism, age-friendly universities and driverless cars while Finland has ambitions to combine ageing and climate change in an integrated strategy with "silver as the next green".
- In the United States, the 2019 AARP/Economist intelligence Unit report estimated that the US longevity economy would surge in value from $8.3 trillion in 2018 to $28.2 trillion by 2050 as America's 50-plus population soars to 157.3 million or 41% of the total US population, creating huge growth opportunities in new and assisted technology, caregiving, real estate and especially banking and finance as baby boomers not only need to plan and organise their own finances but have to consider the financial support that might be needed for both younger generations in their family and for their own ageing parents. Canada, too, has made healthcare and ageing-at-home markets of the future as nearly one in four Canadians will be a senior citizen by 2030 and policymakers are even considering the creation of an AgeTech-Longevity banking system capable of supporting both healthtech and agetech in some sort of intergenerational family chain; a return, maybe, to the family bank of the past but with super-tech as its friendly face.
- Asia is also predicted to *go silver* in the next ten years. According to the consultants Deloitte (2019) by 2030, those aged 50 and over will constitute 32% of the entire Asia-Pacific population and represent 52% of that region's total consumer expenditure with China, Korea, Thailand and Singapore leading the way. This is a $26 trillion Silver Economy of huge national, cultural and ethnic diversity; one with varying degrees of economic readiness ranging

from such *Silver Spotlights* as Singapore and Thailand to such *Silver Adjacencies* as India and Indonesia with the digital revolution and the smart phone as key connectors between corporations and their consumers. By 2020 13 countries in APEC, the Asia-Pacific Economic Cooperation, will be super-aged and *the East Asia and Pacific region will have more older people than anywhere else in the world (2017 APEC workshop)* This isn't just a regional shift in economic demand but a seismic shift in the global economy.

- In the United Kingdom, the Institute of Customer Service (2016) estimated the UK silver economy to be worth some £43 billion annually with utilities (£12.2 billion), travel (£10.6 billion) and insurance (£6.8 billion), some of the largest areas of annual spend with health alone estimated at some £8 billion whilst the 2019 ILC-UK Report Maximising the Longevity Dividend showed that, older households' share of total spending in the United Kingdom is predicted to rise from 54% in 2018 to 63% in 2040 by which time "older consumers could spend more than younger consumers for all sectors".

So, in contrast to the *doomster* scenarios of the old in ageing societies as a crippling economic cost, the Silver Consumer and the Silver Worker look like being the potential Silver Saviours of the future; a rich source of economic regeneration post-COVID just like they apparently did after the financial crisis in 2008 according to the charity SAGA.

New-age marketing

But longevity is not only creating the Silver Economy of the future but inspiring the Silver Consumer of the future too, one that according to the WEF may transform global capitalism by calling it to account, as baby boomers demand a much more socially responsible, trustworthy and compassionate capitalism; one that is adding value, adopting age-friendly strategies and tackling social ills rather than just creaming off profits. After the 2008 crash and the rise of global elite of multi-billionaires, modern capitalism is on trial and under demand to create a fairer, healthier and more inclusive and caring world as well as a wealthier one. And marketers as well as businessmen, economists and governments will have to respond.

In the United States, the baby boomer market is huge – some 73 million relatively affluent Americans; a silver market that marketers such as Mary Furlong, CEO of Third Age Media (2007) have long argued is just waiting to be turned "into gold". To do that she has advocated that businesses need to adopt a *life-stage* approach to marketing and the transitions all ages go through and focus in on baby boomers' search for new identities, new interests and new lifestyles. And at the heart of this boomer revolution are older women; women liberated and emancipated by the first boomer revolution in the 1960s and 1970s: boomer women who are better educated, more financially savvy and who "control about

75% of the family finances, control half of the private wealth (about $14 trillion) and account for at least $2 trillion in annual consumer spending in the United States". Boomer markets, in her view, are the markets of the future and they range from health and housing, through to travel and transport, disability and death; and even sex as a new sexual revolution gets under way. Baby boomers were the first generation to respond to mass marketing and to the "generational" advertising of companies such as Pepsi-Cola and its tagline "Come Alive! You're the Pepsi Generation". And even now, adventurous baby boomers have become what the trade magazine, *Marketing,* called in 2010, DRAGONs-the Divorced, Rich, Aged-65+, Overseas Traveller, and Networker-over 65s who are "on the move, on the go, and on the pull… Highly active Boomers who are looking for 'thrill-seeker' packages, singles city breaks and even medical tourism, combining cosmetic surgery with world travel".

The 2015 Colour Report, cited earlier, similarly described British boomers as youthful and young at heart; as fashion-conscious as their daughters, as tech savvy as their sons and as health-conscious as any other age group with nearly 30% of over 75s, members of a gym or sports club. However, as marketers such as Dick Stroud and his colleagues have argued, many in the commercial sector in the United Kingdom still seem to have a sort of commercial-blindness to the potential this older market; an age-blindness bordering on ageism; possibly because the modern marketer is usually young, male, brash and ambitious, steeped in the latest fashion or fad, living in a major city and divorced from the less exciting and glamorous lifestyles of ordinary people, particularly older people. Instead, Stroud and his colleagues have argued that marketing in ageing societies, such as the United Kingdom, should be ageless, age-friendly and universal in design: "Design for the young and you'll exclude the old. Design for the old, and you'll include the young". Think and act like the elderly and you might just begin to understand what an ageing body is up against; a mantra put into practice by designers and engineers at the MIT Age Lab when they developed "AGNES"; a simulation suit illustrated in Figure 6.1 overleaf and worn by students and product developers, engineers, planners and architects to help them empathise with older consumers when shopping, cooking or travelling.

A new-age consumer, therefore, seems to be emerging that researchers such as I.R. Jones and his colleagues (2008) identified as part of a shift from post-modern society into a second modernity or third age. The post-war baby boomer generation represents a new type of consumer – affluent, secure, dual-income/pension elder households with high levels of disposable income, high levels of savings and assets and the backup support in the United Kingdom of the National Health Service and Social Security/Social Services systems. It is these wealthier boomers that are leading the new images of older age. It is these affluent oldies who are demanding new products, new housing and new lifestyles as they continue the youthful quest for personal fulfilment. The New Old are not passively inhabiting the traditional world of the old age but are actively creating a new one; one with new images, new lifestyles and new identities. The New Old are looking for the

1: The Aged Simulation Set

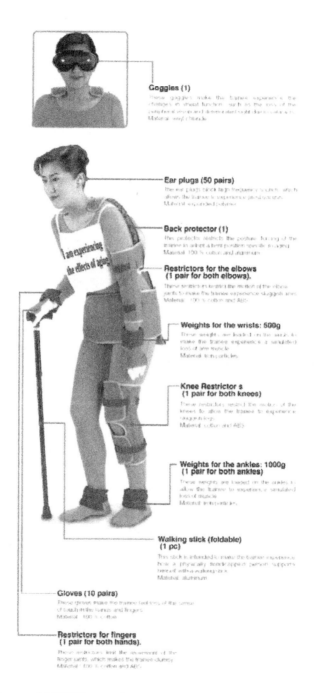

Goggles (1)
These goggles make the trainee experience the changes in visual function, such as the loss of the peripheral vision and deteriorated visibility due to cataracts.
Material: vinyl chloride.

Ear plugs (50 pairs)
The ear plugs block high frequency sounds, which allow the trainee to experience a produced loss.
Material: expanded polymer.

Back protector (1)
This protector restricts the posture, forcing of the trainee in which a bent position typical of ageing.
Material: 100 % cotton and aluminum.

Restrictors for the elbows
(1 pair for both elbows).
These restrictors restrict the motion of the elbow joints to make the trainee experience sluggish arms.
Material: 100 % cotton and ABS.

Weights for the wrists: 500g
These weights are loaded on the wrists to make the trainee experience a simulated loss of arm muscle.
Material: iron particles.

Knee Restrictor s
(1 pair for both knees)
These restrictors restrict the motion of the knees to allow the trainee to experience sluggish legs.
Material: cotton and ABS.

Weights for the ankles: 1000g
(1 pair for both ankles)
These weights are loaded on the ankles to allow the trainee to experience a simulated loss of muscle.
Material: iron particles.

Walking stick (foldable)
(1 pc)
This stick is intended to make the trainee experience how a physically handicapped person supports him/herself with a walking stick.
Material: aluminum.

Gloves (10 pairs)
These gloves make the trainee feel loss of the sense of touch in the hands and fingers.
Material: 100 % cotton.

Restrictors for fingers
(1 pair for both hands).
These restrictors limit the movement of the finger joints, which makes the trainee clumsy.
Material: 100 % cotton and ABS.

FIGURE 6.1   Image of AGNES age-suit

"good life" in older age with as much vigour and ambition as they looked for it in their youth; a DIY, freestyle stage of life is emerging from the boomers' new style of shopping and consuming, one that promotes independence and one that ideally is free from physical or mental decay; a lifestyle and a life-stage that is as diverse as baby boomers care to make it – and the media cares to portray it.

This *Third Age,* however, is not only a period of continued consumption but, in the view of writers such as Peter Laslett (1965) and Anthony Giddens (1991), it is one of reflection and re-orientation, of "reflexivity" in coming to terms with life lived so far and the time left to live in the future. This generation of active and affluent pensioners determined to live their own lifestyles, free from dependency on the state or the family and with an eye to the future, has profound implications too for the Welfare State of the 21st century and the current moves to transfer responsibility for healthcare and social security from the state to the individual and from government to the private sector; a shift of responsibility that is creating a whole new mass market for healthcare and wealthcare for the older consumer to navigate. It is equally a new liberation; a liberation from traditional age stereotypes and role restraints and one that women, especially older women, once again seem to be leading to free themselves from the "tyranny of youth" that seems to pervade modern marketing and design and its uniform images of feminine beauty and lifestyle. As Professor Pat Thane and Dr Lorna Warren (2015) summed it up: "Currently older women increasingly experience double standards in society's attitude towards them. They are expected to follow the ideals of Hollywood and fight or erase all signs of the ageing body, following an impossible ideal of sexualised beauty and youth. The rapidly expanding anti-ageing industry has grown vastly as a result. Women who do not make efforts to conform to this ideal become automatically invisible, can be denied active roles in society and are often subject to abuse". So new images of "ageing beauty" are needed that will inspire and liberate the women of all ages; new images such as the Dove Campaign for Real Women in 2004; a 'game-changer' in female marketing that challenged the traditional youth-only portrayal of feminine beauty and instead offered a kaleidoscope of real life women in real life situations portraying "ageless beauty" in all its shape and sizes, all its ages and angles – even in the nude!

Conclusions

So once again the post-war baby boomer is potentially at the centre of an economic revolution that they have the opportunity and the money to not only landscape but lead, liberate and feminise. And if manufacturers and marketers won't change their strategies, baby boomers will change it for them, go to Amazon in the West, Ali Baba in the East and search online for what they want – "what they really, really want"; and possibly join forces with their younger sisters and siblings in doing so. As the Institute of Customer Service highlighted in 2016, the core values of boomers and millennials are remarkably similar. Both value trust, high standards of customer care and both expect a personalised treatment. As Jo Causon, CEO of the ICS, elaborated "Businesses may think the Millennials and Baby Boomers value different things, but the reality is that they share similar desires: the difference is that they want them delivered in different ways". Boomers tend to prefer phone or face-to-face communication whilst Millennials seem to prefer social media, apps and digital communication.

However, this economic revolution also has its dark side. Along with any new economic opportunity come new forms of exploitation and fraud but this time on an industrial scale. The New Old may well be more educated and more commercially savvy than their predecessors but with assets estimated at £2.9 trillion in property alone by 2036, all older people are increasingly attractive to fraudsters and hackers and, with the onset of disability, dementia and deterioration in hearing, eyesight and memory, increasingly vulnerable. Day-to-day financial management is already increasingly difficult for older consumers as new technology shifts shopping and banking online and away from face-to-face interaction. And although new technology is simplifying such processes and strengthening protections with innovations such as fingerprinting or iris recognition, growing numbers of older consumers are likely to become increasingly dependent on relatives or trusted others to manage their financial affairs and daily living; a burgeoning burden for younger families and an expanding market for fraudsters and scammers. As the Bank of England "Future of Finance" report in June 2020 and the FCA (2017) have both highlighted, the later-life markets offer immense opportunities for the commercial and financial sectors, but if they are not strictly regulated and older consumers fully protected, then the government and families at large are likely to face a financial and social scandal that may dwarf even that of 2008. That really would send a shock-wave through government, through every generation and through every household in the United Kingdom as ageing parents leave their finances in disarray, their wills unmade or contested and fraudsters have a field day at their expense. The New Old have immense economic and marketing potential but only IF they choose to use it and only IF they can be fully protected.

As a young woman in her 20s, Laura was quite astonished by the idea that the world economy was undergoing such an age-shift in orientation. Like most of her age group, she had assumed that the spending power of the Young drove new innovations and fashions. The idea that silver markets rather than those of her age group might be the trend-setters of the future was quite mind-blowing. Now, however, whenever she went shopping in her university and home town, she could see more clearly the age bias – even the ageism – that adorns Britain's high streets. Sexy, sylph-like young models fill every shop window whilst older women tend to be relegated, even herded towards the likes of M&S or Debenhams when it still existed. Even Laura's Mum, glamorous as she was at age 48, would struggle to compete with these "slim, young things" while Laura's grandmother was just grateful that she could still fit into a size 16. Young looks and youthful beauty were apparently the only images for older women to aspire to and whilst Laura felt a natural revulsion at such blatant sexism, let alone ageism, she could now see the "winds of change" that the silver revolution might bring in.

6.2 POLITICAL POWER

Laura was already well aware from her politician grandmother that *grey power* is emerging as a significant political force – if not THE most significant force – across all western democracies and that with ageing, the older voter, the boomer vote, increasingly holds the key to electoral success.

- They have the numbers and they turn out in force at elections.
- They have powerful organisations to lobby for them.
- They hold top political positions nationally and internationally whether it be in the American Senate, the British House of Lords or the European Parliament.
- They own the media and increasingly set much of the political agenda.

As Professor Virpi Timonen summarised it back in 2008, "As the proportion of older people in the population increases, the 'grey vote' becomes more desirable for politicians, especially as in many countries a large proportion of older people vote, in contrast to widespread voter apathy among young adults in particular". Neil O'Brien, director of the "think tank" Policy Exchange put it slightly more dramatically (Telegraph: August 2012), "Politicians used to be famous for kissing babies. Soon they will be sidling up to grannies"; predictions that are now coming to pass in the United Kingdom as older people aged 55 plus will soon represent a near majority of the electorate and continue to vote in much greater numbers than the Young.

This age gap, this chasm in age power and electoral participation in the United Kingdom has been building up for a number of years and generated, in turn, what the Institute for Public Policy Research (IPPR) called in 2014 a "paradox of fatalism"; a self-fulfilling prophecy whereby as politicians pay less and less attention to non-voters – mainly the young and poor – a slow-burning resentment builds up creating a vicious cycle of disaffection and even alienation; one that surfaced in the 2015 General Election by which time the youth vote had fallen to some 35% ; virtually half that of 1992 when 67% of young people voted. Even in the 2016 UK Referendum, only 53% of 18–24-year olds voted compared to 75% of those aged 65 and over; a generational gap of immense political significance given the historic change involved and the implications for the young themselves in future life. Had more young people voted, then a Brexit decision so finely balanced at 52% to 48% to leave the EU, might well have had a very different outcome. The older generations in Great Britain, therefore, increasingly look like a gerontocracy, dominating power in the United Kingdom and using it primarily in their own generational interest while the Young in the United Kingdom still continue to look like the *Generation Lost* described by Demos researchers back in 2015.

Certainly, the 2016 Referendum result sent shockwave through the British establishment, left the political elites in Europe fearing a "domino effect" across the whole of the continent while Donald Trump's election in the same year, again with a strong elder vote, seemed to call into question the whole of the post-war political order as it unleashed a wave of nationalism and anti-establishment sentiment across the western world. The 2017 UK election produced a dramatic – but temporary – resurgence of the youth vote in the United Kingdom in the form of *Jezzamania*, but Boris Johnson's election in December 2019 confirmed conservative dominance of British politics and gave the Tory Party one of the largest parliamentary majorities since the War and Labour, one of the worst defeats since 1935. It confirmed the power of the grey vote and the shift towards age rather than social class as the primary determinant of modern UK elections. "Age is still the biggest dividing line in British politics", and "Class is no longer a key indicator of how people vote" declared YouGov in December 2019 as Conservatives outperformed Labour across all social grades and, even, did better amongst C2DE voters than among their own traditional ABC1 voters. Ultimately, though, the 2019 Election was about Brexit with Boris Johnson leading the charge to get out of Europe with his characteristic vim and vigour whilst Jeremy Corbyn sat painfully on the Referendum fence and like Humpty Dumpty eventually fell off.

The 2019 election finally settled the Brexit Debate, realigned Britain's traditional party platforms and transformed existing party leaderships. However, it also raised significant questions about the fairness and legitimacy of the current British electoral system; a first-past-the-post election system (FPTP) that no other country in Europe continues to use; an election system that the Electoral Reform Society declared in March 2020 "grossly distorts voter intentions and creates exaggerated majorities", leaving millions of voters "voiceless" and huge numbers of young people unregistered. According to the ERS report, the actual conservative share of the vote in 2019 was only 1.3% higher than in 2017; yet, somehow, it delivered an 80-seat majority in the House of Commons and left third parties, like the Lib-Dems and Greens, with substantially less seats than they had before even though collectively they won 25% of the popular vote. This, according to the ERS, is because the FPTP voting system does not require an overall majority in the country at large but simply a majority in each of its 650 constituencies. A winning party can therefore gain a parliamentary majority on less than 50% of the overall national vote leaving a huge swathe of votes counting for nothing in constituencies where the winning candidate was from another party. According to this ERS report: "a staggering 22.6 million people saw their vote count for nothing" in 2019 while only 9.4 million votes (29.2%) "were decisive in securing a candidates election". This is also because almost half the parliamentary seats in the United Kingdom are what are called "safe seats"; seats that tend to always go to the same party, irrespective of its candidate. According to this analysis, therefore, the huge swing to the Tories in 2019 was something of an electoral *sleight of hand* given that in terms of the overall popular vote, the margin of victory was quite small. Had the 2019 election been conducted under an alternative, more representative, system such as the d'Hondt system previously used for electing MEPs in the United Kingdom, then according to the ERS, the 2019 general election would have resulted in a multiparty coalition with no one party in control; certainly not one with an 80-seat majority. As the ERS report concluded, "No government should be able to win a big majority on a minority of the vote" and leave so many votes counting for nothing. The UK's FPTP system is "totally unfit for purpose, leading to warped outcomes, ignored votes, electoral pacts and tactical voting". Replacing the current UK election system might not only restore public faith and fairness in British elections and help many of the disillusioned regions in Britain, once again, feel that their voice is being heard but help re-engage Britain's *Lost Generation* of Young. The UK's FPTP election system seems to be exacerbating Britain's age gap; encouraging its major parties to increasingly rely on age-based coalitions of support, each with contrasting policy priorities; the Young for a better start in life and the older generations for better health and social care. Changing this election system to a more representative one might not only transform the face of British politics but fundamentally change intergenerational relations from confrontation to collaboration. As Laura Gardiner has argued (2019), "The Brexit vote and the 2017 general election put generational politics centre-stage and eclipsed in some ways, the traditionally dominant role of class". As the Independent declared in Jan. 2020, "We need our political leaders to rise to this challenge with an appeal to all generations to deliver the health and care older generations deserve, without asking younger workers to bear all the costs, to promote education and skills especially for those who have not chosen the university route, to provide more security for young people, from the jobs they do to the homes they rent and the houses they aspire to own." Such an appeal across generations is potentially the route to building a better Britain – and a more united one.

So, in this post-COVID/post-Brexit period of national self-reflection, the Age UK appeal in its 2014 Manifesto may still have powerful resonance "When we vote, it is for everyone's future. We are not a voting bloc with interests set apart from the rest of society. We care about our families' and our grandchildren's futures-from schools to global warming. We know that our well-being depends on a strong economy and strong families. And we know that whatever age, everyone should be able to expect a happy and secure later life". Whether this appeal will have widespread and inter-age political support remains to be seen once "normality" sets back in. However, it certainly appealed to Laura and increasingly infused her conversations with her nan about the possibilities of an Intergenerational Manifesto for the years ahead.

6.3 TECHNOLOGICAL POWER

New technology is at the heart of the New Age of ageing and the Holy Grail for any government, family or employer desperately seeking solutions that will liberate their ageing citizens, parents or employees from the costs and strain of an ever-ageing society. However, new technology is developing at such a rate that few governments and even fewer families seem to truly recognise its potential to not only transform ageing lives but to transform ageing societies. As MGI explained in 2015, it is the speed of technological change that is outstripping everybody. "It took more than 50 years after the telephone was invented until half of American homes had one. It took radio 38 years to attract 50 million listeners. But Facebook attracted 6 million users in its first year and that number multiplied 100 times over the next five years" and "as fast as innovation has multiplied and spread in recent years, it is poised to change and grow at an exponential speed beyond the power of human intuition to anticipate".

Laura's introduction to new technology came when she met up with her Uncle Derek and her cousin Dawn at a family BBQ. Derek is an electronics engineer with a passion for putting new technology to the service of older people, notably his parents; while his daughter Dawn is a PhD student from Bath University and MIT, researching robotics whose work placement with the Panasonic Corporation in Japan had given her first-hand experience of the enormous potential of artificial intelligence (AI) and of robotics to transform that most ageing of ancient societies, modern Japan. As Derek explained, new technology is part of everyday life and holds the key to the ageing world of the future and to older people being able to age-in-place rather than in a care home. As the 2018 Ageing in Place Technology report argued, with the cost of residential care in the United Kingdom approaching £40,000 a year, ageing-in-place is now not just a nice idea but a national imperative if governments across the world are not to face unsustainable demands on public services and families are not to collapse under the strain of ageing parents. According to reports such as the WEF (2016), the *Smart-World* of the Fourth Industrial Revolution is already ushering in:

Smart robots as companions, servants or maids providing unlimited 24/7 care and companionship as well as monitoring health and happiness. The "da Vinci" robot, developed for medical operations, for example, has four robotic arms, one for manipulating a video camera and three for precision surgery.

Smart houses operating at the touch of a remote control, dementia-friendly and wired up to alert all of the family to any elderly crisis are already available so that older people will not need to rely on family visiting or neighbours calling in to look after them; rather the "house" will do it all for them, through climate control in every room; effortless replenishment of the fridge, bathroom and kitchen; integrated multi-media and home energy management controlling energy use and charging the electric car.

Smart phones already enable older couples to communicate with family, friends, grandchildren and the outside world through Zoom or Skype-type tele-screens, to order Uber taxis or "driverless" cars to take them

shopping and where they wish; already have apps and sensors to monitor their health, order food and clothing and pay bills and purchases
automatically.

Smart health care programmes will provide that will continually diag-
nose "elderly" health, give early warning of illness, detect cancer and
ensure that older people adhere to their medication schedules. Robo-
doctors will soon not only diagnosed patients but treat them.

As described in Chapter 4, *a paradigm shift* is underway within the field of elder
healthcare, with the step-change from treatment to prevention, from specialist
doctors to personal self-help, from illness and disease to well-being and wellness.
Anti-ageing drugs such as Senolytics and revolutionary new developments in
medical science using AI and robotics that enable doctors to probe deep into the
human body as well as into the human mind, develop new ways of attacking cancer and heart diseases, conduct complex virtual experiments at speeds far beyond
human analysis, employ see-through surgery using a Microsoft HoloLens headset
that can scan below the skin and prescribe 3D personalised pills to treat patients,
especially children with rare diseases. The whole person – their psychological,
emotional and even spiritual well-being – will be as much part of the diagnosis as repairing the physical bits that are "faulty" or threatening to drop off.
With longevity, with more and more people living into their 80s, 90s and even
beyond, a revolution in thinking and practice in patient care is on the horizon
created by the advances in personal technology and the opportunity to put the
individual at the centre of future healthcare programmes designed to promote a
new, active life. Through the Internet and new forms of interactive technology,
the elderly even today can explore the outside world, visit where they wish and
meet whoever they want from the comfort of their own armchair and the safety
of their own home. They can shop online, learn online and socialise online, not
only with real friends and relatives but with virtual ones and even avatars. And
the new technologies just keep on coming, each with the potential to elevate and
liberate later life be it in the home or in the car, the shop or the travel agents.

Japan is already on the cusp of a ***Robot Revolution*** – a revolution that will
not only create robots that are intelligent but super-intelligent; that are not only
rationally intelligent but emotionally intelligent too. The government is investing huge sums in mechanical staff to man coffee machines, welcome visitors to
sports events and serve customers in banks. The glamorous actroids on recep-
tion at the Henn-Na Hotel in Nagasaki are the first step in this transformation
and robots are fast spreading through Japan's care homes as the ultimate solution to the dramatic shortfall of 380,000 care workers predicted by 2025. As
Camilla Cavendish illustrated in 2019, robo-pets are fast becoming the Japanese
solution to the epidemic of loneliness that pervades many care homes throughout the world; a farmyard of elderly-friendly "companion robots" ranging from
RoBoHoN or "robby" – a cute 8-inch tall monkey-like figure that sits on an
elderly person's bedside – through to Pareto the soft seal and Pepper, a 5-foot

humanoid used to lead exercise classes for the elderly. Many elderly Japanese, particularly those with dementia, are apparently so devoted to their care-bot companions that they prefer talking to their mechanical friends than to each other or to their care workers.

Professor Kaku (2012) has even predicted that by 2100 we will not only have very intelligent robots everywhere in our everyday lives but that "we will be part of them". We will be part-robot, part-human; cyborgs or man–machines capable of living forever in super-bodies into which even our personality can be download according to futurologists such as Ian Pearson. From such perspectives, physical ageing may soon no longer be an issue. We will have moved from inhabiting an ageing body into living in an ageless one; one that is linked to a computer and to other people across the planet in a global *virtual* reality. Free from the physical limitations of the human body and with advanced technology to vastly expand and augment the human mind, the only limitation on human development will be the human imagination. The elders of tomorrow – our grandchildren and great grandchildren – will, according to such futurologists, be able to live without fear or constraint, be as young and active as they wish to be, able to travel the universe by mind or matter with a robot as an intelligent companion, servant or slave. They will be immortal and unstoppable. Fantastic, though such visions might seem, the forces behind this "super" scientific revolution – the internet, the global economy, the global media and the new global middle classes – already exist and interplanetary travel is already a real prospect with Richard Branson, Jeff Bezoz, Elon Musk and other "space tycoons" seeking to open up space to the travelling public while internet billionaire Dmitry Itskov plans to go further and through his 2045 Initiative create an Avatar or Robot with a human personality so he never "dies"; a later-day "Iron Man". So, explained Dawn, AI is about to take over the universe; take over the world of work, of transport, of health, of communication and even the world of later life. It will, she explained, not only be embedded in all our new gadgets but inside our daily lives – and probably, increasingly, in our heads. As Professors McAFee and Brynjolfsson of MIT has predicted, robots and AI are not just replacing – and potentially liberating – human labour from routine and repetitive tasks, but they are likely to be "man's" future workmates, working alongside human beings rather than ousting them altogether. Alexa is already at home in houses across the world, Uber predicts that robo-taxis will soon be so available, accessible and cheap that there will be no reason to own a car – or need a parking space – while the advent of Sexbots in the sex industry may not only wipe out the oldest profession in the world, transform marriage and personal relationships but provide companionship for many of both sexes in older age to come.

So, new technology is advancing at breakneck speed. It offers an immense opportunity to liberate ageing and the aged from the bonds of their ageing bodies and the baby boomer generation will certainly not be backward in getting their hippy hands on whatever new technology becomes available; redesigning it for their own use and enjoyment and in so doing contributing to its future development. The keys, explained Derek, are adaptation and protection; adaptation to the emerging needs of the older generation and protection from its dangers. And here his thinking drew heavily on the insights of Joseph F. Coughlin (2005; 2017) and his view that *active ageing* in an ageing society needs more than a never-ending toy shop of new wonder gadgets. It is about a new way of life, a new style of life, one that requires the right IT platforms and the proper infrastructure for new technology to become an asset rather than a liability and promote healthy living not only for the elderly but for all ages. We need to move away from focusing on individual developments, such as driverless cars or personalised computers, and look instead to developing technology platforms and infrastructures that are future-proof, that can support and co-ordinate new technology in the long-term and so provide a new way of life for all of us. We need to focus first on *ageing-in-place and* creating age-friendly communities.

So, the challenge for the Derek and Dawn is not just to identify new technologies that might be helpful to older people but to develop a secure and sustainable Active Ageing Strategy and well-protected household platform that was robust and personalised enough to meet the specific needs of any elderly couple seeking to enjoy their remaining years together and yet stay independent and in control. Elderly couples, such as Derek's own Mum and Dad, Wilfred and Wilma, who are both quite keen on what new technology can do for them and who use their laptops and smartphones quite regularly, but who are equally, quite sceptical about where all this technology is leading us. As an ex-trade union official, Derek's Dad, Wilfred detests anything that smacks of "Big Brother"; be it government surveillance or corporations trawling for "big data" and fears the trolls and fraudsters trawling the internet for vulnerable victims. Designing an appropriate technological platform that would fit in with and adapt to his parents, changing later-life lifestyle and priorities, identifying the particular SMART technologies that they might need now and in the future – be they a driverless car or home communication, sensors and aids to make daily living lighter but with control systems that were not too complex; that put his parents clearly in control but also allowed for the loss of memory and the aching limbs that inevitably would "kick in" later on in their retirement, was a massive challenge for Derek and Dawn. The idea of a home robot, of a family-friendly Robo-companion acting as his parent's housemaid, butler, chauffeur and shopper now became Derek and Dawn's commercial mission but with the default button to ensure that such electronic elves never start to overstepped their technological mark and attempt to become a *Big Sister* or worse a *Big Brother* deciding for his parents what is best for them, making them hostages in their own home and turning their retirement dream to a later-life nightmare. Home robots are already at work in super-ageing nations such as Japan while Sophia, shown below in Figure 6.2, is an illustration of just how sophisticated – and possibly scary – today's robots are becoming. "Team Grandad" in contrast is an inspiring and real-life example of what family and technology can now do together to make later life both more comfortable and more human. At age 81, diagnosed with Parkinson's disease and advanced dementia, Albert Powley was facing the prospect of an ageing decline into a care home. That is until his family stepped in – all 14 of them – and with the installation of sensitive technology in his home to monitor his health and help around the house and with their personal commitment to become part of his daily life and company, they enabled him and his wife to continue to live comfortably at home, saving both them and the British Welfare State, huge sums of money in the process (For a more detailed review of the array of technologies emerging to support ageing-in-place, see Laurie Orlov's 2021 Market Overview referenced below).

Governments are slowly waking up to the potential – and the dangers-of new technology in an ageing society. The United States has a taskforce dedicated to developing an age strategy based on the six primary functional capabilities of independent living, cognition, communication and social connectivity, personal mobility, transportation and access to healthcare as target areas for emerging technologies. In the United Kingdom, the government's industrial strategy now has new technology as one of its grand challenges with the aim of putting the United Kingdom at forefront of AI and data management in tackling the diagnosis and treatment of chronic diseases and in using innovation to help people can enjoy at least five extra healthy, independent years of life by 2035 while "narrowing the gap between the experience of the richest and poorest". A competition to launch the "Home of 2030" is now underway. Greater Manchester aims to soon become a WHO-accredited age-friendly city while a new National Innovation Centre for Ageing is being set up in Newcastle. And, in response to the fears above, the UK Select Committee Report on AI in 2018 proposed an AI code based on five key principles, principles that AI should only be developed for the common good, be intelligible and fair, be citizen-friendly and work for all citizens. In particular AI should never be developed or used to diminish or undermine the data rights or privacy of individuals, families or communities; "the autonomous power to hurt, destroy or deceive human beings should never be vested in artificial intelligence". European Initiatives on Smart Ageing have included the Ambient Assisted Living Joint Programme on ICT solutions for ageing well, the eHealth Action Plan on products, services and inter-communication between patients and professionals and the More Years Better Lives Joint Programme Initiative on such areas as the quality of life, health and wellbeing during the life course, lifetime learning and healthy employability, governance and institutional integration. The Europe 2020 Strategy – *Together for Health* – sought to bring together such initiatives with a focus on health data and security, health workforce skills and training and strategies for reducing health inequality.

As a non-technologist, Laura was entranced by this brave new world; as a sociologist, she was increasingly concerned about the multiple warnings emanating from leading scientists that this brave new world might not be entirely a human world; that AI and developments in robotics may soon raise not only ethical questions about the use of such technology but existential questions about its potential impact on humankind and the future of man as a species. The MGI concluded in April 2019 that AI is "a double-edged sword" offering, on one hand, $13 trillion of additional global economic output and on the other hand huge new risks for humankind that include data theft and violations of privacy regulations, security black holes that fraudsters, terrorists and foreign governments might exploit and automated systems that overrule human judgement with potentially disastrous results be it a plunging plane or a self-driving car out-of-control. And if the Young are increasingly at risk, who will protect the elderly and the vulnerable from the dark net; from the hacking and identity theft that are already rife through new technology and putting even the most sophisticated government agencies under strain? Online shopping, online working and Zoom communications have thrived during lockdown but so too have hackers and scammers, as they develop and employ their own version of "track & trace". What the world will look like post-COVID awaits to be seen but certainly the shift towards the digital society has been accelerated by COVID-19 and its potential as the primary solution to the ageing world ahead has been significantly enhanced. As Stephen Hawking concluded in 2018, "Our future is a race between the growing power of our technology and the wisdom with which we use it. Let's make sure that wisdom wins". In the meantime, watch and wonder on YouTube and elsewhere at the explosion of new technologies for the life ahead and that might make the New Age of Retirement an adventure, a voyage of discovery for your parents and grandparents – and eventually yourself – rather than the downhill drift into disability, isolation and "old age" on offer for many old people today. And if they have any problems about how any of it works, I am sure that you or your children will tell them; particularly if they are already friends with the family robot or if you get chatting to "intelligent" robots like Sophia in Figure 6.2 below. Sophia is one of the latest generation of Humanoids and one of the most sophisticated. She is capable of holding an interview with a human being although she is only three years old while her co-bot AI-DA has learnt to paint portraits that apparently have been on exhibition in the London Design Museum.

FIGURE 6.2 Image of Sophia, the sophisticated robot

6.4 THE JUDICIAL & MORAL POWER OF HUMAN RIGHTS AND SOCIAL JUSTICE

Laura now had three very powerful potential forces at the disposal of her *Sociological Superhero* – the baby boomer generation; three sources of silver power to do battle with the Governments, tech-giants and super-robots of tomorrow. But that's all they were – potential powers, latent powers; not actual ones. They had, as yet, no cause, no spark that might engage and enrage them. They need, argued Laura's tutor, Jonathan, a cause and a mission so powerful that it galvanises this *Rebellious Generation* back into action, even in their older age; a cause and a moral mission that would over-ride complacency, conservatism and self-interest and convert baby boomers' latent powers into political power on a scale no government or business could resist; one that unites not only their own age group but age groups from all generations. But what was that cause; what might be that mission?

For Laura's Grandparents, Polly and David, the answer was quite simple. It is the same moral mission that inspired the silent generation to fight World War Two and to set up the British welfare state; the same political cause that inspired baby boomers when younger to march for women's rights or against the War in Vietnam; the same idealism and sense of fairness that has imbued the British character with its thirst for social justice, freedom and human rights. These were the causes that had brought boomers out onto the streets when they were young; these were the causes that had defined and inspired them in the past; these were the causes that might stir boomer consciences in the future. They have fought for a better world for themselves; now they had a chance to fight for a better world, a fairer world for their children and grandchildren. And the two "evils"; the two classic sociological beasts to be slayed that came out in these family discussions were **ageism and inequality**; ageism because it is an affront to the human rights of older people; inequality because it is an affront to the right of all ages to enjoy a fair distribution of wealth and opportunity. These twin towers of evil, Polly and David believed, would stir the heart and boil the blood of any red-blooded baby boomer and inspire them to put aside their comfort blankets and join in common cause for the sake not only of themselves but also for that of their children and grandchildren. If politicians like Boris Johnson and Nigel Farage could rally and rouse the British electorate – particularly the older electorate – to fight for Brexit and freedom from the EU, why couldn't politicians like her grandmother lead the fight against ageism and inequality and the fight for a new intergenerational social contract for the British welfare state?

Ageism: Age rage or age resignation – or just old people moaning?

Initially, Laura had not seen ageism as a major issue. In fact, she had not even seen it at all. To her getting old is just getting old so where's the discrimination – what's the problem? In fact, from a young person's perspective, ageing seems to make many older people more human and considerate, kind and caring – or maybe that's just their grans. Grandads still seem to enjoy being grumpy and constantly complaining about the youth of today – at least that is until you get them reminiscing about the war and their teenage adventures in the past. This cosy and sunny image, however, was soon shattered once Laura began reflecting on her visits to her great-nan's care home and talking about her thesis to her grandparents, Polly and David. Though they were both still enjoying active careers as an MP and GP respectively, they quickly gave Laura a lesson in the evils of ageism that she never forgot and that changed her views of later life forever. Baby boomers, like Polly and David, had fought against every form of social discrimination during their lifetime from sexism and racism through to homophobia. They had campaigned for every form of human right, for every type of social minority and now as ageing baby boomers they had hit that final obstacle to realising and releasing the full potential of humankind – the scourge of Ageism: the great obstacle to realising the full potential of those in older age and what they might contribute to society if they were encouraged and supported to do so.

So, what is ageism?

What is this great social slur that gets old people so riled up and so offended? The term ageism was coined by Professor Robert Butler in 1969 when he became the first director of the National Institute for Aging in the United States. He defined ageism as: "a process of systematic stereotyping of and discrimination against people because they are old…old people are categorized as senile, rigid in thought and manner, old-fashioned in morality and skills….Ageism allows the younger generation to see older people as different from themselves; thus they subtly cease to identify with their elders as human beings". However, unlike sexism or racism, ageism is not lifelong; it is not a permanent feature nor a physical characteristic inherited at birth. Rather, it "comes with age" and so is not so easily identifiable or recognised in the way gender or ethnicity are, even by the victims themselves. It sort of creeps up on you as you get older and approach later life.

Professor Butler outlined the four main categories of ageism as he perceived them:

- **Personal ageism** – ideas, attitudes, beliefs and practices on the part of individuals that are biased against persons or groups based on their age.
- **Institutional ageism** – missions, rules and practices that discriminate against individuals and/or groups because of their older age.
- **Intentional ageism** – ideas, attitudes, rules or practices that are carried out with the knowledge that they are biased against persons or groups based on their older age, including practices that take advantage of the vulnerabilities of older persons.

- **Unintentional (or inadvertent) ageism** – ideas, attitudes, rules or practices that are carried out without the perpetrator's awareness that they are
  biased against persons or groups based on their older age.

As Polly and David explained, all four types of ageism can be found in the media
or marketing today, ranging from condescension in advertising through to negative images on TV with the old depicted as decrepit, demented and in decline.
It may even occur unintentionally in normal conversation or social interaction,
when, for example, trying to help an older person finish their sentence, eat their
food or cross the road; all on the assumption that they can no longer do these
tasks themselves. Yet to reject such help, however patronising it may feel, would
seem churlish and ungrateful and only confirm the stereotype of older people as
cranky and awkward. The Centre for Ageing Better report in *Doddery but Dear?*
(2020) found ageism to be rife in modern Britain with attitudes to ageing "overwhelmingly negative" with stereotypes ranging from "benign indifference" to
mocking, infantilising, patronising and even demonising older people as a burden on society rather than a benefit. As Geraldine Bedell commented back in
2011, "Ageism is so deeply ingrained that most of the time we don't even notice
it… It is acceptable to speak of old people in a way that would be unthinkable
about race or disability". As Polly and David explained, we live in an age of ageism. Ageism is the hidden –ism, the –ism people rarely see and rarely discuss yet
it is all around us.

It is the invisible age

As Nicca Gerrard (2014) so poignantly put it in describing the "twilight" of her
father, "The old can imagine what it is like to be young but the young cannot
imagine what it is like to be old, frail, full of loss (of hearing, eyesight, status,
loved ones, recognition) and full of memory and the past. To imagine it, is to
acknowledge one's own journey towards decay and death". As she went on, "My
father has always been courteous, proud, honourable and reticent, and he still
is, but now he is old, white-haired and furrowed, and very vulnerable….People
don't call him Dr Gerrard any more but 'dear' or 'darling', and refer to him as
'we' instead of 'you' (how are 'we' today) Quite often they don't call him anything at all, because they don't address him….What they tend to see, when they
see him at all, is age. He has become an old man and his past lies behind him,
unknowable, and his future is short. He has become invisible as a person in his
own right".

Worse, it is often the old who are the main perpetrators of ageism either
because they tolerate it or because they collude in it, agreeing that they are too
old for this job or that task and voluntarily withdrawing from mainstream society;
a *"self-fulfilling prophecy"* and a downward spiral into dependency and inactivity.
Many older men simply accept that their time is up and simply withdraw into

retirement at home and into life in front of the TV. Other men respond to ageism with denial. They reject their status as an older person, insist on looking young, have hair transplants and cosmetic surgeries, seek out younger women and drive sports cars. Denial of ageing is an especially common response amongst the New Old. As the Demos researchers reported back in 2003/2004, this eternally youthful boomer generation detests and fears the onset of ageing and all that goes with it: "They were terrified of the physiological changes which are irreversible and which accompany old age…women talked about their fears of wrinkly skin and grey hair.…the possibility of senility raised a chill, as did the thoughts of illness and protracted pain or suffering.(they) talked about becoming 'trapped' by their physical dependence on others, and their genuine desire to avoid becoming a burden".

Modern capitalist societies are by nature institutionally ageist. In their relentless search for new talent, new markets and new profits, companies and corporations have promoted the young and retired the old. There is an overwhelming assumption that after a certain age, the older ages are no longer "fit for purpose"; a "burden" on society and their families; unhealthy and incapable of living active and independent lives *within* society so they are retired to the margins, dependent on the generosity of the young and the middle-aged for their income, healthcare and social support. The State Pension Age – currently age 65 – reinforces and legitimises the public image of the older generations as *decaying* human beings entering their "second childhood" and becoming an increasing burden on society and on their families. The old as a cohort, even as a class, face social isolation, segregation and deprivation as powerful and as "accepted" as any other form of social discrimination and, even today, it seems to be rampant in the workplace, as companies across almost every sector of industry still seek to pay off older workers to make way for younger, possibly cheaper ones.

It is the "abused age"

As Age UK has persistently highlighted, for many OAPs, later life is miserable not only because of loneliness and isolation but also because of fear; fear of abuse and neglect even by agencies tasked with protecting them. Even today, elder abuse is more widespread and more all-pervasive than anyone cares to admit. The 2011 Eurage Survey concluded that according to the best estimates "350,000 older people in the UK are abused in their own homes (primarily by their carers or relatives) and that a further 150,000 are abused in institutional settings". The NHS, in particular, has hit the headlines with several horrific examples of elder abuse while the 2017 Care Quality Commission Report identified a 40% rise in serious injuries amongst elderly people in care homes in England in the period 2012–2016 and declared a quarter of care homes in England to be unsafe. The WHO Report in 2021 on preventing elder maltreatment estimated that "at least 4 million older people" aged 60 and over suffer physical, sexual, mental or financial abuse or neglect every year in the WHO European Region with the most vulnerable at risk more from their carers or family members than strangers. While child protection is now a social priority, elder protection still is not.

It is the isolated and excluded age

According to Age UK (2018), half of all people aged 75 and over live alone and 17% of older people has less than weekly contact with family, friends and neighbours. As the WRVS has highlighted, isolation can be so bad that on occasion, elderly people die without anyone noticing. But ageism is not simply about physical or social exclusion; it is also about psychological exclusion, about the loss of social self-confidence and sense of purpose that leads older people to exclude "themselves". As Joan Bakewell (aged 81) – a television celebrity in the 1970s and later "The Voice of Older People" – so poignantly described it, women in particular often suffer the double whammy of ageism and ageing bodies: "whilst old men are thought to be ruggedly attractive, old women are deemed to be beyond allure, devoid of sexual chemistry, a worn husk of their juicier, former selves".

Ironically and almost perversely, it is in the **healthcare industry**, David's own profession, where ageism is often at its worst and at its most damaging; a health ageism that some have described as a "silent killer" in western societies because elder healthcare is often:

- **Temporary** rather than permanent with treatments limited to repair rather than replacement.
- **Over-medicalised** with products prescribed to keep the elderly docile and dependent rather than restoring them active life.
- **Reactive** rather than proactive with a focus on remedial treatment rather than using screening or regular monitoring to forestall chronic or fatal diseases by for example extending breast cancer screening to women over 65.
- **Under-regulated** with numerous cases in recent years exposing the institutional abuse and mistreatment that seems to be quite widespread even in the NHS and which in some cases has bordered on the scandalous, if not the "criminal".

Age discrimination in healthcare is at its starkest, however, when issues arise over the allocation of expensive or limited medical treatment; notably through the use of QALYs or "quality adjusted life years" which according to Professor Sarah Harper (2006) discriminate against older people because older people have lower life expectancies, higher levels of chronic disability and what is seen as a lower quality of future life. This age discrimination appeared most forcefully in the early days of coronavirus when *Do Not Attempt Resuscitation (DNAR) notices* were put on many elderly bed posts in hospitals and care homes, as under-equipped medical staff desperately tried to cope with overwhelming numbers of patients and limited ICU equipment and hospital beds. As Tessa Harding of Help the

Aged concluded in 2006, "We **expect** older people to be treated unequally and to be treated worse than their younger counterparts. That is how policies are constructed, how services are shaped and how the environment is arranged. Age discrimination is so integral to our thinking, so much part of the accepted way of doing things and so taken-for-granted in how we see and interpret the world around us, that our judgement is coloured, our perceptions affected and our experiences shaped whatever age we are". Ageism is often institutionalised and justified as the natural and fair way of allocating resources-a perception of "natural justice" that often even the elderly themselves subscribe to.

Age rage and the "fight back"

In the view of the WHO, age discrimination has to be tackled as a human right. While the 20th century was the age of the rights of women and children, the 21st century needs to become the age of the rights of the elderly – not just for moral or political reasons but as simple economics and self-interest. The idea that societies should invest in children is taken for granted; the idea of investing in older people apparently still seems absurd despite the fact that within the global economy of today, no developed or developing country can afford to "lay waste" to the enormous experience, skill and talent of its older population. As the AARP and EIU report in 2020 illustrated, while ageism cost some $850 billion to the US economy in 2018, rising to some $3.9 trillion by 2050, the longevity economy has the potential to contribute some 40% of the US GDP rising to 61% during the same period. So, in the interests of all ages, age discrimination needs to be challenged just as forcefully and just as politically as racism and sexism. As Age UK argued in its 2014 manifesto, the key is Equal Respect: Forget about Age-See Us as People: "We are still seen as second-class citizens (and) a fundamental change in attitudes is needed. We want opportunities to live better lives and make a contribution; we want equal rights as workers, as consumers and as users of public services; we want to be treated with dignity and respect, especially when times are tough; and we want decisions that affect us to take account of our needs and our views. We resent being patronised, talked down to and excluded from decision-making. As active, self-confident citizens we expect equality". Yet, despite this, ageism and disrespect remain rife in our society, leading writers like Baroness Julia Neuberger (2008) to argue for a "Rage against Age" in the UK and even the creation of a grey power movement while in America, Ashton Applewhite (2016) has drawn up a manifesto against ageism, arguing that ageism is "the last socially sanctioned prejudice". It encourages age-segregation. It pits Young versus Old, robs society of an immense accrual of knowledge and experience and poisons our futures by framing longer healthier lives as problems instead of the remarkable achievements and opportunities they represent. *Agefulness,* in her view, should be the new battle cry and *radicalising ageism* the new strategy. However, advised Polly, as in all these battles for human rights, traditional stereotypes and traditions about age are deeply held and well embedded in the "fabric" and even the language of society, so they are very open to subtle and low-level perpetuation whatever the law might say. While the state can give a lead and set an example or a sanction, ultimately responsibility for confronting age discrimination lies with the "victim" themselves – the New and the Old Old. As women, ethnic minorities and gays have shown, it is only in the "small battles of daily combat" that ageism will eventually be put to rest.

By the time Polly and David had finished their *Tale of Ageism* today, Laura was not only better informed, she was furious; furious for being so blind and prejudiced herself; furious at such ill-treatment of so vulnerable an age group, especially older women like her great-nan Christina caged-up in a care home where she was treated like a child and where her past identity and monumental achievements were simply erased and forgotten. Laura's "blood boiled" but what could she, as a young person, do except use her dissertation to help highlight this social evil and maybe convince her own age group to also take up this cause given that one day in the future, they too may face being belittled and ignored in this way. As the 2014 UCL report commented; "A key aspect that separates age discrimination from other forms of unfair treatment is that everyone is potentially at risk or experiencing it at some point in their lives". Certainly, coronavirus has brought the state of today's elderly into the public eye and into everyone's living room; and confronted the government with what now looks, to many, like institutionalised ageism. As the statistics in Figure 6.3 below illustrate, the COVID-19 related death rate in the UK has been one of the worst in the world, hitting older age groups hardest and leaving many of them to suffer some of the worst practices in age discrimination as shortages in intensive care equipment, protective clothing, facilities and staffing led to widespread use

Global Deaths:	2,978,935
National Deaths:	
USA:	559,010
Brazil:	361,884
India:	174,308
United Kingdom:	127,191
Italy:	115,937
Russian Federation:	104,795
Norway:	707
Vietnam:	35
Singapore:	30
New Zealand:	26

FIGURE 6.3   COVID-19 death rate: April 2021

Source: Sample from WHO Coronavirus (Covid-19) Dashboard: April 16th

of the DNAR notices mentioned earlier. Many elder patients were sent back to care homes without COVID-testing and care homes became breeding grounds for the virus as well as being locked down like prisons, leaving residents isolated and in many cases dying alone cut off from their families and loved ones. As this report concluded, "Covid-19 recovery is an opportunity to set the stage for a more inclusive, equitable and age-friendly society, anchored in human rights and guided by the shared promise of the 2030 Agenda for Sustainable Development to Leave No One Behind" – a statement and an ambition that could apply as urgently to Great Britain as to any developing or super-ageing nation.

Inequality: *Unequal, unfair and socially destructive*

While ageism might well be the "cause célèbre" for the New Old, social justice and intergenerational fairness are currently the rallying points for many of the New Young. Social justice and the search for fairness, for equality and for equality of opportunity both *between* generations and *within* generations are at the heart of the democratic dilemma of trying to liberate and reward all citizens on one hand, but harness the potential contribution of each and every citizen for the common good on the other. Equality and equality of opportunity, however, are not necessarily the same thing. In fact, as political philosophies they have generated ideologies, societies and economic systems at both ends of the political spectrum with communist and capitalist societies, for example, both claiming to be both democratic and fair. However, where inequality is so extreme that it is clearly not serving the interests of the people but serving the interests of the few at the expense of the many, then even the most capitalist of societies – and the most communist or socialist – struggle to justify it, and it was here that Laura and her grandparents began to find common cause in uniting the power and aspirations of both the New Old and the New Young through some form of new or revised intergenerational social contract that might make the ageing societies of the future, fairer, age-inclusive and more harmonious. If her readings about ageism generated an age rage, Laura's research into inequality ignited her socialist soul and unleashed an outrage even stronger. It informed her emerging thesis but equally inspired her to join her grandmother's election campaign in Suffolk East.

Global inequality

Inequality is clearly a huge issue on its own and one that has risen to the top of world agendas in recent years, not only because of the rise of the *super-rich* but also because global capitalism seems to be out of control. Governments seem powerless to regulate it – and even to tax the giant corporations that are driving it. The *super-rich* seems to be getting richer at a time when the vast majority of the world's population are getting poorer, opening up a chasm in wealth and opportunity that is undermining the very legitimacy of capitalism itself; a chasm starkly illustrated by the Oxfam report "Time to Care" in 2020 which claimed that the richest 1% in world have more than twice as much wealth as the remaining 6.9 billion people on the planet. As Oxfam explained "The social and economic consequences of inequality are profound and far-reaching: a growing sense of unfairness, precarity, perceived loss of identity and dignity weakening social fabric, eroding trust in institutions, disenchantment with political processes, and an erosion of the social contract". As the OECD put it more forcefully in 2012, "Youths who see no future for themselves, feel increasingly disenfranchised. They have now been joined by protesters who believe they are bearing the brunt of a crisis for which they have no responsibility, while people on higher incomes seem to be spared". In the OECD's view, inequality is seriously undermining economic growth because significant sectors within the working population are being "excluded" from the wealth-making and wealth-sharing process through under-employment or unemployment and low pay, thus dramatically reducing the capacity of the poorest 40% to contribute to productivity and to national income earning. Even the super-rich themselves have become quite concerned and at a conference on *Inclusive Capitalism* in London in 2014, Mark Carney, the then Governor of the Bank of England, argued that the old social contract is breaking down and "virtually without exception, inequality of outcomes both within and across generations has demonstrably increased".

According to the World Bank in 2018, globalisation produced a massive 66% increase in global wealth to $1,143 trillion in the preceding four years, yet, apparently, little, if any, of this additional wealth "trickled down" to ordinary people or even to national governments. As Thomas Picketty and his colleagues summarised it in 2018, while "countries have become richer, governments have become poorer"; an astonishing revelation at any time; a scandalous conclusion, ten years after a global financial scandal and one that means that instead of increases in national wealth going into the public purse for public use, they are increasingly going into private hands for personal profit. Inequality, however, is not inevitable, argues Picketty. It could be dramatically reversed if governments across the world simply introduced more progressive taxation and more public investment in better healthcare, better education and better-paid jobs. A simple global financial register of the ownership of financial assets alone, would, he suggests, "deal a severe blow to tax evasion, money laundering and rising inequality"; a hidden source of wealth that Gabriel Zucman (2015) calculated amounts to some $8.7 trillion worldwide. Unfortunately, according to Nick Shaxson (2018), many modern businesses and banks today seem more concerned with extracting wealth from the economy for themselves than creating wealth for the nation, their clients or the economy, "Britain owes its pre-eminence as a financial centre to the combination of a strong legal system which stops people stealing your money with a weak regulatory one which allows you to steal other peoples"; a conclusion reflected in the BBC Panorama revelations in 2020 about HSBC and other leading British banks' involvement in money laundering. Hence, the moral outrage, the "angrynomics" claimed by writers like Longeron and Blyth (2020), against an economic system that no longer seems fit for purpose and that fails to deliver a fair distribution of economic wealth and social justice. As the UN and UNICEF have consistently argued, inequality is one of the greatest challenges to Human Rights in the 21st century, one where multiple deprivations generate layer upon layer of discrimination and injustice so that "patterns of powerlessness, marginalization and exclusion persistent over time". As the UN (2015) concluded, all this inequality and exclusion emanates from an "unequal control over assets"; one that "needs to be countered by explicit policies seeking a more equal distribution". A conclusion that even Karl Marx might have applauded. Moreover, UN Secretary General Antonio Guterres declared in Sept 2018 that, "Trust is at a breaking point. Trust in national institutions. Trust among states. Trust in the rules-based global order". Restoring trust and stability is critical to re-directing the global agenda back towards inclusion, shared prosperity and economic and environmental sustainability.

Inequality in the United Kingdom tends to be at the higher end of any international scale of inequality but less overt and less conspicuous than in nations such as the United States, Russia and Saudi Arabia. The distribution of wealth in the UK today is illustrated in Figure 6.4 below and Oxfam claimed in March 2014 that the richest five families in the United Kingdom own more wealth than the poorest 20% of the entire population (some 13 million people) and that one family alone, the Grosvenor Family, owns more than the whole of the bottom 10%. The 2019 IFS report showed that the Top 1% in the United Kingdom are overwhelmingly male, middle-aged and most live within 65 parliamentary constituencies mainly around London and the South East while the 2020 Sunday Times Rich List confirmed that the United Kingdom is still

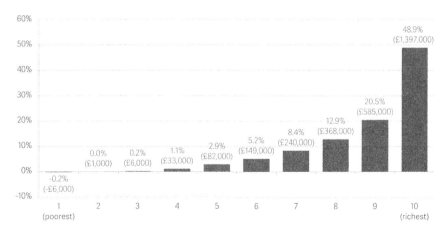

FIGURE 6.4 Distribution of wealth in UK

Notes: Wealth includes net property wealth, pension wealth and financial wealth. It does not include physical wealth. Deciles are calculated on total net family wealth per adult

Source: RF analysis of ONS, Wealth and Assest Survey

home to more billionaires (147) than any other country in the OECD except America and China. They have a combined wealth of some £742.6 billion and London remains the billionaires' capital of choice. Moreover, according to recent Resolution Foundation reports (2020 and 2021), "For those households who have become richer over the past decade, most of these gains were not as a result of active saving (but) rather passive accumulation in the value of wealth for those families who were already lucky enough to be well-off".

The 2018 IPPR report concluded that "the UK economy is not working" for the majority of the population. Instead, it argued that economic justice needs to be 'hard-wired' into the way the economy works" through labour and wage bargaining, the ownership of capital and wealth, the governance of firms, the operation of the financial system and the rules that govern the markets. The IPPR ten-point plan for prosperity and justice ranged from the establishment of a new National Investment Bank, the creation of a National Economic Council and a more "active, decentralised and purposeful state". *Muddling through is no longer an option* in face of the hugely disruptive challenges of the 2020s. It is time for a paradigm shift, argued the IPPR report, towards a fairer, more inclusive economy and a new consensus that could bring a divided United Kingdom back together again; an ambition reflected in Boris Johnson's promise of *levelling-up*; though whether a Tory government can deliver such a radical agenda remains to be seen. Moreover, as Richard Wilkinson and Kate Pickett argued in 2014, this debate isn't just about the redistribution of wealth or income but about the quality of human life and the pursuit of happiness, not just profit, materialism and ever-growing GDP. As the climate change agenda is dramatically illuminating, our planet cannot take continued, exponential growth and untrammelled exploitation; nor can our social structures.

Finally, inequality in the United Kingdom, is not just about unequal income or unequal wealth. It is equally about unequal lives and unequal opportunities across all areas of life. Numerous reports in recent years have identified the *Chasm of Inequality* that has been slowly splitting the United Kingdom apart and one that COVID-19 has now brutally exposed. The Marmot Review "10 years On" in 2020, for example, concluded that "The more deprived the area, the shorter the life expectancy with the largest gap being that between North & South England, between the most deprived 10% of neighbourhoods in the N/E and least deprived 10% of neighbourhoods in London" while Public Health England's report in 2020 showed that BAME groups have suffered disproportionately from the pandemic with death rates from COVID-19 significantly higher for Black and Asian ethnic groups; groups who are more likely to work in occupations with a higher risk of COVID exposure such as nurses, security guards and cab drivers, more likely to use public transport and more likely to suffer from "historic racism and poorer experiences of healthcare". As Paul Johnson of the IFS commented, despite government claims "We are not all in this together when it comes to the social and economic consequences of the virus". The better-offs have been protected by home working, home-schooling and greater access to space at home and outside. Low-earners, especially the young and ethnic minorities, are most likely to be exposed as key workers, living in crowded conditions with limited outlet and inadequate support for their children's health and education. The UK2070 or Kerslake Report (2019) concluded that "The UK is the most unequal country amongst the major developed nations". It isn't just that England has a North–South divide but rather that London and the South East tend to be the economic and political powerhouses while large parts of the North and Midlands tend to be the "poorhouses", devoid of a voice, deprived of investment and employment; part of an economic and social "Rift Valley" that galvanised much of the Brexit debate and led to the Labour Party's loss of its "Red Wall" in the 2019 General Election. Britain, argues Lord Kerslake, needs a long-term plan to "re-align power" and tackle the "deep-rooted regional inequalities", marginalised communities and the vast gap between the living standards of the better-off and least well-off in the United Kingdom today; a strategy that would extend opportunity and social mobility right across the United Kingdom. Unfortunately, as the 2020 Social Mobility Commission report revealed, social mobility within Great Britain has "stagnated" in recent years with the UK coming a woeful 21st in the WEF 2020 Global Mobility Survey; well behind most of Europe. Britain may not be entering the New Class War suggested by Michael Lind (2020), but the rise of populism and the widespread sense of *being left behind* certainly reflects a heart-felt reaction against the new technocratic elite that has emerged in recent years – London-based, university-educated, professionally employed, global in orientation and smugly self-satisfied in what they have achieved, according to the LSE/Sutton Trust report in 2020.

So divided and unequal is Great Britain today that the Institute of Fiscal Studies (IFS) set up the Deaton Commission in May 2019 to produce a definitive review of inequality in the United Kingdom today and to find ways to stop Britain "tearing itself apart". The Commission's initial report revealed that the United Kingdom is one of the most unequal nations internationally with the share of national income going to the richest 1% nearly tripling since the 1980s. "Deaths of despair" from suicide, drug and alcohol overdose are escalating and a chasm in wealth, lifestyle and opportunities for social mobility is emerging between London and the rest of the country. Each of these inequalities are bad enough; collectively they reinforce each other and create "myriad forms of privilege and disadvantage". Such inequalities, argued Professor Deaton, "have sparked worldwide protest movements and been linked to some of the most important political events of our time, including the vote for Brexit and the rise of populism across the developed world". The taking of wealth seems to have replaced the making of wealth "enriching the few at the expense of the many, taking the free out of free markets" and in the process "making a mockery of democracy". In that world, "inequality and misery are intimate companions" and "democratic capitalism is broken". Devastating conclusions for a country that prides itself for its "fair play"; dynamic evidence for any political party proposing radical change and a detailed agenda for any Tory administration serious about "levelling-up". In light of these revelations, the Wealth Tax Commission's proposal in 2020 of a one-off Wealth Tax in the United Kingdom on all individual wealth above £500,000 to raise an estimated £260 billion over the next five years, no longer seems fanciful, but increasingly fair.

So, the United Kingdom today appears to be a sadly divided and highly unequal society splintering apart socially, economically and politically with the SNP campaigning once again for Scottish Independence, the Brexit Protocol threatening to undermine the Good Friday agreement in Northern Ireland and a "lost generation" of unemployed or under-employed young people unable to get on the "housing ladder" and move their lives forward. Britain appears to be at a *democratic tipping point*. There appears to be a crisis of confidence in government, a collapse in social solidarity and potentially, the death of the nation as national identity begins to fragment and fall apart. Globally – and nationally – we now appear to be close to the edge of what economic growth can do for us materially and physically. Rampant capitalism and the "gross" inequalities of wealth and income evident in the emergence and elevation of the new global elite, now threaten to undermine the *quality and the spirit* of human life rather than enhance and enrich it. As Richard Wilkinson and Kate Pickett highlighted in the "Spirit Level" back in 2009, the more egalitarian a society is, the happier and more united it is likely to be; the more unequal a society is, the more disunited and discontented it is likely to be. At present the United Kingdom, sadly, falls into the latter category and coronavirus has not only laid such inequalities bare but exacerbated and accelerated them. Whether the conservative government under Boris Johnson can *build back better* and reunite Great Britain in the post-COVID decade ahead remains to be seen. Certainly, as the Centre for Ageing Better (2020) has argued, not only have existing inequalities exacerbated the impact of coronavirus across the country but coronavirus has, in turn, exacerbated existing inequalities and in so doing "set people in mid-life on a path to poverty and ill-health; set to die younger and spend longer in ill-health in old-age". Ageing for too many in the United Kingdom remains a continuing "accumulation of disadvantage" rather than the promise of a new later life to be enjoyed with:

- Three in every four who died from COVID-19 related reasons aged 75 or older.
- People's sense of connection improving during lockdown – but mostly for the better-off.
- A million more pensioners living in poverty than there were in 2014–2015.
- Women in the wealthiest parts of the country set to live 16 years longer in good health than those in the poorest.
- Those potentially most in need of help during lockdown were least likely to access it.

Conclusions

Laura's debates with her grandparents, Polly and David, on ageism had been sad and bad enough. Her debates with them and her visits to the foodbanks of Lowestoft and the tower blocks of Sunderland where her uncle Wilfred and his wife Wilma lived, shattered Laura's rosy picture of a United Kingdom as a wealthy, healthy and harmoniously nation at one with itself. Inequality is clearly eating away at the fabric of the United Kingdom and the ageing of Great Britain is fast approaching a point where age either adds a further social, political and economic divide or it becomes a bridge to reuniting and rejuvenating a nation just starting to recover from national lockdown and just starting to face the realities of life after Brexit. Inspired and outraged by her reading, Laura had in many ways moved beyond just writing an academic thesis into feeling the urgent need to "do something" – something beyond the usual student rant and rage; something of substance to make a difference and give her dissertation some real meaning and lasting purpose rather than being just a nice, neat academic qualification. So, she and her grandmother began debating the potential for age and ageing to become a new and unifying political platform; for ageing to build on the huge intergenerational goodwill inspired by COVID-19 after the polarisation of Brexit and for ageing to generate a fundamental shift in political debate in the United Kingdom away from personal material advantage onto one about the political and social health of the nation, about "re-uniting" the generations, strengthening social solidarity and inspiring a new social contract based on greater social justice and a fairer distribution of wealth and opportunity; a new-age intergenerational manifesto that looks to the future for future generations as well as to the present for today's elderly not just in terms of material benefit but increasingly in terms of the quality of life and the quality of society that our grandchildren will inherit when the baby boomers have gone; a legacy and an epitaph to the generation, many claim, have had it all.

But would the baby boomers of the 21st century respond to such calls for social justice now that they were retired and looking back on society as much as looking forward to the future? And why should the New Old reunite with the New Young in common cause when their lifestyles, locations and ambitions are so different. Her grandparent's and mum's responses astonished and inspired her – and totally changed her perception of the older generations. As Polly, a Labour MP and leading-edge baby boomer explained, Laura may well be banging on an "open-door". The baby boomer generation has changed the world before. They now have longevity on their side, giving them 20 more years of life, so giving back, especially to their children and grandchildren but this time with the wisdom of age and a concern for both the quality of life and the future of a planet, is exactly the sort of cause and campaign that many baby boomers might again rise to if the leadership is charismatic enough and the communication clear enough. If David Attenborough and Greta Thunberg can rally generations worldwide to support climate change, why can't we find politicians and celebrities of similar ages and persuasions, to rally generations across the United Kingdom in support of an Intergenerational Britain and a new Social Contract for the 21st century?

So, is **generational power**, possibly, the *fifth and final power* in driving this Age Agenda forward and in releasing the true gift of longevity? The older generations cannot do it on their own; nor should they or else the Young would inherit a 21st-century "retirement" that they had no part in designing but one that they have to pay for; a tax bill for the future that will cripple them for life. An intergenerational partnership, in contrast, would at least let them have the opportunity to help shape any new social contract to fulfil their own needs as well as those of their parents; to share its costs and to more fully understand and engage in the opportunities of ageing as well as the potential burdens it inevitably might bring. Certainly, it would also force young people to think and plan ahead for their own retirement, their own extended "life-plan". As UNICEF concluded in 2018, the United Kingdom is one of the least family friendly countries in the 72 countries it surveyed, and British teenagers are some of the least happy. If ever there was a case and a cause for an intergenerational manifesto, then maybe this should be it.

Bibliography

6.1 Economic power

AARP/Oxford Economics: *The Longevity Economy* (2019)

APEC Tiva Workshop: *Summary Report* (2018)

Bank of England: *Future of Finance Report* (June 2020)

Deloitte Monitor: *The Silver Avalanche* (2019)

EC: Technopolis/Oxford Economics: *The Silver Economy* (2018)

Financial Conduct Authority (FCA): *Ageing Population and Financial Services* (2017)

Furlong, Mary: *Turning Silver into Gold*: FT Press (2007)

ILC-UK: *Maximising the Longevity Dividend* (2019)

Institute of Customer Service: *The Service Generation* (2016)

Jones, I.R. et al: *Ageing in a Consumer Society*: Policy Press (2008)

Laslett, Peter: *The World We Have Lost*: Methuen & Co. (1965)/Giddens, Anthony: Modernity and Self-Identity: Polity Press (1991

OECD: *G20 Principles on the Silver Economy and Active Ageing*: Turkey G20 (2015)

Thane, Pat; Warren, Lorna: *The British Academy Debates* (2014)

WEF: *How the 21st Century Longevity Can Create Markets and Drive Economic growth* (October 2015)

6.2 Political power

Age UK: *Age Manifestos* (2014/2015)

Bell, T; Gardiner, L: My Generation, Baby: The Politics of Age in Brexit Britain in Kelly G & Pearce N (eds), *Britain Beyond Brexit: Political Quarterly*, Vol. 90, Issue S2, pp. 128–141 (2019)

Demos: *Tune In: Turn Out* (2015)

Electoral Reform Society: *The 2019 General Election: Voters Left Voiceless* (March 2020)

Independent (January 2020)

Institute for Public Policy Research (IPPR): *Divided Democracies: Public Inequality in the UK and Why it Matters* (2014)

Neil O'Brien, Director of the 'Think Tank' Policy Exchange: Telegraph: (August 2012)

Timonen, Virpi: *Ageing Societies; A Comparative Introduction*: OUP (2008)

YouGov: *How Britain Voted in the 2019 General Election* (December 2019)

6.3 Technological power

Cavendish, Camilla: *Extra Time: Ten Lessons for an Ageing Society*: Harper Collins (2019)

Coughlin, JF: *Technology and the Future of Ageing (2005); The Longevity Economy*: Public Affairs (2017)

Dept. for Business, Energy & Industrial Strategy: *The Grand Challenges* (January 2021)

EUC: *Together for Health: a Strategy for the EU 2020*

Hawking, Stephen: *Brief Answers to the Big Questions*: John Murray (2018)

Kaku, M: *Physics of the Future (2012); The Future of Humanity*: Penguin (2019)

McAFee, A; Brynjolfsson, E: *Machine Platform Crowd*: W.W. Norton (2019)

MGI: *Confronting the Risks of Artificial Intelligence* (April 2019)

MGI: Dobbs, R; Manyika J; Woetzel J: *No Ordinary Disruption*: Public Affairs/Perseus (2015)

Orlov L.M: Technology for Ageing: 2021 Market Overview: Ageing and technology Watch (Jan.2021)

UK Select Committee Report on Artificial Intelligence: *Ready, Willing and Able?* (April 2018)

WEF: *The Fourth Industrial Revolution* (January 2016)

6.4 The judicial & moral power of human rights and social justice

Ageism

AARP & EIU: *The Economic Impact of Age Discrimination* (2020)

Age UK: *2014 Manifesto* (2014)

Age UK: *All the Lonely People* (September 2018)

Applewhite, Ashton: *This Chair Rocks: A Manifesto Against Ageism*: Network Books (2016)

Bakewell, Joan (aged 81), a television celebrity in the 1970s and later appointed as 'The Voice of Older People' by the Labour government in 2008.

Bedell, Geraldine: Observer (August 5, 2011)

Butler, R.N.: *Age-ism—Another Form of Bigotry*: The Gerontologist: Vol. 9 (1969)

Care Quality Commission: *Elder Abuse* (2017)

Centre for Ageing Better: *Doddery but Dear?* (March 2020)

Demos; Huber, J; Skidmore, P: *The New Old* (2003); Harkin, J; Huber, J: *Eternal Youth* (2004)

Eurage: *Grey Matters-A Survey of Ageism across Europe* (2011)

Gerrard, Nicci: *The Twilight Hour*: Penguin books (2014)

Harper, Sarah: *Ageing Societies*: Hodder/Arnold OUP (2006)

Neuberger, Julia: *Not Dead Yet: A Manifesto for Old Age*: Harper Collins (2008)

Tessa Harding: Help the Aged Farewell Speech (2006)

UCL/Pubmed: Rippon Isla et al: Perceived age discrimination in older adults: *Age & Ageing*, Volume 43, Issue 3, pp. 379–386 (May 2014)

UN (DESA): *Covid-19 and Older Persons: A Defining Moment for an Informed, Inclusive and Targeted Response* (May 2020)

WHO: *Ageism is a Global Challenge*: UN (March 2021)

Inequality

Carney, Mark: *Inclusive Capitalism*: Bank of England publications (May 2014)

Centre for Ageing Better: *The State of Ageing* (November 2020)

Health Foundation: *Health Equity in England: The Marmot Review 10 Years On* (February 2020)

Institute for Fiscal Studies (IFS): *Deaton Review of Inequalities* (May 2019)

Institute for Fiscal Studies (IFS): *The Characteristics and Incomes of the Top 1%* (August 2019)

IPPR Report: *Prosperity and Justice* (2018)

Johnson, Paul (IFS): We May Be in this Together, But That Doesn't Mean We Are in this Equally (April 2020)

Lind, Michael: *The New Class War*: Atlantic Books (2020

Longeron, Eric; Blyth, Mark: *Angrynomics*: Blackstone Publishing (2020)

LSE/Sutton Trust: *Pulling Away? A Social Analysis of Economic 'Elites' in the UK* (January 2020)

OECD: *In It Together: Why Less Inequality Benefits All* (May 2015)

Oxfam: *Even It Up: Time to End Extreme Inequality* (2014)

Oxfam: *Time to Care* (2020)

Picketty, Thomas et al: *World Inequality Report* (2018)

Public Health England (PHE): *COVID-19: Beyond the Data: Understanding the Impact on BAME Communities* (June 2020)

Resolution Foundation: *Rainy Days* (June 2020)

Resolution Foundation: *The UK's Wealth Distribution and Characteristics of High-wealth Households* (January 2021)

Shaxson, Nick: *The Finance Curse: How Global Finance Is Making Us Poorer*: Bodley Head (2018)

Social Mobility Commission: *State of the Nation-2018 to 2019* (2020)

Sunday Times *Rich List* (2020)

UK2070 Commission (Kerslake Report): *Fairer and Stronger: Rebalancing the UK Economy* (June 2019)

UN Secretary General Antonio Guterres Address to the General Assembly (September 25, 2018)

UNDESA: *World Social Report* (2020): *Inequality-Bridging the Divide* (2016)

UNICEF: Innocenti Report Card 14: *Building the Future* (2018)

Wealth Tax Commission: *A Wealth Tax for the UK* (December 2020)

WEF: *Global Social Mobility Index* (2020)

Wilkinson, R; Pickett, K: *The Spirit Level*: Penguin Books (2009)

Wilkinson, R; Pickett, K: The world we need: The challenge of inequality, *International Journal of Labour Research*, Volume 6, Issue 1, pp. 17–34 (2014)

World Bank: *The Changing Wealth of Nations* (2018)

Zucman, Gabriel: *Hidden Wealth of Nations*: University of Chicago Press (2015)

PART IV

Towards a new sociology of ageing for the 21st century

FIGURE IV.1 Image of the 100-Year Life

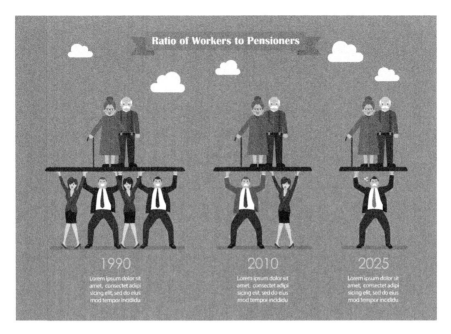

FIGURE IV.2(a)   Image of soaring dependency ratios

FIGURE IV.2(b)   Image of happy families

7

TOWARDS A NEW-AGE PARADIGM, MANIFESTO AND INTERGENERATIONAL SOCIAL CONTRACT

The longevity paradox

I have coined this phenomenon "the longevity paradox". Billions of dollars have been invested to enable us to live longer. We have better health. We have better health delivery. We have better nutrition….However, we are not prepared, because we did not expect all of that investment, be it public or private, to actually work. Now that we are living longer, we have not even begun to think about the physical infrastructure of an aging society. Perhaps today will be the beginning.

Joseph F. Couglin (2000)

If I had known I was going to live this long, I would have taken better care of myself.

Arthur Krystal (2019)

Social theory and the sociology of ageing

As outlined in the Foreword to this reader, ageing is now considered part of a global revolution; part of what the WEF has called the Fourth Industrial Revolution; a mega-force reshaping life in the near and far future as **grey power** becomes a major force in political life, the "**Silver Economy**" an emerging driver of the global economy and **age-technology** the silver solution to later life at home. We seem to be at the forefront of a new type of society – an age-friendly or even "ageless society" – as super-ageing societies such as Japan and Singapore begin to plan for the 100-Year Life ahead; a life in which the old move from the margins of society back to the centre and begin to represent and live out a new philosophy of human life, a more spiritual, less materialistic one based on ideas

DOI: 10.4324/9781003029373-12

such as generativity in devoting their later lives to improving the world about them as much as enjoying it themselves. A new sociological paradigm seems to be emerging; a new theoretical framework upon which a sociology of the 21st century might be built; a new-age sociology in which senior culture is as important and prominent as youth culture.

And this was the basis, too of Laura's initial dissertation presentation to her fellow tutees for the peer reviews that her tutor organised prior to any formal presentations to academic exam boards. Laura began her presentation by setting out the central theme of her thesis and the main arguments behind it, namely that:

> **Ageing is not just a new phase, a third stage in a longer human life but rather one that, alongside the other great global forces of globalisation, urbanisation and new technology, is the forerunner of a New Age and a New Stage in human social and economic development; a new social paradigm, a new social order where Longevity and the 100 Year Life are the norm and where the Ageless Society is the future.** "Less than a hundred years ago, the average Western life expectancy was 40; now it is 80. And, there is no end in sight: the first person who will reach 135 has already been born...Our average life expectancy has increased dramatically, but society has not yet adapted to that development...This will require a revolution in the way people live, and society as a whole, think (and plan).
>
> *Professor Rudi Westendorp (2015)*

Although ageing is sweeping across the world at breath-taking speed and will engulf all continents except Africa by 2050 and the whole world by 2100, this demographic revolution is still described under the limited lifespan paradigm of the last century, not the unlimited one of the 21st. Worse, ageing is still usually perceived as an economic liability restricted to the older age groups, rather than as the gift of longevity described by the UN and WHO for all ages. The rise of super-ageing societies such as Japan and Korea and the emergence of studies such as the 100-Year Life (2017) and the Longevity Economy (2017), however, have taken the ageing debate onto a whole new sociological plane and highlighted the longevity revolution as possibly the forerunner of a new age and a new stage in human and social development; and one that now needs a new social and economic structure to support it and a new approach to life to exploit it. From this perspective, longevity is no longer just an extra lease of life for older people but a new age of longer life for all ages; a new stage in social evolution that policymakers need to recognise and plan for rather than continue to contain and restrain it within a traditional three-age and three-stage social framework that dates back to the 19th century. Today is the age of the Fourth Industrial Revolution and the 100-Year Life. One for which we need a new vision of life, a new "map of life" and a new social and political paradigm if we are to fully exploit this *demographic dividend*; this gift of longer healthier life that, at present, few governments seem able or willing to see or plan for, despite the best efforts of the WHO and EU.

From this perspective, the 20th-century age paradigm seems increasingly outdated and under strain as the digital revolution gathers pace, challenging and transforming every aspect of modern life. As outlined in in Chapter 4, even in societies as prosperous and stable as the United Kingdom, every area of modern life seems to be under challenge and under strain from ageing, inequality, globalisation and new technology. All our traditional assumptions about healthcare, work, retirement and even death and dying are under scrutiny and that most fundamental of social institutions, the family, is being reconstituted right before our eyes. Even the New Old are not the Old Old. They are not the "silent generation" of the past. They are the baby boomer generation of the present; a generation well used to making their voice heard, well able to rewrite the *age script* and well able to reshape society if the message is clear and the cause is right. Whether they will fulfil Karl Mannheim's concept of generation or Howe and Strauss's historic mission as an agency of social change remains to be seen but certainly, the concept of generation is increasingly informing academic and political debate; although at present, more in terms of intergenerational conflict and unfairness than in terms of intergenerational collaboration and common purpose. Finally, the 20th-century paradigm has rested largely on economic growth, on the material standard of living and the distribution of wealth. The *21st-century paradigm*, in contrast, may well focus more on the quality of life than the quantity; on wellbeing and happiness more than simply on material possessions; on the meaning of life and the preservation of the planet rather than endless and relentless material growth.

COVID-19, for all its devastating effects, has given humankind a moment and an opportunity to reflect and rethink its traditional lifestyle; to reconsider the meaning of life in an age of both longevity and apparent plenty. It has accelerated economic and technological change by five, maybe ten years, ruthlessly exposed the institutional ageism within society today and unveiled the deep and divisive inequalities that lie beneath the social and economic surfaces of most modern societies. In its own brutal way, coronavirus may prove to be the great catalyst for change that the longevity revolution needs, exposing the weaknesses and inadequacies of the old social structure and accelerating the pace of change towards the new; accelerating the shift to living, learning and working online, to strengthening and reforming the healthcare and social care services, to investing in new technology in every sector of life, to fundamentally tackling systemic social inequality and to rethinking the current way and pace of life after a lockdown that has given everyone the opportunity to reconsider their priorities, their way of life and the relationships that really matter. In particular, by hitting the lives of the Old and the livelihoods and futures of the Young the hardest, COVID-19 may have helped generated the intergenerational movement needed to replace the post-war social contract that underpins most western societies and help design a new one fit for the century and the longevity society ahead.

Finally, to personalise and enliven this sociological leap in lifestyles, Laura invited Jonathan and her fellow students to imagine, on one hand, what their own life might be if they knew that they might live to 100 years and beyond, and on the other hand, to consider how lockdown had affected their lifestyles and views of the future. Challenging stuff at any age. Exciting stuff when as a student in your early 20s, you start thinking of the life ahead of you and all its possibilities and opportunities of living into the 22nd century. Frightening stuff, when you wonder whether in a post-COVID-19 and ageing society, you will ever have a career, a family or own a house of your own while having to pay massive taxes for all these older people, watching dementia stalking every street and "grey" fashions filling the shop windows once coronavirus has been wiped out and normal life – whatever that might be – restored once again. Emotional stuff when recollecting the havoc and distress that COVID-19 has brought to every household in every country and wondering what sort of world we will have left once the pandemic has subsided.

Not surprisingly, Laura's opening presentation left Jonathan and her study group somewhat dumb-struck by its audacity, breadth and ambition. It forced them to rethink all their previous personal as well as sociological assumptions about life and society in the century ahead and so with the study group's enthusiastic agreement, Jonathan agreed to incorporate three additional seminars into the weeks leading up to the end of term; three extra opportunities to challenge and road-test Laura's thesis.

Firstly, in light of the age-challenges ahead as described in Parts I and II, what might an all-age political manifesto or a new intergenerational social contract actually look like?

Secondly, how might the New Old and the New Young described in Part III get involved in its construction and actually deliver this new agenda?

Thirdly, what might a new sociological paradigm for the longevity society ahead actually look and feel like?

These would have been tough questions for a postgraduate student let alone an undergraduate facing her first dissertation. The timeline alone was pretty daunting and had Laura not had extensive family backup, she might possibly not have met it. However, having campaigned with her grandmother Polly – MP for Suffolk East – in the 2017 and 2019 General Elections for a New Age Manifesto and having a mother, Hannah, as a media specialist, Laura not only had the inside knowledge to support her thesis but outside experts who would not only give her presentation substance but also sufficient drama to stop even *Nodding Nigel* thumbing through his Facebook entries, and have him actually listening to the arguments and engaged in debating them.

Seminar 1: The challenges ahead and possible solutions

For this first seminar, Laura introduced her grandmother Polly, MP for the newly formed constituency of Suffolk East, a constituency that combines some of the most heavily deprived boroughs in the East of England such as Lowestoft with some of the wealthiest, such as Southwold, a retirement centre, with some of the most expensive beach huts in the United Kingdom. This area of East Anglia is a classic economic backwater that desperately needs hefty investment to staunch the flow of youngsters to the bright lights of London and to stop those left behind feeling that they had no hope and no future. Rich territory for Brexiteers; worrying landscape for intergenerational tension.

Polly opened her presentation with a quote from Stephen Burke, Director of the Charity, *United for All Ages*; a quote and a fear, explained Polly, that first inspired her interest in Ageing and that has nurtured it ever since. "If you landed in Britain today for the first time, you could be forgiven for thinking that we are a country where there is a civil war between the generations. That is what the media and many policy-makers would like us to believe as they pit young people against older people and seek to divide the generations…We should not be stoking up a war between generations. We should be focusing instead on the distribution of income, wealth and opportunities within and across generations and how we create a society where people of all ages prosper…It's time to build a Britain for all ages with a new contract "between the generations…a national strategy from cradle to grave".

Polly then briefly summarised the key challenges facing ageing Britain by drawing on the government's own Future of an Ageing Population Report in 2016 as well as Laura's briefing notes from the chapters above.

Firstly, the challenge of an ageing workforce as the proportion of those aged 50–64 rises from a quarter of the working population at present to 35% by 2050 – an increase of approximately 8 million people.

Secondly, the challenge of ageing households with the number of households headed by someone aged 85 and over alone projected to increase by 1.42 million – an increase of 161% in 25 years.

Thirdly, the challenge of the modern British family – its diversity, its fragility and its capacity to provide the quality and quantity of eldercare likely to be needed in a future where long-term care and care of the disabled elderly become urgent issues.

Fourthly, the healthcare challenge of adapting the UK's health and care systems to the chronic and long-term needs of an ageing population by both supporting care in the family and by investing in new assistive technology.

Finally, the challenge of social, physical and technological connectivity in integrating the emerging Old into supportive social structures to offset isolation, ill-health and worse the sort of wave of silver suicide seen in super-ageing countries such as Japan.

As this government report concluded, ageing needs a national strategy that engages all government departments, all age groups and all sectors of the economy and society. It is not a departmental, age-related issue solely about old people. It is a whole-society, all-age, lifetime issue that affects us all and that we must prepare for and plan now for as a matter of urgency. Moreover, the challenges of ageing and intergenerational tensions now sit alongside the uncertainties of life post-Brexit; a roller-coaster world of digital change and post-COVID existential rethinking for all ages and all societies; a cocktail of societal challenges for the United Kingdom in the next five years that is tense, if not toxic. The future is deeply uncertain and whilst ageing Britons might enjoy "Longer, healthier and wealthier lives over the next ten years"; they might equally face "Too Little for Too Many", according to the ILC-UK Summit in November 2017; a nightmare scenario of intolerable pressures on the health and social care services due to under-funding and shortages in trained staff, spiralling house prices due continued shortages in house building and the provision of specialist retirement homes, the financial time-bomb of retirees running out of savings and surviving solely on a State pension for daily living, and the "cliff-edge" loss of workforce experience and skill for employers who have failed to adapt their workplaces to an ageing workforce. The post-Brexit picture painted by the Institute for Public Policy Report for *Future Proof-Britain in the 2020s* (Dec. 2016) is even more depressing; an apocalyptic vision of a deeply divided union facing declining economic growth, escalating inequality and an ethnic and generational diversity that the current FPTP electoral system would be unable to contain. "Without reform, our political and fiscal system will struggle to build a more democratic, healthy society in the decades ahead, even as Brexit accelerates us towards a radically different institutional landscape…The old political order cannot cope and we need to be the architects of a better future". As the website Future Timeline described it in 2015, "The world of 2050 will be a world of contrasts and paradoxes. On the one hand, science and technology have continued to advance in response to emerging crises, challenges and opportunities. This has created radical transformations in genetics, nanotechnology, biotechnology and related fields. On the other hand, many of these same technologies have been so disruptive that it has led to a more frightening, unpredictable and chaotic world than ever before. Humanity is at a cross-roads that will determine its future path for centuries to come – survival or destruction, prosperity or collapse". And all this before that most disruptive of global forces to date, coronavirus, even reached Britain's shores and paralysed its economy, health service and way of life.

Having shocked Laura's classmates out of any complacency about the challenges ahead, Polly set out the age manifesto that she had trialled in campaigning in Suffolk East; an age manifesto inspired by the quotation from Stephen Burke, above and by an all-age family conference earlier, which helped her appreciate that any one-sided, old-age policy programme was a non-starter. It would leave a bad taste and leave the younger ages feeling that, once again, the selfish oldies were raiding the welfare state at their expense. Instead, this family gathering gave the *Voice of the Young* centre-stage and led Polly to conclude that it is the young who are the future not just the New Old. It was the ideas and the engagement of Laura and her cousins; their energy and their enthusiasm that most impressed Polly and led her to conclude that the New Young might be the key to releasing baby boomers' latent generativity and be the allies they need in leaving one last and lasting legacy for a better world. To Polly, such a two-pronged, two-age strategy hit all the right political, ideological and media buttons. A social contract for all ages for the multigenerational society ahead reflected the plea of the World Economic Forum way back in 2012 for a fundamental change of government mind-set, moving from a "challenge mind-set to an opportunity mind-set; from focusing on self-interest to focusing on shared benefits and long-term objectives and reinforcing a sense of moral responsibility and leadership". The family conference had equally been an opportunity for breaking down some generational barriers and challenging certain generational myths and stereotypes. The *Generation Game* that involved teams from both "ages" dressing up and acting out their images of the other worked particularly well. Baby boomers, inevitably, were mimicked as long-haired and mini-skirted teenagers bopping away on Top of the Pops to T-Rex, Adam Ant and other pop groups from the 1960s while Generations X, Y and Z were portrayed as iPhone zombies, tied to their smart phones and locked in a box, devoid of any human contact. As you can imagine, this generation game broke down a whole host of misunderstandings and generational stereotypes in a stroke – and with howls of laughter that would resonate thereafter in the family memory. It is a generational game that Polly and Laura recommended for any "family get-together"; a suggestion that two of the study group later took up, turning up at the next seminar in Grandad's leather jacket and winkle-pickers and Grandma's Afghan and mini-skirt.

So, as Polly explained, this was how the concept of ***mutual support for mutual benefit***, was born and how it became the backbone of the intergenerational manifesto that the family finally drew up. It wasn't that intergenerational support doesn't already exist. It clearly does exist and in "bucket-loads" through the "Bank of Mum and Dad", the chain-gangs of childcare that exists in many families and the rise of the multigenerational businesses. It was, however, that at present, such support is entirely informal and often unnoticed. It operates entirely out of familial ties and sentiments and so it can collapse-and often does – as easily as it is set up. It has no strategic support from government or big business. There is no policy framework that might take the principles of intergenerational support to the next level, no incentives for generational collaborations as part of a national strategy for the future and as a driver of the national and global economy of the 21st century. Yet, the opportunities and the potential for underpinning generativity, for combatting ageism and for promoting the harmony of an ageless society seem endless and endlessly inspiring. It may even, offer the principles needed to inform and inspire an intragenerational strategy for moderating inequality **within** generations as well as **between** them; particularly at a time when after the divisions of Brexit and now devolution, the United Kingdom seems to have lost its sense of social solidarity, its sense of collective identity even if coronavirus has temporarily revived intergenerational kindness and support.

A new-age manifesto

With these thoughts and ambitions in mind, Polly then explained that the drafting of an agreed intergenerational manifesto had been undertaken in two stages. Firstly, an outline of the underlying *Needs of the New Old* and those *of the*

New Young and the common ground in-between; and secondly, the design of a detailed manifesto covering the huge range of intergenerational issues such an ambitious document might encompass.

The Needs of the New Old that emerged essentially focused on policies and programmes to:

★   keep older people healthy and independent throughout later life and to give them the opportunity and incentives to continue to keep healthy, contribute positively and pro-actively to the community and the family around them and not be a burden on either.
★   support and promote the productivity and well-being of the Young as the working population who will be funding the British welfare state and the generation that is likely to be caring for the Boomer generation in Old Age.

The Needs of the New Young (Generations X, Y and Z) highlighted the need for policies and programmes that:

★   promote and support their own *life-long planning* in terms of employment, health, finance, housing and child/eldercare and that contribute to a comfortable and fulfilling retirement for them too.
★   keep the (New) Old, healthy, active and independent and so reduce the potential Burden of Age Dependency on the Young, their families and the welfare state.

These two statements quickly revealed the blindingly obvious conclusion that, despite apparent differences, the Old need the Young as much as the Young need the Old. The Old and the Young are simply at different stages on the Age-Journey and so see it from different perspectives – the Old looking back and the Young looking forward. All ages, however, need each other to survive and thrive; they need each other's support particularly in early life and later life. They simply need to recognise that explicitly and enshrine it in a new social contract with a clear set of agreed principles, responsibilities and policy actions for making it happen in the same spirit of generational collaboration set out by Lord Beveridge back in 1944. The vision statement that the family group finally chose was that of New Labour back in 2009; a vision of an ageing Britain that was not only ambitious but also included the sort of moral dynamic that the family had been looking for, notably by proposing to outlaw age discrimination and promote age equality. It set out a strategic framework of responsibilities for making this happen within and outside government. While it wasn't the finished product and needed much more on intergenerational relations and possibly a greater commitment to a new intergenerational social contract, it, nevertheless, offered a strong starting point given that it had come from a government in power and so reflected both Whitehall and Westminster thinking. For Polly in particular, this vision statement was something of an emotional "blast from the past", harking back to the political principles that inspired her to join New Labour in the first place back in the late 1990s.

A DRAFT INTERGENERATIONAL MANIFESTO OUR VISION OF A SOCIETY FOR ALL AGES AND ALL GENERATIONS

Our Vision is a Society for all Ages, where people are no longer defined by age, everyone is able to play a full part and where the spirit of Intergenerational Collaboration and Mutual Support that has defined Britain to-date is set out in a renewed and refreshed Social Contract designed for the Century ahead. This will require a major cultural change which includes the creation of a National Plan for the Challenges of Ageing facing Britain today; with the first step being to outlaw "unjustifiable age discrimination".

*This **strategy**:*

*For **individuals, families and generations,** it will mean planning for later life (early) so that they can fulfil their ambitions in work, leisure and in their communities.*

*For **government,** it will mean generating and leading a national debate on ageing and developing a vision and a manifesto for a better Britain for all ages. It will mean supporting individuals, families and generations in doing this but also enabling older people to continue to play an active and important role at the heart of family life and in their local communities in promoting their own wellbeing and the wellbeing of the younger generations around them.*

*For **businesses,** it means recognising and engaging the skills, abilities and experiences of older workers, investing in the new Silver Economy and in promoting Silver Enterprises and multigenerational projects that might best deliver the goods and services needed by an ageing population.*

*For **public services,** it means working with older people to design services that are right for people of any age, as well as recognising the specific needs that older people often have, for example, in healthcare.*

*Finally, for **government and communities**, it means ensuring that there are safe, accessible and attractive neighbourhoods to enable people of all ages to participate and be involved in.*

On the basis of this vision, the Family Working Party called on the Government of the Day to adopt and commit to the Principles of Active and Independent Ageing adopted by the UN and EU and draft a Bill of Human Rights for the Elderly as advocated by the WHO, outlaw ageism as rigorously and relentlessly as racism or sexism and appoint a Minister of Ageing to draw up a National Strategy for Ageing in Britain 2022 with a specific focus on:

- **The silver market and the silver economy** and their integration into National Economic Planning with a specific focus on the UK dependency ratio and on the potential for the Silver Economy to drive all-age employment, enterprise and innovation particularly after Brexit and COVID; a strategy that should include a review of current business and financial regulation in terms of its capacity to protect the elderly against fraud, mis-selling etc. and its ability to promote and protect the silver markets of the future.

- **The development of new technologies** that will encourage and enable active, outgoing and independent later life, ageing-at-home and family/community communication; technologies that would include artificial intelligence and robotics as steps forward in promoting active and independent ageing and in offsetting social isolation as well as contributing to society at large and reducing the UK dependency ratio.
- **The creation of local plans** by city councils, local authorities and devolved nations within the United Kingdom for addressing ageing in their communities from 2022–2035 and beyond such as that by Portsmouth City Council.

With this intergenerational framework in mind, Polly now broke the study group into small groups of mixed ages and invited each group to choose one or possibly two policy areas to draft proposals of their own; an exercise that generated intense activity in which even *Nodding Nigel* got involved, and during which the study room walls became festooned with policy proposals ranging from retirement and work through to lifelong education, housing and even sex, death and dying. The final results, outlined below, were amazingly similar to the family manifesto below with the powerful addition of a radical reform of the United Kingdom's current FPTP election system; a recommendation that Polly reflected afterwards was possibly the key to re-engaging all ages – and notably the young – in designing and deciding the Great Britain ahead.

AN ALL-AGE INTERGENERATIONAL MANIFESTO

1. **Retirement and work:**

   ⋆ Raise the age of state pension in line with longevity rather than simply on a fixed age.

   ⋆ Incentivise longer working lives through, for example, attractive deferred pension incentives and later-life work schemes with pensionable incentives, health benefits and/or tax breaks particularly in such shortage areas as teaching, nursing, medicine and care.

   ⋆ Incentivise and support silver entrepreneurs and particularly, intergenerational new businesses especially in the emerging "silver" markets.

   ⋆ Create a comprehensive National Retirement Service for all ages at all stages of life's transitions: a one-stop shop along the lines proposed by Lord Wei but with a broader brief than just retirement planning for the Old but life-long planning for the Young too.

2. **Pensions and life-long financial planning:**

   ⋆ Raise the State Pension to 60% of average earnings to equalise income in later life and remove pensioner poverty altogether, funded partly from progressive taxation on wealthier pensioners and partly by the withdrawal of current pension benefits for those under 85 years of age.

- ★ Create more attractive and secure pension saving schemes for the Young with, for example, a single tax relief rate on pensions of say 30% to encourage long term pension saving by all young people not just the "better-off".
- ★ Create more attractive pensioner saving schemes for the Old to help stabilise pensioner incomes and to release billions of pounds in zombie or low-interest savings accounts as new investment funds for such mutually beneficial projects as New Build Housing schemes for Old and Young alike.
- ★ Promote high quality and fully regulated all-age financial planning advice and guidance including financial education and entrepreneurship schemes in schools

3. **Healthcare:**

- ★ Raise spending on health and social care by 2% in line with GDP spend of leading European nations such as France and the Netherlands with the emphasis on preventative and active health.
- ★ Radically and comprehensively redesign and fully fund social care and integrate it within the NHS on the basis of Personalised Care Plans and Budgets as proposed by the Barker Commission and King's Fund with far stricter regulation and quality standards and with much greater involvement of families as proposed by the ILC-UK. As the Nuffield Trust (2018) has argued, the Japanese long-term care system might well offer a model for the future.
- ★ Raise recruitment and training into geriatric medicine and into social care by elevating their pay and professional status and standards accordingly.
- ★ Create healthcare saving schemes with progressive or, at least, equitable tax relief to incentivise long term healthcare funding in the same way as pension saving.
- ★ Provide greater promotional and preventive health schemes for all ages with pensionable incentives for good health as employed by many private health insurance schemes.
- ★ Secure low-cost financial schemes to support the cost of later-life care with tax relief throughout working life-and into early retirement.
- ★ Set up eldercare incentive schemes for young and middle-aged volunteers (e.g. volunteer credits) to reduce pensioner isolation and promote intergenerational support and contact.
- ★ Promote investment in new technology for supporting ageing-in-place, active engagement outside the home and for ongoing communication and monitoring of the elderly by the family.
- ★ Set up a national campaign to raise funds to combat age-related diseases, and specifically to raise the status and research funding into dementia as the emerging cancer of the 21st century.

4. **Education**:

   ★ Put ageing and longevity on the school curriculum to promote longer life planning and early pension saving.
   ★ Promote intergenerational volunteering and support (e.g. in secondary schools with residential homes).
   ★ End higher education fees or cut interest rates on existing student loans and incentivise life-long learning and training for all ages.

5. **Housing**:

   ★ Develop a *single chain* housing strategy and associated financial packages, including trustworthy and value-for-money equity release schemes to promote downsizing by the Old and support upsizing by the Young with reduced stamp duty to encourage both.
   ★ Design and develop a new generation of housing schemes for both retirement and multigenerational living.
   ★ Design saving plans to attract pensioner savings for investment in new build housing for Young and Older People alike and so stimulate both ends of the housing chain.
   ★ Promote ageing-at-home through research, subsidies and planning approvals for new technologies that will support and encourage independent living in old age at home.

6. **Family**:

   ★ Create an affordable, accessible and high-quality childcare system across the country to support early learning and relieve and release working mums or dads.
   ★ Create family care schemes to incentivise the Young to support older relatives and relieve "care sandwich" (e.g. volunteer credits as pension savings and/or offset student loans).
   ★ Promote grandparent incentive schemes to support family childcare/school travel, to enhance their role in the family and add income to their pensions.
   ★ Promote visitor/volunteer schemes and incentives to offset the epidemic of loneliness in many residential homes getting volunteers – and families – in and pensioners out into the community.
   ★ Consider legislation as in other parts of Europe to "encourage" and incentivise greater family responsibility for the elderly.

7. **Volunteering**:

   ★ Undertake a major overhaul of charity and community support sector to bring it into the 21st century to help develop a more business-like approach but one that nevertheless retains and strengthens its voluntary mission, spirit and ethos, and develop incentives and simpler schemes to attract the baby boomer retirees and more young people, especially post-education and/or as part-time pay while studying.

★ Create a national volunteer service to mobilise the over-50s comparable to Marc Freedman's Encore programme in the United States and Lord Wei's ideas in the United Kingdom.

8. **Death and Dying:**

   ★ Generate a national debate on euthanasia, organ donation and concept of living wills and legislation to follow.

   ★ Create a policy framework to regulate, stimulate and control the financial market in *death and dying* products including the cost of funerals and the creation of family financial plans.

   ★ Research and regulate the emerging *ever-lasting life* industry and its promises of life after death.

Finally, for comparison (and as homework), Polly distributed copies of the Intergenerational Commission's recommendations in 2018 for a **New Intergenerational Social Contract** for the 21st century; a framework that included:

- **Sharing care costs** by introducing a new council tax on the housing wealth of the older generation but with a limit on care costs themselves so that "no-one can be asked to contribute more than a quarter of their wealth for their own care".

- **Raising more funds for the NHS** by re-imposing National Insurance charges on those still working after pensionable age but with most of this money coming from the richest fifth of pensioners.

- **Strengthening young people's income and job security** by establishing the right to a regular contract for those doing regular hours on zero-hour contracts, to extend statutory rights to the self-employed and set out a minimum notice for shifts to reduce the current levels of job insecurity.

- **Setting up a £1 billion better jobs deal** to support young people seeking work and training and £1.5 billion to support the development of high-quality technical education funded by cancelling 1p of the forthcoming corporation tax cut.

- **Protecting tenants** from escalating rent increases and to increase the supply of housing for first-time buyers by introducing community land auctions and a time-limited capital gains tax to incentivise owners of additional properties to sell to first-time buyers.

- **Encouraging pension saving** by lowering the earnings threshold for auto-enrolment, flattening rates of pension tax relief to say 28% for all and reconsidering the current ratio of State pension to median earnings which at 32% is half the EU and OECD averages.

- **Developing a framework for a collective defined pension scheme** to reduce risk for younger workers and develop a guaranteed income product purchased at age 80.
- And finally – and most controversially – **abolishing inheritance tax** and replacing it with a lifetime receipts tax that generates sufficient revenue to support a £10,000 citizens inheritance for all young adults from age 25 to support skills, entrepreneurship, housing and pension saving.

This was an amazingly rich feast of intergenerational proposals; so rich that several of Laura's study group found it too much to take in, in one gulp, and so they asked Jonathan for more time to digest and debate it – possibly at the next seminar. However, while the study group overwhelmingly agreed with the ethos, ambition and virtually all of the proposals in Polly's all-age manifesto, the IGC proposal about abolishing inheritance sparked off an all-mighty row between those who saw inheritance as a "natural right" and those who agreed with Torsten Bell (2018) that inheritance is the root of the inequality in British society and should be abolished or at least severely restrained. The resultant discussion quickly escalated into a Brexit-type stand-off not only about what is right and fair but also about what makes a society stable and at one with itself; an argument that Polly eventually had to mediate by reminding the group that in a technological age of plenty – and especially after a global pandemic – health and human happiness are as critical to human and societal wellbeing as the creation and distribution of wealth. According to the 2019 Origin of Happiness Report, the United Kingdom is one of the least happy societies in the world despite being one of the richest. As the OECD report Well-Being in 2020 concluded, those "OECD countries with higher average levels of well-being tend to have greater equality between population groups and fewer people living in deprivation". Norway, Netherlands, New Zealand and Switzerland might make far better role models for British politicians, suggested Polly, than trying to compete with the rampant materialism of the United States.

So, a seminar that began by looking at political solutions to ageing, ended up with an intense debate about inequality, the distribution of health, wealth and even the future of happiness. A big leap in intergenerational debate and one that led Laura's study group to give Polly a rousing round of applause and many heartfelt thanks. For most of them, this was the first time that a politician had spoken directly to them and to their emerging needs and aspirations. This was the first time that most of the study group had even considered the idea of an all-age manifesto and they were now quite inspired by the idea of a new intergenerational social contract that sought to improve their own futures as well as those of the older generations. They were inspired too by Polly as a person and a politician and by her final quote from Professor Sarah Harper in her speech to the ILC-UK Conference in November 2016: "We have a wonderful opportunity with all these generations being alive at the same time for the experience and understanding of older generations to be passed down to younger generations. Imagine being able to draw on the experience of five generations at the same time".

Seminar 2: The new old and the age revolution

Although Polly's presentation provided Laura's study group with a framework for both an age manifesto and a new intergenerational social contract, they had no idea of who and how this new age agenda might be driven and delivered. Laura had suggested in her briefing notes that the New Old might be the primary agency for such political and economic change but that left hanging the question of who might lead this transformation and how the older generation might be motivated and inspired to so act; a question that Alex and Geraldine – two hardened baby boomers from the 1960s – willingly agreed to respond to. Alex and Geraldine set the strategic scene by asking the study group to describe their impressions of old and older people today. While several of the boys choose the road sign image below (Figure 7.1), most of the girls were far less stereotypical and less ageist. Instead, they highlighted the diversity amongst older women, identified their own mothers and even their grandmothers as still being both

FIGURE 7.1 Image of old people road sign

FIGURE 7.2 Image of ageing celebrity (Jane Fonda at age 83)

active and glamorous. They were more likely to choose celebrities such as Helen Mirren, J.K. Rowling and even Jane Fonda (Figure 7.2) as their role models not just for their enduring glamour but for their achievements and enduring presence on stage or in public life. And although Victor Meldew (or Mildew as Nigel called him) from the sitcom *Til Death Do Us Part*, remained the archetypal grandad, some of the girls, at least, accepted the vague – very vague – resemblance of their dads to the silver, smooth images of Mel Gibson, Alec Baldwin, Donald Sutherland and even, in one case, to George Clooney himself. They all accepted at the end of this *image-breaking* exercise that the Old today are nothing like the old of yesterday and likely to be even less like the *old* of the future – their own age group.

Alex and Geraldine now added their own memories and experiences – along with ancient photos – of their time as teenagers and students during the late 60s and early 70s; experiences that included demonstrating against the War in Vietnam, sit-ins over Women's Rights and concerts featuring Bob Dylan and The Who at the Isle of Wight. The extract from the Top of the Pops show of that era had at least one of the girls in the study group shrieking in delight at the sight of a teenager she was sure her mum alongside her aunt Maureen while Alex and Geraldine's personal reminiscences had the study group in disbelief at just how radical many of the baby boomer generation had actually been – and as Alex and Geraldine believed could be in the future. They both agreed with Laura that baby boomers today possibly still have an appetite for radical change, for political campaigning and for the sort of Intergenerational Manifesto being proposed by Polly, provided that the cause is right and that they have the right leadership, inspiration and organisation to make it happen. They agreed too that baby boomers today have more powers at their disposal to put life right than any generation before and that human rights and inequality remain for many baby boomers the two great post-war challenges, the two great causes and "longest running sores"; ones that that they thought that they had put to rest in the late 1960s and that even today would inspire many of them to take to the streets yet again. COVID-19 has brought ageism brutally to public attention while equally exposing the rampant inequalities between the wealthy and healthy; the vulnerable and the deprived.

Where Alex and Geraldine possibly disagreed with Laura's analysis, however, was whether the New Old was yet at the point of actively joining any intergenerational cause and though they could both see the possibilities of a Grey-Green Alliance, at present, such a cause lacked the sort of charismatic leadership needed to thrust it forward into the public limelight in the way that Nigel Farage had galvanised the Brexit campaign in the United Kingdom and Donald Trump had used "Making America Great Again" in 2016. So, in contrast to the *political way* proposed by Polly and the Grey Vote, and the *economic way* reflected in the rise of the Silver Economy, Geraldine and Alex suggested a third way, one that reflected both their own professional backgrounds in social services – Alex as a housing officer with Shelter, Geraldine as CEO of the Samaritans – one that reflects much that is at the heart of the British way of life and one that has been dramatically resurrected by lockdown, COVID-19 and people's underlying concern for and kindness to others. This **third way**, this voluntary way, has motivated and mobilised a national movement in the United States, pioneered by such American Age gurus as Mark Freedman and Ken Dychtwald, and to illustrate their thesis, Alex and Geraldine streamed Marc Freedman's recent ILC-UK London lecture to a distinguished audience of academics, politicians and industrialists.

Marc Freedman began by setting out the primary aim of his volunteer campaign; his call for baby boomers to take up an encore career; to come out of retirement and go back into mainstream society not this time for personal profit or advantage but as a payback to society for what it had given them and as a contribution to the next generations for the life ahead; an intergenerational altruism to combat the selfish image many have of this charmed generation; a generational *legacy* and a new social contract fit for the 21st century and for the generations to follow.

In Freedman's view:

- *We fear* the future, instead of embracing and engaging in it.
- *We fear* mortality and we remain obsessed with youthfulness, our own youthfulness rather than that of future generations and the future of mankind.
- *We fear* the loss of life and the time ebbing away rather than planning for a "new life", a life free of daily demands and material needs; a life free to explore our true selves and the world around us; a time to look forward with hope and renewed ambition rather than with nostalgia and longing for "times past".
- *We* **worry** about our children and our grandchildren and the "state" of the world they are about to inhabit.

Now, however, through the gift of longevity, he argued, we have the time, the energy, the experience and the *wisdom* to think ahead, to see where we might make a difference – and to actually do it, and so help make the future, the future of our grandchildren and great-grandchildren-better. The gift of longevity has created a *demographic dividend*, an opportunity for a third act, a *later life* not as part of the traditional passive passage into retirement from society and then off into the "hereafter" but as an active and adventurous climax or culmination of life to date, one beyond the demands of everyday existence and self-interest; one on the higher moral plane of service to the community and particularly to improving the quality of life for the generations to follow; and in so doing leaving a legacy "and leaving the world a better place than we found it". This third act or third age "isn't simply a better phase of life than commonly thought; it's the culmination, the new 'crown of life, the age of fulfilment'. It's a time when individuals are liberated from the practical concerns and requirements of midlife yet years from old age. It's an opportunity for new pursuits, for learning and growth, for perhaps the most important contributions of one's life'; for becoming what the historian Peter Laslett, called the "trustees for the future".

This third age therefore offers the potential for a ***generative revolution,*** a revolution, or evolution, in human development that would enable humankind to realise its full potential as individuals and as a species. As the psychologist Carl Jung wrote, "Mankind cannot reach a state of true fulfilment until late in life....a state of 'individuation'; a state of being all that you can be". Erik Erikson went further and argued that "The most actualized, or fully developed, adults reach the point where their greatest satisfaction in life is giving back". "I am what survives of me" declared Erikson and the withdrawal of the elders or older populace en masse from modern society after a lifetime of challenge and contribution, is a social and an individual waste that has to be reversed if mankind as a species is not to stagnate and to fail to rise to its highest level of development. And the beauty of the concept of generativity is that it foresees man-individually as well as collectively – living forever; it provides, "a way of thinking about the end of one's life that suggests that the end is not really the end. I may die, but my children (and grandchildren) will live on".

So, for Mark Freedman, the concept of generativity offers the *vision*, the *hope* and the *opportunity* for a generational legacy that will inspire generations ahead and contribute to raising mankind to a higher level of values, behaviour and development; "a shift, a **big shift** to the dizzy heights of Generativity". And leading that "Revolution", believes Freedman, will be the boomer generation, a unique generation with the appetite and the energy, **if** only they can step outside "their generational tendency toward self-centredness and wield this power with wisdom and generativity" and so perhaps they will be remembered not just as "the 'largest' generation in history, but the finest". As Marc Freedman concludes, ***the choice is ours and the moment is ours***; there will be no second chance and soon we will be too old to march, too old to lobby, too old to make a difference. Marc Freedman concluded his presentation with the words of his own inspiration and colleague in age-arms, Jimmy Carter, President of the United States 1977–1981: "When I was in my fifties, I thought the things that mattered most were the things you could see—an expensive car, a big, beautiful home, status and wealth. Now I see that it's none of that. What truly matters in life are the things that you cannot see; deep love you share with your family and close friends, your spiritual faith, the contributions you make to other people's lives, and your wealth of lifetime experiences are what really matter"; a philosophy and way of life neatly summed up in the title and sub-title to Marc Freedman's most recent publication as illustrated in Figure 7.3 below.

Marc Freedman had a standing ovation at the London Conference and he inspired a round of spontaneous applause too at Laura's seminar. The study group was blown away by Marc Freedman's ideals and inspiration – not least because COVID-19 had thrust public altruism to the fore, created folk heroes such as Captain Tom and Marcus Rashford and inspired the public at the beginning of the pandemic to communally applaud the beleaguered staff of the NHS and UK care homes. By the end of Marc Freedman's talk, many of them not only

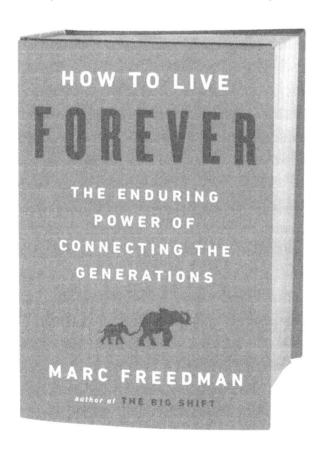

FIGURE 7.3 Cover of *How to Live Forever*

appreciated what it might be like to be a baby boomer but even half-wished that they were one. He had shown what an Age Evangelist could do to inspire generational consciousness and intergenerational engagement; but he had equally raised the question of who might play Marc Freedman in real life; who might be the poster person for the older generation in the United Kingdom; a debate that generated a rich and boisterous conclusion to Alex and Geraldine's presentation with suggestions ranging from Prince Harry to Jeremy Clarkson, from David Attenborough to Dame Judy Dench and even their tutor, Jonathan, was in close contention.

Marc Freedman's presentation, however, also raised the question of whether the voluntary sector in Great Britain today has the vision and the capacity to lead a generational revolution and mobilise a mass movement. The NPC/ILC-UK Report on *Ageing and the Voluntary Sector* in 2014 – of which Geraldine was a member – concluded that currently the United Kingdom's voluntary sector is ill-equipped to meet the challenges of an *ageing Britain* of the future. It is still stuck in the past, still stuck in the Victorian era of philanthropy and paternalistic concern for the elderly and the poor; still organised around the charity shop, the coffee morning, the food bank and the third world appeal. In the Commission's view, there is "a collective failure of imagination and innovation" of the sort needed to meet the age of opportunity that longevity is now creating. Instead, there is a need for a "sea change" in strategy and approach, a radical rethink of the role, image and organisation of volunteering in the United Kingdom to make it fit to meet the changing needs of ageing Britain. Such a paradigm shift would, in the Commission's view, involve a much more professional and business-like approach, particularly to fundraising and to relations with employers; a dramatic and much more up-market image and a much more appealing offer to potential recruits, especially baby boomers with so much else on offer to engage their time. The *volunteering buzz* that currently inspires and sustains volunteers needs to be turned into a *volunteering bug*, into an urgent and infectious lifelong commitment, an ongoing desire to help others, one that generates that very special and uniquely uplifting sense of personal fulfilment and human purpose, that sense of achievement and emotional wellbeing, that sense of having made a difference that is gained from helping others and the overwhelming gratitude it often generates in response. The United Kingdom has a rich history of charity work and a rainbow of charity organisations ranging from those patronised by the Royal Family such as the Prince's Trust and Prince Harry's Invictus Olympics through to the NHS Helpforce, RSVC and the foodbanks mushrooming across the country. The need is certainly there, explained Geraldine – and it's likely to escalate exponentially post-COVID, but, as the 2018 Centre for Ageing's Review of Community Contributions in Later Life highlighted, the obstacles to mass engagement are still considerable not only in terms of the cost involved but because of transport, language barriers, the digital divide and people's lack of self-confidence in actually volunteering. David Cameron's "Big Society" and Theresa May's Civil Society Strategy were attempts by national government to encourage community work but as The Guardian commented at the time (August 8, 2018), "There is something sad and ridiculous in the launch of a 'civil society strategy' imagining new institutions to support local communities when the existing political structures, the democratically mandated authorities that have always fulfilled that purpose are collapsing in a fiscal famine imposed with ideological motive by central government".

However, despite this public image, volunteering in the United Kingdom today is, in fact, big business and growing. As government retreats from welfare services and hands huge contracts over to the private and charity sector, a £24 billion a year project is emerging employing some 23 million volunteers annually. And that's without including unpaid childcare that the ONS has valued as a £343 billion contribution to the UK economy; about three times the contribution of the financial services sector. Volunteering in the United Kingdom today therefore is a mass market and one that is likely to grow exponentially as the over-65s age group in the United Kingdom rises rapidly from 16% of Britain's population in 2010 to 23% by 2030 – with the over-80s set to double in number and centenarians to grow "five-fold" in the same period. In the face of such a massive growth, a dramatic restructuring of the voluntary sector is slowly taking place and the 2014 NPC Commission predicted that by 2033, whilst big charities with over £10 million turnover are likely to expand to nearly 60% of the sector, small charities will have to become more specialist and age-niche at the local level if they are to survive. This is a seismic shift in the structure and provision of the voluntary sector and a direct outcome of the outsourcing of numerous public services as both national and local government respond to the pressures of ever-increasing "austerity cuts" to their budgets. The past ten years, alone, have seen voluntary sector income from government contracts soar and a "three-way" relationship emerge between the public, private and voluntary sectors as the public sector "steps back" and uses commissioning and outsourcing rather than providing services itself. However, with this shift towards big business and a focus on income streams comes real dangers as a sector built on 19th-century ideals of selfless, community service now enters the mainstream of 21st-century business, competing with and working alongside huge corporations, like Capita with global reach and multiple income streams. It may look like economic suicide as well as an ethical sellout as the voluntary sector is in danger of losing public trust if its unique selling point of altruism, integrity and traditional honesty is ever questioned. A new-age voluntary sector could help lead the British Silver Economy into the 21st century but with a heavy health warning that "getting into bed" with big business can turn even a *saint into a sinner* as such well-known and highly respected charities as Oxfam and Save the Children found to their immense cost after revelations in 2018 about aid workers in disaster areas consorting with local prostitutes. Nevertheless, inspired by coronavirus, the United Kingdom's appetite for voluntary work is probably at a post-war high and with it the opportunity to inspire Encore careers amongst all ages and to campaign fervently for the sort of intergenerational social contract being proposed by the

FIGURE 7.4 Image of Joanna Lumley and quote: "I love old. I love old people and I always knew old would be good for me and would contain great glories". (Mail Online: October 5, 2018.)

ILC-UK and IGC. The issue, nevertheless, remains of who might lead it and how, and whether a celebrity like Joanna Lumley (Figure 7.4) might have more public appeal – and public trust – than any current politician?

So, as Alex and Geraldine concluded, ageing has its cause and potentially its campaign manifesto. It has a huge range of intergenerational forces at its disposal politically and economically, socially and morally and it could possibly combine ageing and climate change under a joint green and silver banner as in Finland. The opportunity is there but, at present, the bandstand is bare. Coronavirus has shown what the State can do in a national crisis. It has shown what the British people can do for each other. So, what can politicians do to capture this national spirit? How might British political parties capture the spirit of coronavirus and use it in 2024 to reunite and rejuvenate Great Britain after 14 years of austerity and viral lockdown? An inspiring question to end this seminar. A challenging question for Laura and Polly to take away for their future presentations.

Seminar 3: Towards a new sociology of ageing: A new-age paradigm

This was to be the climax to Laura's study group scrutiny; the summing-up that convinced her peers – and her tutor – that her thesis had sociological substance and real meaning for all of them now and in the future. She began by briefly reminding the group of the three main themes underpinning her thesis, namely that:

- Ageing now constitutes one of the great global forces of the 21st century; one that sits alongside globalisation, urbanisation and new technology in driving the ageing societies of today towards the ageless societies of tomorrow, forcing them to adapt or redesign their economic, social and political structures to cope with the new realities of the 100-Year Life in a technological world of such intense and immense change that there is no "normal" anymore. Japan may currently be leading the way but eventually, every continent, even Africa will follow.
- Age and generational power in the form of the silver economy, grey vote and possibly now the voluntary way, now represent sociological forces capable of driving such social change through intergenerational harmony rather than, as many fear, through intergenerational conflict, in unlocking and unleashing the demographic dividend on offer and in preparing 21st-century societies properly for the age of longevity ahead.
- This demographic journey, however, isn't just a sociological and economic shift towards longer life and making society more age-inclusive. It is also, according to age gurus such as Marc Freedman and philosophers such as Erik Erikson, part of a shift towards higher human values and a higher way of living and thinking. It is part of a shift towards generativity and benevolence where altruism towards others and contentment with oneself have supplanted competitive materialism and self-interest and where the desire to leave an intergenerational legacy rather than an intergenerational debt is the ultimate inheritance and this generations' enduring last wish. As Professor Chris Phillipson argued back in 2014, "The twenty-first century will without question be a time when all societies take stock of the long-term impact of demographic change .... A different approach would separate out the issue of Individual Ageing-where some element of decline and eventual death is inevitable-and Population Ageing-where the idea of a new type of life-course is beginning to emerge".

A **new-age paradigm** would therefore, argued Laura, necessitate a wholesale reconstruction and redesign of social thinking involving some or all of the following:

- A redefinition of age and the underlying assumptions and perceptions behind it.
- A redefinition of the life-course and the traditional stages defined by chronological age, distinct lifestyles and social expectations ranging from childhood through to adulthood and retirement.
- A redefinition and a redesign of the current notion of retirement and all its underlying assumptions about work and leisure, lifestyle and engagement with society at large.

- A redefinition of the role of the State – and of employers – within an age-ing – or ageless society and the extent to which the State can or should bear all the cost and responsibility for leading and supporting the burden of dependency.
- A redefinition – and re-examination – of the role of family in a multigen-erational society and of the employer with a multigenerational workforce.
- A redefinition of the social contract that currently underpins post-war democracies and their various welfare states.
- A redefinition of the current notions of social equity and social fairness as part of the drive to eliminate – or at least moderate – intergenerational and intragenerational inequality and conflict.

A new-age paradigm would therefore need to incorporate within it:

The concept of an *ageless society*, one in which **stage** not age is the defining characteristic determining life-stages, lifestyles and career paths; one in which instead of the predetermined linear pathway of today, the life-course is much longer, richer and varied involving multi-ple *careers* and ongoing personal development; one in which retirement is no longer seen as a step "downhill" but as part of the staircase of pro-gression through Maslow's Hierarchy of Need onto Erikson's "altar" of generativity and its foresights into the future.

The concept and complexity of new, more fluid and extended social structures such as the emerging *multigenerational, multi-ethnic fam-ily* that is emerging today alongside a new generation of grandparents and their growing contribution to future family life, childcare and relationships.

The concept of *multistage welfare stretching right across the life-course of a 100 Year Life with the* costs and responsibilities rebalanced between the Individual and the State, the family and the employer.

The power of the *silver markets and the silver vote* on both the economy and the polity of ageing societies in the future and on the direction and pace of social change.

The elimination of *ageism* as a social evil and a structural and cultural obstacle to creating an "age-free" society in which the old as well as the young can fully contribute and yet be protected from discrimination and exploitation at a time when they are most vulnerable.

The moderation of extreme *inequality*, and the creation of a fairer dis-tribution of wealth and power not only *between* generations but *within* generations to prevent the emergence in later life of two "classes" of pensioner-the wealthy and the poor.

Such redefinitions and paradigm change, Laura argued, would release the full potential of the longevity dividend and in the process:

★ **Transform healthcare** and our current notions of *good health*, keeping the elderly active and independent and enjoying happiness in their later life by promoting healthy living much earlier on.

★ **Transform the workplace** and our current concepts of career and employment with older workers retained as treasures of experience and multigenerational workforces blended and bonded to work in harmony with AI and automated robotics in the jobs of the future.

★ **Transform technology** and make it more age-friendly, more universal in design, developing products that no longer depend on physical strength or perfect sight and that help older people lead more independent lives: smart-homes, telehealth, assistive technology, driverless cars and of course "age-friendly" robots.

★ **Transform our environment and especially our cities** and make them more age-friendly and age-accessible; make transport, shopping and even walking more comfortable and welcoming not only for the elderly but also for the disabled in a wheelchair or the young mother with her buggy. As the McKinsey study in 2016 highlighted, cities are becoming the powerhouses of growth in the 21st century and the old as much as the young will be the power-consumers of tomorrow.

★ **Transform our financial services** and make their products simpler, fairer and more able to protect the elderly than exploit them. The current range of financial products available to older age groups are generally complex, poor value and the source of numerous scandals or mis-sellings in recent years.

★ **Transform the role and status of the senior citizen** from the senile and the segregated into the "wise and the caring" – the family "godfathers"; the *grandfather* and the *grandmother*, of future life whose "words of wisdom and lessons of life" are taken as important and considered worthy of listening to and whose contribution to family or community life is taken as essential and beneficial, to be neither ignored nor patronised.

This was the theoretical framework for Laura's thesis; and to illustrate it in more detail, Laura streamed into the classroom an online TED talk by Professors Lynda Gratton and Andrew Scott on how the **100-Year Life** might actually work in practice. Firstly, to illustrate the growing tension between the current three-stage life cycle and the longer life emerging, Gratton and Scott used the life-plans of three representative characters, Jimmy, Jane and Jack. Under today's 3.0 cycle – life, work and pension plan – by living 100 years, all three characters would be out of money by the later stages of retirement and worse, they would have run out of the skill needed to obtain later-life employment. In tomorrow's fast-changing technological world, old skills learnt during formal education in a person's 20s are likely to be obsolete 40 years later. Retraining in later life (scenario 3.5) is one solution for those brave enough to embark on it. Retraining throughout life (scenario 4.0) to extend your current occupation or to prepare for a new one, or even to start your own business in later life, is a far better solution for both coping with future life and exploiting it to the full. A 100-Year Life requires a youthfulness and plasticity or adaptability that the authors refer to as "juvenescence" – a sort of older person's adolescence and active anticipation, embracing future change, rather than fearing and withdrawing from it. This multistage, almost adolescent approach to life, argue Gratton and Scott, may also help reverse the contemporary segregation of the generations as multiple generations increasingly live and work together as life gets longer.

Secondly, Gratton and Scott highlighted the massive challenge of inequality to the quality of life in any age of longevity. They identify two key sources of inequality. Firstly, the huge variances in the length of life enjoyed by the well-to-do compared to the poor; and secondly, the inequalities in terms of skill, education and social networks inherited by the richer sections of society that enable them to take full advantage of later life opportunities while their poorer counterparts languish in shorter lives, poorer lives lacking the skills or opportunities to continually regain work and offset the limited savings and poor pensions earned earlier. Future society in an age of longevity could be characterised as a Hobbesian Horror of a *War of All Against All* just as easily as it could be characterised as one of multigenerational harmony. Which vision and which pathway prevails will depend as much on the quality of government leadership and employer foresight as action by ordinary people on the ground. Either way, Gratton and Scott hope life with longevity will be lively, exciting and a whole new experiment in human living but only if we start discussing it now. And to help generate just such a national conversation they have set up their own website: www.100yearlife.com.

Gratton and Scott's follow-up publication The New Long Life (2020), however, was even more explosive and, in many ways, far more frightening. Their argument here was that new technology is far outstripping social ingenuity, leaving people increasingly feeling overwhelmed by the speed and scope of technological change. We fear losing our jobs, losing our way of living and "even our sense of what it is to be human" as automation increasingly takes over our jobs, robots start to become part of everyday human life and worse, start to control it. New technology, they postulate, has become the new *Frankenstein*, a monster created by man but now wreaking havoc across the world reshaping future society, redesigning life itself and generating mass anxiety and uncertainty in its wake as governments seem unable to control it and populist politicians seek to exploit it by offering simple solutions to highly complex problems. Like Laura's theoretical framework, Gratton and Scott's solutions represent a radical shift in thinking about life in the future, one that involves:

- **Reimagining age and restaging life**, moving away from the automatic assumption that chronological age determines biological, sociological or personal age and move to an anatological age whereby age is not determined by how long you have lived since birth but how much longer you still have left to live, how you feel about it and how healthy you are to enjoy it. You determine your age not the State; a step that a Dutchman, Emile Ratelband, took quite literally when he applied to the Dutch courts to have his age changed from 69 to 49 so that he could be re-designated as middle-aged rather than old-age; an application that so far the Dutch courts have turned down. We need to rethink too, our traditional measures of wealth and economic development, argue Gratton and Scott. GDP may be the standard measurement of national economic wealth but at present it ignores "happiness" as a measure of socio-economic success although the UEA, for example, has now appointed a Minister of Happiness and New Zealand's Finance Minister has delivered the country's first *wellbeing* budget.

- **Shifting from a three-stage to a multistage life and career**, working on tasks and project contracts for a variety of companies rather than a single life-time career; a shift towards life-time training and learning, from STEM to STEAM in terms of technical and digital skills towards interpersonal and creative skills and from academic institutions and degrees towards lifetime and online learning, accreditation and learning support. China is already investing heavily in lifetime education, Singapore's SkillsFuture programme offers every citizen over the age of 25, $500 (around £320) credit to pay for approved courses while Andy Haldane at the Bank of England has long been calling for a UK multiversity for all ages, one that teaches technical and emotional skills as well as traditional cognitive ones and one that has multiple entry points for all ages. The shift from a single lifetime career to a multi-stage one will also require a new social support framework insuring the person not the job such as the UBI scheme mentioned earlier or the sort of *flexicurity system* being developed by the Danish government to aid job transition and retraining. Automation threatens to replace jobs but in the long-term, automation promises far greater productivity, job satisfaction and a better work life balance as digital slaves do much more of the *dirty work* and so generate a whole new generation of jobs; up to 20–50 million according to MGI (2017). We will need what Professor Laura Carstensen (2018) has called a *new map of life*; one that reflects our changing life span and promotes a better quality and pace of life, the shift from today's lifespan sprint to tomorrow's 100-year marathon with breaks in-between to raise children or a later start to working careers following extended education and child-rearing when still young.

- **Addressing head-on rising intergenerational tensions** about the potential damage ageing may do to the future prospects of young people – a fear or resentment called "rougai" in Japan. The three-stage life actually encourages age segregation, separating out young and old not only at work but also where they live and so fuelling generational stereotypes that generate and exacerbate misunderstanding and conflict rather than support and harmony. In contrast, multi-stage societies bring generations together for such mutual benefits as multigenerational volunteering and multigenerational housing.

- **Personalising the longevity challenge** by adopting a longevity life plan that involves planning ahead on the orientations of the future not the trends of the past; developing your future self, being open to new ideas and new opportunities and investing in relationships especially those involving family, community and intergenerationality.

Both books have become best sellers and the Japanese government has set up a Council for Designing the 100-Year Life with Lynda Gratton as a special advisor. The Japanese even renamed Gratton & Scott's book, The 100-Year Life as *Lifeshift* and republished it in comic format to encourage even the very young to think of life in the future as a silver opportunity rather than a grey doomsday. As Lynda Gratton explained, "When people read our book in the US, the concern was that people will not be able to afford to get old. In Japan, it was never seen as a book about pensions. It was seen as a book about opportunity" (August 2018). As these authors conclude, "We are all in the early stages of a profound shift in how individually and as a society we structure our lives and learn to flourish". We will need *social pioneers* to test out this new world and bring our social and political structures into line with this technological revolution if we are to avoid the *Frankenstein future* that the world seems to be spiralling towards. The 100-Year Life offers the opportunity to rethink the foundations of modern life; its assumptions about economic growth, wealth distribution, human relations, happiness and the quality of life particularly for our children and future generations. Just as global warming has fundamentally challenged humankind's relationship to and exploitation of the planet and COVID-19 has brutally exposed the inequalities underlying many advanced industrial societies, so too longevity and ageing are fundamentally challenging our current way of life and our relationship to each other. As the McKinsey Global Institute has argued (2020), while capitalism, especially American capitalism, has delivered untold wealth, it has equally generated growing discontent, heightened inequality and stimulated increased competition from alternative economic models in the developing world and generated existential threats from climate change and increasingly, from new technology. If capitalism is to survive and thrive, if it is to deliver the American dream, argue the authors, it needs to evolve toward greater inclusiveness, resilience and fairness, to consider the future balance between technology and empathy, artificial and human intelligence and to reconsider the balance between the market and the State, the working population and the economic and political elites, the health of the nation as well as the wealth alongside America's relations with the emerging and ageing world outside. Donald Trump, an arch-capitalist, unleashed the well of discontent of those millions feeling left-behind by American capitalism and democracy today. Rebalancing it, let alone reforming it, will be a herculean challenge for any new President if America is not to inexorably, permanently and racially fragment into the "haves & have-nots", the included and excluded, but one that Joe Biden seems determined to address.

Finally, asked Laura, are we, as Stephen Sigrist's (2015) has argued, on the dawn of a new social era? Are transhumanists, such as Aubrey De Grey and the "race for endless life" being pursued by Google's Calico project and numerous other tech-billionaires, actually on the right lines? Fantastic as such claims may now appear to be, can these tech billionaires yet again go where no man has gone before? Can the human body can be endlessly transformed and repaired by technological replacements and humans rejuvenated by continuous intervention in biological ageing. Is aging as Brian Kennedy, Director of Singapore's Centre for Healthy Ageing, claims, "the climate change of healthcare"? Is senolytics the new science of ageing and senescence the new adolescence? As the French President, Emmanuel Macron has declared, "This is not the time for falling back on comfortable ideology. We need to get off the beaten track, reinvent ourselves, find new ways of living". Coronavirus has forced everyone from the youngest and poorest to the richest and most powerful to reconsider life itself and how we live in an uncertain and even life-threatening world. It has inspired the spirit of generativity and community collaboration so brilliantly displayed in the United Kingdom by Captain Tom. It has equally exposed the deep-seated inequalities within the United Kingdom with the low paid often having to be at the forefront of living with and fighting this pandemic while those living in the most deprived or multiracial areas are most likely to catch or die from it. Age has become the defining feature in the fight against COVID-19 with the oldest in society the most likely to lose their lives from it and youngest most likely to lose their livelihoods and potentially their futures. It has simultaneously polarised and isolated society and yet generated a spirit and a need for all-age collaboration not seen since the Second World War. It has forced government to think completely out of the traditional box and spend astronomic sums combating this disease and its economic aftermath. Whether it will inspire a national recovery plan, a long-term strategy for an ageing Britain or ageing world, where health and lifestyle are at the heart of the 100-Year Life ahead, remains to be seen. "There is no doubt that Covid-19 has hurled us into a future where our work and relationships are shaped by technology, where we wrestle with supporting a healthy economy and an older population, and where we recognise our enhanced individual and collective responsibilities. In doing so, it has exposed our own and society's vulnerabilities. Yet at the same time these experiences have provided us with experiments and stress tests that have clearly revealed our values and our needs. In doing so, it has given us the chance not just to be prepared for the future challenges of technology and an ageing society, but also to seize the opportunities it brings" (Deloitte: 2020).

The whole study group had never before experienced such an intellectual voyage of discovery. For some it has been an exciting adventure, for others a funeral of fear. For young students in their 20s with possibly 80 years of life ahead of them, the thought of planning now for a 100-Year Life was way out of their comfort zone and far beyond any of their current horizons. Until, that is, baby boomers Geraldine and Alex once again stepped in and began to illustrate how a *life road map* might well help them all navigate the life ahead and avoid many of the pitfalls and bad decisions they felt that they had made. Such thoughts, such personal examples, calmed the discussion down and even inspired some of the group to later try to *track and trace* their own parent's life maps; an exercise that made many of them realise just how big a part chance plays in everyone's life; in who they meet, who they marry and what job(s) or career(s) they end up in. Meanwhile, to finish their presentation off on a humorous note, Laura put up a photoshoot of every member of the study group now and in 50 years' time; a generational display of ageing that literally almost brought the roof down as each and every student swore that like baby boomers of the past they would die before they got old; an intragenerational photoshoot that many of these students took back home and still have today.

So, Laura's embryonic thesis came to an end with much laughter and heartfelt thanks from the group to all Laura's family as well as to Geraldine and Alex. The age manifesto from Laura and her grandmother Polly, the visuals from Hannah of the Ageing Kingdom ahead and the wise words from Alex and Geraldine had the study group bubbling for weeks afterwards – not least when *Nodding* Nigel appeared on Instagram looking just like Victor Meldrew at Glastonbury. They all knew, and now appreciated, so much more about the dangers of ageing if nothing changes and on the other hand, they now had a glimpse of what the gift of longevity could potentially offer if the generations work together rather than continue to drift apart. Laura's Team presentation had inspired immense and intense interest in the sociology of ageing and in the notion that it might possibly represent a new sociological paradigm capable of informing if not directing sociology in the 21st century. So much so that Jonathan now decided to include the sociology of ageing as a course in its own right in future academic programmes and he asked Polly to do a presentation to the whole Social Science Department after her forthcoming Parliamentary Working Party's visit to Japan, the oldest nation on earth; the nation at the forefront of the ageing revolution.

So, that was Laura's draft thesis; a thesis that contributed significantly to the first-class honours degree that she gained later that summer; a thesis that inspired her lifetime interest in Ageing not just as the basis of her future PhD and academic career but also as the inspiration to her decision to join her grandmother after graduation as a researcher for the Labour Party in developing an Intergenerational Manifesto for the 2024 General Election. However, while all this reading and debate had satisfied her academic need, it had not quenched her desire to see what an ageing society actually looks like in real life; an ambition given reality by her grandmother's offer of an internship with the parliamentary working party that Polly was taking to ageing Japan that summer; a trip that would open up Laura's eyes forever and transform her perception of life hereafter.

Bibliography

Bell, Torsten: *How to Solve the UK's Wealth Inequality Problem*: New Statesman (February 2018)
Burke, Stephen: Director of the Charity, 'United for All Ages' (2016)

Carstensen, Laura: *A New Map of Life*: WEF (2018)

Centre for Ageing Better: *Review of Volunteering and Community Contributions in Later Life* (2018)

Coughlin, J.F.: *The Longevity Economy*: Public Affairs (2017)

Couglin, J.F. (Director of Technology for Healthy Living: M.I.T): The Fourth Wave of Technology and Aging, *Public Policy & Aging Report*, Vol. 30, Issue 4, pp. 138–141 (2020)

Deloitte Centre for Healthy Solutions: *Covid-19 as a Catalyst* (November 2020)

Freedman, Marc: *Prime Time* (1999); *Encore* (2007); *The Big Shift* (2012); *How to Live Forever* (2018): Public Affairs.

Future Timeline *Report* (2015)

Government Office for Science: *Future of an Ageing Population Report* (2016)

Gratton, L.; Scott, A.: *The 100 Year Life*: Bloomsbury (2017)

Gratton, L.; Scott, A.: *The New Long Life: A Framework for Flourishing in a Changing World*: Bloomsbury (2020)

Gratton, Lynda: *Financial Times* (August 2018)

Gratton, Lynda; Scott, Andrew: *The 100 Year Life: Living and Working in an Age of Longevity*: Bloomsbury (2017)

Harper, Sarah: *Speech to the ILC-UK Conference* (November 2016)

Helliwell, J.; Layard, R.; Sachs, J.: *World Happiness Report*: Sustainable Development Solutions Network (2019)

ILC-UK: "*Too Little for Too Many*": ILC-UK Summit on the Future of Ageing in the UK (November 2017)

Institute for Public Policy Research (IPPR): *Future Proof: Britain in the 2020s* (December 2016)

Intergenerational Commission's Final Report: *A New Generational Contract* (2018)

Krystal, Arthur: *Why We Can't Tell the Truth about Aging*: New Yorker (October 28, 2019)

McKinsey Global Institute (MGI): *Rethinking the Future of American Capitalism* (November 2020)

MGI: *A Future that Works: Automation, Employment, and Productivity* (January 2017)

New Labour: *Building a Society for All Ages* (2009)

NPC/ILC-UK Report: *Age of Opportunity: Putting the Ageing Society of Tomorrow on the Agenda of the Voluntary Sector Today*: (2014)

OECD: *How's Life? 2020. Measuring Well-being* (2020)

Phillipson, Chris: *Re-thinking ageing populations*: British Academy Debates (2014)

Scott, Andrew: *Ageing and New Technology*: ILC-UK: 2020

Sigrist, Stephen: *The Dawn of a New Social Era*: W.I.R.E (2015)

Sinclair David A: *Lifespan*: Thorsons (2019)

The Guardian (August 8, 2018)

Westendorp, Rudi: *Growing Older Without Feeling Older*: Scribe (2015)

World Economic Forum (WEF): *Global Population Ageing: Peril or Promise?* (January 2012)

World Economic Forum (WEF): *The Fourth Industrial Revolution: What It Means, How to Respond* (January 2016)

8

TOWARDS THE AGELESS SOCIETY OF THE FUTURE AND THE AGEING WORLD AHEAD

While Laura had thoroughly enjoyed the twists and turns of debating the ageing world of the future with her fellow students and tutors, she was well aware that it had been an artificial debate, an intellectual exercise within the safe confines of a university with mainly young people of her own age about new sociological paradigms or new intergenerational social contracts in which problems could be freely debated and instantly solved. This, however, was not the real world, not the ageing world of people actually living to a hundred years or more; nor the reality of a society facing real-life crises of immense economic and political consequence as a result. A research PhD and a modern political career would certainly require a much deeper understanding of the challenges of longevity and life in a 100-Year Society, so the offer of a research internship after Laura's finals, working with the parliamentary working party that her grandmother Polly was putting together to tour ageing Japan, was "manna (or nanna) from heaven"; a life-changing experience for the young social scientist and a chance to test her thesis in real life in the oldest society in the world.

Ageing in ancient Japan: Life in a super-ageing society

Is Japan today the future for all of us?

Ageing Japan is still one of the top five economies in the world, but it now faces the monumental challenges of both ageing elders and an "imploding population". As illustrated in Figure 8.1, Japan today is literally super-ageing and demographically shrinking at the same time as it downsizes from its current 127 million people down to a mere 95 million in the next 30 years. It is en route for the grey nightmare feared by so many in an age of ageing, but it equally faces the possibility of *"the dawn of a silver age"* as the Japanese government accelerates its technological revolution in response. Japan is fast becoming an age laboratory

DOI: 10.4324/9781003029373-13

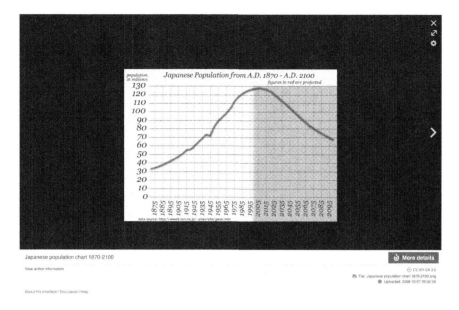

FIGURE 8.1 Image of Japan's demographics

for the longevity revolution ahead and the land of the rising sun is working desperately towards transforming itself into the "land of the silver sun" rather than becoming the world's first "grey graveyard". According to the Statistics Bureau of Japan 2020, Japan today has a population of some 126 million people, a fall of nearly 1 million people since 2015 with a projected fall to 95.2 million by 2050 and to 87 million by 2060; a cliff-edge collapse in population of some 31% or one million people a year over the next 36 years; a demographic disaster that economists at Tokyo University have called a "countdown to national extinction". With average life expectancy in 2019 at 87.5 for females and 81.4 years for males, Japan currently has the highest proportion of those aged 65 and over (28%) and the lowest ratio of those under 15 years old (12.1%) in the world. By 2060 those aged 65 and over are projected to rise to 40% of the total population, the percentage of over 75-year olds is predicted to more than double from 11% to 27%, and Japan already has over 68,000 people over 100 years of age. Meanwhile, the working population in Japan is projected to shrink to 53.6% of its population by 2050, from 66 million in 2013 to 38 million by 2060, with a dependency ratio of 1:3 and a fertility rate of 1.4 well below the natural replacement level of 2.1. Japan is super-ageing as the reality of the 100-Year Life fast approaches and the associated costs escalate. "Japan's gross government debt has risen to close to 220% of GDP, the highest level ever recorded amongst OECD nations with age-related spending on health and long-term care projected to rise by 7% of GDP between 2020 and 2060 unless drastic measures are taken", according to an OECD Briefing in April 2018.

So, Japan faces an age Armageddon, a ***population implosion*** of catastrophic dimensions and monumental challenges; challenges that include:

How to respond to hyper-ageing? How to raise the birth rate and rebalance the population in a society where the birth rate is currently only 1.36 children per woman, well below the replacement level of 2.1 and where, on average, young women delay child-rearing until aged 28–30 or stay single for life as a means of enjoying high levels of disposable income? They live at home and focus on their careers rather than seek marriage. While single women are labelled as parasites by the Japanese media, single young men are often referred to as herbivores because they too seem equally reluctant to engage in marriage, long-term relationships – or even sex. This declining birth rate is considered by many to be a national crisis threatening the very existence of Japan as a nation.

How to rebalance a dependency ratio that is already approaching 3:1 by 2025. The working population is shrinking, but there is a national aversion to immigration as a replacement source of labour. Immigrants are seen as a threat to the purity of Japanese culture. It is difficult for foreigners to become Japanese citizens, although two million foreigners live in Japan currently. A UN study in 2000, however, found that Japan would need to admit ten million immigrants annually to maintain its current "worker to retirees" ratio.

How to transform post–war employment practices that now obstruct social and economic transformation; practices such as the traditions of lifetime employment by one company and total loyalty to it, of payment systems based on seniority rather than on merit and trade unions with membership restricted to one company rather than spread across an entire industry. Women in particular face discrimination for taking time off to have children – hence the declining birth rate – while Japanese men rarely take paternity leave or share in childrearing.

How to engage and reactivate the elderly as they retire from work and live apart in the mushrooming towns and cities or live alone and abandoned in the countryside. While the Japanese elderly are living longer, many of them are living alone and giving up on life. Senior shoplifting has soared ten-fold in the past 20 years and one in five inmates in Japanese prisons is elderly, many of whom have deliberately sought incarceration in preference to the loneliness of life outside. So much so that with 20% of Japan's prison population aged 60 and over, Japan's prisons are fast becoming their new care homes. According to the 2019 Ipsos Global Advisor Survey on Ageing, 87% of Japanese – especially 45–54-year olds – fear ageing; fear shrinking social benefits, old-age poverty, the loss of mobility, memory and money and the sense of being a "pesky nuisance" or rougai – the expression increasing used to describe the elderly for delaying trains or dressing-down young people for lack of respect as generational friction ferments.

The government's response has largely centred around the following:

Abenomics. The economic strategy launched in 2013 by the Japanese Prime Minister Shinzo Abe to resurrect the Japanese economy after two decades of low growth and the financial crash of the early 1990s. Abenomics is based on three key strategies: reflating the economy through quantitative easing or cash injections; investing in infrastructure to stimulate employment and consumption and deregulation to free up Japanese markets and encourage foreign investment. In particular, the government aims to raise the working population by encouraging higher labour participation by women, encouraging the newly retired back to work and even by reconsidering the country's retirement age of 60. Japan's female labour participation rate is amongst the lowest in the advanced economies at 50%, compared with 60% in the United States and United Kingdom. It reflects both the priority given by families to childcare – and now eldercare – the impact of a male-dominated working culture and the glass ceiling facing Japanese women seeking entry to the top professions. Finally, and very cautiously, given the traditional Japanese resistance to immigration, the government has recently relaxed its immigration control laws to allow a limited number of manual labourers from abroad to enter the country. The longer-term solution, however, lies with automation and the adoption of service robots across all sectors from hospitals to care homes, factories to food deliveries and schools to transport offering on one hand greater productivity and on the other greater contact and comfort for those isolated by remote learning or living alone especially the elderly and very young.

Promoting "womenomics" campaigns to liberate Japanese women and pressure corporations to employ and promote more females, become more gender-friendly and inclusive and replace their systems of promotion from seniority to meritocracy.

Promoting childbirth initiatives. In 1994–1999 the Japanese government launched the Angel Plan, with the aim of trying to improve work-life balance and so encourage couples to have more children by improving childcare and improving family life. However, this failed to stem the country's declining fertility rate, which fell dramatically from the 2.07 in the 1970s to a record low of 1.26 in 2005, rising slightly to 1.36 in 2019 partly because child-support payments remain low but fees for education and health remain high. The Japanese government's latest initiative – an advanced AI matchmaking system to promote marriage as well as its birth-rate – has yet to bear fruit.

Transforming national health and social care. As described in Chapter 4, the Japanese long-term care (LTC) system is considered one of the best in the world. Until the year 2000, it was assumed that the family would look after older relatives, as part of the Confucian ethic of filial piety and as part of the duties expected of children. However, with Japan's economic miracle and the economic boom of the 1970s, health-care expanded but so did the nuclear family and the rise in female labour participation. Traditional values were under threat as the young started to enjoy new opportunities and the abuse and poor treatment of elderly relatives included the abandonment of elderly parents in hospitals and residential homes. The shame of this pattern of behaviour led in the year 2000 to Japan introducing a new compulsory long-term care insurance system with the motto *our family our society*; a new form of social contract through which everyone pays healthcare insurance. This brought long-term peace of mind and a sense of security to the elderly alongside, a dramatic expansion in service use and a reduced burden on family carers. The demand for improvements in the quality and level of care, however, soon led to increases in both taxation and insurance premiums. In 2005 the government introduced measures like means-testing to ensure that the new system was more sustainable, comprehensive and proactive. It is now accepted that care is a collective social responsibility led by the state and funded by taxation. It is equally recognised that isolation is one of the greatest dangers of ageing. To that end, the number of residential homes is severely restricted to encourage care in and by the community, mainly by volunteers, many of whom are pensioners themselves, acting as part of an "age circle of care". Inevitably, however, as costs rise so do taxes, while shortages of nursing homes and care staff are creating inequalities in provision and putting a heavy burden still on poorer families. Japan now has an age tax levied on every worker over 40 – paid too by pensioners – to fund long-term care; a strategy that the UK government, amongst others, is currently looking into and a system that Britain could well learn much from, according to the Nuffield Trust (2018).

Investing in new technology and the robot revolution as the primary means to raising productivity and the national GDP. New technology is being developed to service the rapidly expanding elder market, with products as wide-ranging as intelligent toilets that can literally lift the elderly up off the loo, analyse their waste and report to their GP; intelligent cars with enlarged dashboards and computer controls that can curb erratic or dangerous driving, care beds that can transform into wheelchairs or even turn the sleeper over during the night; a robot bath that can put an elderly person through a wash and rinse cycle and walking sticks with inbuilt SatNavs to guide the elderly home or alert carers in the event of any falls they may have. Japanese mega-corporations such as

Panasonic are aiming to develop the ***total solution*** to the silver society, not only for Japan but also for the ageing world at large with robots as the ultimate solution, whether as workers or servants, pets or partners, in the battle to raise productivity for the young and combat loneliness and isolation for the old; "in a society that remains resolutely anti-immigration, robotic technology is seen as the answer to the lack of human beings". Companion robots have not yet led to dramatic reductions in healthcare costs, but as Camilla Cavendish found in her study of *Extra Time* (2019), they do apparently boost the morale and sense of community of both care home residents and their staff. Many elderly find robots like RoBoHoN – an eight-inch tall black and white figure with a cute monkey-like face – much easier to talk to than humans, and even more soothing in reducing anxiety and depression.

Promoting the silver economy, particularly with Japan's elderly spending "like there's no tomorrow", buying luxury goods, travelling abroad and indulging their tastes for expensive food. They are no longer saving to support their children financially, and parents now have few inhibitions about spending their children's inheritance. The unspoken family contract is no longer quite as firm as it once was. In 2019 Japan launched its Moonshot Research and Development programme, a $963 million initiative to not only address such major social problems as its ageing population, climate change and inequality but also such lofty goals as developing community-based Open Energy Systems, creating sustainable care systems to overcome major diseases by 2040 and even freeing people from the limitations of body, brain, space and time by 2050. These are extremely ambitious research programmes that have attracted huge interest from the major Japanese corporations and led more specialist start-ups such as MELTIN to literally reach for the stars by creating humanoid avatar robots controlled by thought instructions from their owners. The mobility industry alone has the potential to become a $61 billion market and offers the opportunity for older people to move around safely and seamlessly whatever their mode of travel using driverless technology and a data-driven integrated transport system, using smartphone technology to simplify payment, ease congestion and mitigate not only the spread of coronavirus but pollution of the urban atmosphere.

Creating a more age-free society along the government guidelines issued in 2018 by which people 65 and older will no longer be automatically considered senior citizens but will be encouraged to stay healthy and keep working into their 70s. Age-friendly communities such as Yukarigaoka in the city of Sakura have been designed so that residents have everything at hand through well integrated transport and have families close by to support active ageing and ageing in place. Japan is now developing self-driving robot shuttle buses in rural communities and highway rest stops to ferry the elderly to and from medical, retail and banking services. Senior "super-heroes" or silver-athletes are emerging such as Mieko Nagaoka who set a world record for swimming or the master-class sprinter Hidekichi Miyazaki nicknamed the "Golden Bolt" after the Olympic Gold medallist Usain Bolt. Perhaps the key to growing old gracefully now is simply to embrace the no meiwaku mentality and reject the *I am a nuisance philosophy* hard-wired from birth in Japan.

And this too was one of Laura's most abiding memories. Wowed as she was by all the technological wizardry that the Japanese government and corporations were throwing at the ageing challenge, what stayed with her most was the attitude and demeanour of the older and elder Japanese people that she and her grandmother met; an attitude and demeanour summed up in the WHO survey of 95-year olds living near Tokyo in 2015; an attitude that would have struck a strong cord with many people during the coronavirus pandemic and one characterised by:

- Diligence and compassion "we should never forget that helping others helps ourselves" with family ties especially important "My children are my treasures. They make me very happy".
- A natural acceptance of self and of others; acceptance of life and all that it had thrown at them.
- A profound appreciation of the precious moments in everyday life: simple routines and living moment to moment give elderly people perceived control over their lives, help them maintain their individual beliefs and social ties and find pleasures in simple moments; a positive and contented attitude that has underpinned their longevity and their moral code that "if you do good for others, it will return to you".

Their visit to the ancient people of the island of Okinawa, in particular, introduced Laura to the concept of **ikigai,** the Japanese word meaning *having a reason to live; having a reason for being*; a way of life where self-realisation and a sense of oneness or commitment to the group underpin every aspect of this community's way of life. Here, the people enjoy exceptionally long lives living on a very healthy diet, and they specialise as master craftsmen in skills that collectively contribute to the way of life of the whole community, whether it be as master fishermen, farmers or karate experts. Laura found their sense of purpose and their community spirit truly moving and, given that many of this island's inhabitants were over 100 years old, their example of positive and purposeful ageing stayed with Laura long afterwards and heavily influenced her ideas on generativity and the ageing societies of the future. Okinawa, however, is not alone. It is one of the growing number of *Blue Zones* around the world that includes Barbagia in Sardinia and the Nicoya peninsula in Costa Rica, where communal living based on healthy natural eating and communal rituals that include destressing exercises underpin some of the longest and healthiest lifespans in the world. Dan Buettner,

Blue Zones founder, has now attempted to set up Blue Zone projects within urban environments in the United States to try and combat the hectic, stressful and unhealthy lifestyles that such manmade environments seem to generate. The results, he claims (WEF: 2017), have been dramatic, with local people living nearly three years longer, healthcare claims falling by 49% and absenteeism from work declining by some 20%. Changing the lifestyle of a whole nation, however, may prove another challenge altogether, but at least such Blue Zone living offers an alternative model for arriving in later life fit enough to enjoy it and with a happier philosophy of life after the ravages of COVID-19.

Post-visit reflections

So, Laura had now seen for herself the impact of ageing. She now had personal experience of some of the realities of living in an ageing society – a super-ageing world where the old are exploding and the young are shrinking. She had met with young and old and seen first-hand how one of the richest nations on earth is using the latest technology and the most *human* of robots to tackle the greatest challenge to the future of Japan since Second World War. She had equally come across a philosophy of life, a silver philosophy of life, practised in the mushrooming communities of the Blue Zones, that had offered inspiration not only for how to live to 100 or more but also how to do so with purpose. It had been a life-changing experience as well as a fact-finding expedition that had not only profoundly affected Laura herself but also her grandmother Polly and all of her fellow MPs. This visit equally inspired Laura to look across at Europe, the oldest continent on earth today and only a channel tunnel away from the United Kingdom, to see how it was now preparing for ageing. At her mother's suggestion, Laura contacted her cousin Robert, previously a member of the British delegation in Strasbourg, to try and arrange a research visit to the EU even though the United Kingdom is no longer part of the Erasmus and other student study exchange schemes. To her great delight, Robert not only arranged a visit but also a three-month research scholarship; a European age-tour that not only gave her invaluable material for her doctorate but also huge insight into the way Europe, the oldest continent in the world, is preparing for ageing.

Ageing in an ancient continent: The ageing of the European Union

Ageing Europe faces a demographic bomb, declared the World at Five on January 20, 2020. Europe, the oldest continent in the world, is facing a *demographic implosion*. According to the European Commission 2021 Ageing Report, by 2070:

> **Europe will be the "senior citizen of the world"** as people aged 65 and over are expected to account for 30.3% of the EU's population of nearly 450 million; an astonishing increase from the 20.3% in 2019; while

those aged 80 years plus will have more than doubled from 5.8% in 2019 to an estimated 13.2% by 2070. By 2050 Eurostat estimates that the EU will have nearly 130 million people aged 65 and over 27 million people aged 85 years and older and nearly half a million centenarians, most of whom are and will be women, although males are gradually catching up. It is and will continue to be the oldest continent in the world with a median age by 2050 of nearly 50 years (48.2) with Germany and Italy leading the way. The total EU population of the 27 countries of the EU, now that the United Kingdom has left, is projected to fall by 5% between 2019 and 2070 from 447 million to 424 million.

Life expectancy at birth for males will have risen by 7.4 years from 78.7 years in 2019 to 86.1 by 2070, and by 6.1 years for females from 84.2 to an astonishing 90.3 years reflecting some closing of the traditional age gap between men and women. Life expectancy at age 65 in 2019 was 21.4 years for women and 18.1 years for men but women have a shorter time proportionately in good health.

The total fertility rate is expected to rise slightly, from 1.52 in 2019 to 1.65 by 2070, across the EU but still be well below the replacement level of 2.1; and the annual net migration across the EU is expected to decline, from net inflows of about 1.3 million people in 2019 to one million by 2070.

The old age dependency ratio will have nearly doubled, from nearly 3:1 in 2019 to less than 2:1 by 2070, a *demographic shift* of volcanic proportions, partly offset by a projected rise in labour force participation in this period by both older workers aged 55–64 and younger women. GDP across the EU is projected to grow by 1.3% annually in the 2019–2070 period, but clearly this baseline scenario is subject to severe modification in light of the economic impact of COVID-19 and the onset of the "deepest economic recession" in the EU's history. In addition, an *age-faultline* is emerging as Europe splits into two demographics with the populations in Southern and Eastern Europe ageing faster than their Western and Northern counterparts. Fourteen EU member states face old age dependency ratios of 2:1 or less over the next 30 years mainly in the East but with Portugal and Greece equally vulnerable; a fragmentation and demographic shift that has huge economic, social and even military implications as Russia lurks hungrily on the borders of eastern Europe eager to offset its own "demographic downfall".

Environmentally, according to the EC Report on the Impact of Demographic Change (June 2020), the EU also faces immense environmental challenges as these population changes threaten to generate huge increases in the global need for food, energy and water at the very time that climate change requires a dramatic reduction in carbon emissions and consumption. Severe climate change may equally generate a dramatic increase in global migration as some 143 million people in sub-Saharan Africa,

South Asia and Latin America seek refuge from desertification and coastal erosion in their own countries. The EU's Green Deal and new Climate Law are therefore now part of a combined strategy for transitioning to a climate neutral and resource efficient economy alongside strategies towards "Green Cities" and a circular economy.

Globally, the EU's share of the world population will have shrunk by 2070 from 5.7% in 2020 to 3.7% at a time when Africa's share will escalate to some 32% and Asia's fall to around 50%. These are seismic shifts in the balance of world population with huge implications too for the balance in global power economically and politically, particularly for the EU and the whole of the western world.

Europe, therefore, is at something of a demographic and political crossroads, with a dependency ratio projected to rise from nearly 28% now to over 50% by 2060: a 2:1 ratio that Vítor Constâncio, Vice-President of the European Central Bank, has described as "collective demographic suicide" unless addressed immediately. Spain, for example, has the lowest fertility rate in the EU, with an average 1.27 children per child-bearing woman and a mass exodus of young people abroad in search of work. Germany and Italy are also shrinking demographically, while Portugal faces the prospect of soon becoming "unsustainable in terms of economic growth, social security and the welfare state", according to its own demographic commission report in 2015. Sweden is one of the few countries that is, likely to weather this demographic storm, aided by its generous parental leave and childcare system, its stable economy and its high net immigration. Every one of these issues, however, is bound to lead to intense political debates in every member state about the fair, as well as affordable, levels of age-related spending each country can provide to support and protect the older age groups. It is equally likely to impact profoundly on what the Europeans call *social solidarity*, on intergenerational relations, as the younger working-age groups face escalating taxes to pay for their elder relatives, while facing cuts in areas that they need help with, such as education, training and childcare. The full impact, though, is expected to hit home from 2030 onwards as the baby boomers across Europe retire en masse and fundamentally shift the balance of the remaining workforce and the focus of the economy from the young to the older populations. At which point the European models of welfare state, ranging from the Social-Democratic model of most Scandinavian countries, the Corporatist-Bismarckian model of Northern Europe, the Beveridge-Liberal model of Anglo-Saxon democracies and Familial-based model of Southern Europe described in Chapter 4, are likely to come under very severe strain unless they move towards the common blueprint, the Social Triple A being advocated by the EU Commission. This proposal for a welfare state for the whole of the EU is based on trying to achieve an "upward convergence" in welfare provision across the continent as a pathway towards equality of outcomes as well as equality of opportunity, generating greater social solidarity as well as greater economic progress within and between countries.

This is an immense challenge given the North-South divide between richer and poorer EU members and the emerging intergenerational tension between young and old over who pays. The debate on the escalating costs of welfare ageing is, in turn, inspiring a search for a new and fairer intergenerational social contract, a fairer distribution of cost and benefit and fairer models of measuring who gains and who loses in Europe's welfare states. According to the EC Ageing Europe report, old age pension benefits accounted for 10.9% of GDP in 2016, some EUR 1.89 trillion with Europe's wealthiest pensioners living in Luxembourg and the poorest in Romania with some 14.5 million older people in the EU at risk of poverty in 2017. Loneliness and social isolation are more prevalent in Northern EU states than the Mediterranean countries and while older Europeans are more likely to be wary of globalisation and more anti-immigration than younger age groups, generally, they seem happier with life than most middle-age Europeans. Similarly, while, the OECD Perspectives on Global Development in 2019 rated Europe as a world leader in terms of quality of life, the EU's external relations are in something of a state of turmoil not only with the United Kingdom post-Brexit and with the United States, post-Trump but also increasingly with the developing nations of Asia and Latin America. A *demographic war* threatens to break out between the wealthy West and the Asian Tigers both searching and competing for the young talent, energy and ideas that will be central to economic growth and prosperity in the mid and late 21st century; a competition that might soon involve Africa as its expanding Youth Dividend offers rich "new blood".

The EU's response to the age challenge

The response of individual members of the EU has ranged from the proactive planning of the Nordic and Northern nations of the EU through to the less progressive response of many nations in the poorer regions of Eastern and Southern Europe; ironically, those most exposed to ageing. This "peacock parade" of preparation and forward thinking was captured quite well in the coloured clusters used in the 2018 edition of the EU's Active Ageing Index (AAI) cited in Chapter 2; coloured clusters that ranged from the yellow badging of the Netherlands and the Nordic nations through to the red, blue and green clusters representing countries like France, Germany and Bulgaria respectively.

The collective response of the EU, however, seems to rest with three main strands:

> **Firstly,** while the EU has fallen behind both the United States and China commercially and has no global super-tech companies comparable to those in South East Asia, China and the United States, it does have one of the largest Silver Economies in the world, it is a world leader in such areas as sustainability, welfare and data protection and it has leading universities in such fields as engineering and technological research. What it needs, according to the McKinsey Global Institute (MGI: 2020), is a

mission-led innovation strategy, initiated and led by business in partnership with government, galvanising European companies and governments in such common projects as space exploration, decarbonisation, congestion, healthcare and environmental sustainability. The future of work in Europe, argues the MGI, lies in supporting and resourcing the acceleration in all sectors towards automation-adoption and a shift towards expanding telecommunications, finance, education and health, developing a select number of high growth economic centres clustered around such megacities as Paris, Amsterdam and Madrid and supported by such emerging economic hubs as Budapest, Lyon and Riga. The MGI report estimated that up to 59 million European jobs – 26% of the total – are at risk in the short-term from COVID-19, mainly in the three low-wage sectors of customer service and sales, food services and building occupations alongside jobs most vulnerable to displacement by automation and where workers are without a tertiary degree. The authors further estimate that under a mid-point scenario, about 53 million jobs across the EU could be automated by 2030 and although emerging sectors such as education, ICT and human health and social work could replace many of these jobs, the ageing of the EU population could leave employers with a serious shortage of suitably skilled and qualified employees, especially in what are currently low-paid jobs. They predict that the demand for technological STEM skills and socioemotional skills such as nursing and care work will rise exponentially while manual and physical skills will decline sharply. Post COVID-19, MGI predict 21 million European workers will have to leave declining jobs and 94 million will have to upskill as automation takes over many of their current tasks or roles. "Helping individuals connect with new opportunities and prepare for the jobs of tomorrow will challenge every community across the continent". The EU should be a vanguard in the AI revolution argued MGI in 2019 and the EU's own report on the Future of Work (2019) proposed that a university dedicated to AI be created along the lines of America's MIT, that new vocational and technical education systems such as Switzerland's VET (Vocational education and training) programme be introduced and that *Digital Europe* create a structured collaboration between industry, research and education. In addition, it proposed the development of a co-ordinated strategy to recruit and retain AI specialists, a universal social protection scheme or personalised account to support job transition and retraining, stronger collective occupational representation such as the guilds in France and official bodies authorised to monitor potential risks from AI as part of a Digital Europe Mission Statement and investment package for 2030.

Secondly, while the Age Platform Europe argued in its 2014 Manifesto for Europe to move to a more age-friendly philosophy, towards "a society for all ages, free from age discrimination and stereotypes, and based on solidarity and cooperation between generations", its 2019 Age Platform Manifesto focused specifically on challenging ageism, arguing for "equal rights and dignity for older persons" through more (age)inclusive labour markets, adequate pensions and old-age income, person-centred healthcare and elder empowerment in social and political life. Such a strategy, argued MGI (2018) could help convert ageing from an economic liability into a social asset and elevate the EU back to world prominence; not so much as an economic or military power but as a social and moral example of a continent where the full potential of all ages is being exploited for the common good and where the quality of life and the harmony of its intergenerational relations make it the greatest continent to grow old in; one where the older age groups feel valued and engaged, able to contribute as well as be supported and one where they no longer discarded onto the margins of society as before. That would be a true European legacy and a European example of how human civilisations, and continents, can progress through generativity and solidarity rather than through war or Darwinian economics. Such a strategy, claims MGI, would require a more inclusive European growth strategy based on increasing public social spending, tackling rising income inequality between and within member states and renewing the post-war European social contracts between employers and workers, citizens and government. The existing intergenerational social contract certainly needs radically rewriting argued Leonardo Quattrucci in 2017 or else "The future is becoming a burden young people are indebted with, rather than a public good to inherit". If today's generation of 20-somethings are not to end up poorer than their parents, then more countries need to incorporate the principle of intergenerational equity in their constitutions and/or, like Sweden, create a Ministry of the Future. The EU Commission's most recent green paper on ageing, launched in January 2021, sets out a whole series of proposals for "fostering solidarity and responsibility between generations" based on a life-cycle approach to highlight "the universal impact of ageing on all generations" and to strengthen intergenerational solidarity.

Thirdly, immigration is still a possible solution but only if it is far better managed than in 2015/16. While the flood of refugees into Europe at that time, initially seemed like manna – or manpower – from heaven in rebalancing Europe's OADR and in providing vitally needed new young labour, particularly for such ageing nations as Germany and Italy, it quickly turned toxic as a wave of anti-immigrant sentiment and fears about being ethnically swamped swept across the continent. Countries such as Hungary, Croatia and the Baltic States began closing their borders and the United Kingdom voted to leave the EU altogether. Some, like Christian Bodewig of the Brookings Institution (2015), believe that this lack of leadership lost the EU a golden opportunity to rejuvenate its population, rebuild its dependency ratio, regenerate its economy and regain its international reputation for compassion and humanity. However, according to the UN World Population Report in 2015 and the Federal Statistical Office of Germany in 2016, immigration alone would not solve either Europe's demographic divide or Germany's. Germany's elder population aged 67 and over, for example, is set to skyrocket, from 15.1 million in 2013 to 21.5 million in 2040, a 42% increase, while its working-age population, aged 20–66, is set to drop dramatically by nearly 25%, a potential loss of 13 million workers. Bridging this demographic chasm would require nearly half a million new immigrants every year for the next 25 years and that would require a complete rethink of Germany's demographic strategy, let alone that of the EU as a whole. What the European refugee crisis illustrated, however, is that global migration and global greying are intertwined; and that as they play out on the continent of Europe, "doing nothing" may well prove the worst strategy of all. Europe is in severe danger of becoming an *ancient continent* left behind by the subsonic speed of globalisation, its failure to nurture tech giants capable of competing with those in America and Asia, and its failure to manage immigration in a controlled way so as to infuse "new blood" into its ageing workforce and generate a new *baby boom* amongst its young in the way that the other "united states", the USA, continues to do.

Finally, COVID-19 has clearly had a devastating effect across the whole of Europe with the largest and oldest economies suffering some of the worst effects – notably Italy, Spain, Belgium, France and, across the channel, the United Kingdom. The pandemic has ruthlessly exposed underlying weaknesses in what appeared to be some of the world's best healthcare systems. Care homes, in particular, have been left exposed, and healthcare systems across Europe have had to divert huge resources into prevention, protection, *track and trace* as well as into developing new vaccines and propping up hospitals under immense and relentless patient pressure. Like the United Kingdom, the EU has huge lessons to learn from this pandemic; and from the governments of South East Asia who contained and controlled this pandemic much more swiftly after their experiences with MERS and SARS. Combining this COVID Recovery Plan with its strategy for both healthy ageing and for climate control may be both the EU's greatest challenge and – if successful – its greatest post-war achievement.

The ageing world beyond

Laura now had an in-depth perception of the oldest country and the oldest continent in the world. Now, she embarked on a "whistle-stop" tour of the other major continents to try and identify their individual stage of ageing and how far their experiences supported or challenged her overall thesis and therefore needed further investigation. A brief summary of her findings is discussed in the following sections.

Ageing Asia

Asia and the Pacific nations are ageing fast and the UN (2017) has predicted that one in four of the region's population will be over-60 by 2050; 1.3 billion compared to the 535 million over-60s in 2015. The over-65s alone are projected to increase from 6% in 2000 (209m) to 18% overall by 2050 (870m) with Korea, Singapore, Thailand and China (26%) approaching "super-ageing" status as old age dependency ratios skyrocket. According to the OECD (2020), by 2050 11 Asia-Pacific countries are projected to have achieved "super-aged" status compared to only 1 (Japan) in 2020. This region now hosts some 60% of the world's older population aged 60 and over, and about 50% of those aged 80 and over globally, with females being the predominant gender. With China at some 230 million, India approaching 130 million and the Russian Federation over 30 million, ageing is a huge challenge for emerging nations hoping to "get rich before getting old". As the 2017 UNESCAP report explained, the Asia Pacific region faces a race against time as this ageing "tsunami" approaches its shores at the same time that these countries are attempting to digitalise their economies, build up their health and social protection services while also preparing for the silver economies ahead in a more age-friendly society. As in Japan, the Asian "Tigers" have responded by turning to new technology with AI and robots fast becoming familiar features of both the workplace and the care home. They are using ageing to drive up rather than drive down their economies, incentivising senior citizens to stay in work longer or retrain for new employment. Meanwhile, their silver economies are starting to boom and with longer life spans, greater literacy and internet use, hundreds of millions have been lifted out of extreme poverty and the breakneck pace of urban growth and super-cities has helped create a middle class soon to be over 3 billion.

The Asian nations are also shifting the centre of gravity of the world economy. The "Asia century has begun" declared McKinsey and Company on July 15, 2019 as Asia's tech-giants multiply and expand with China, Japan, Korea and Singapore amongst the most digitally advanced nations in the world. By 2040 Asia could drive 50% of future global consumption with the region's seniors alone "adding $660bn to what they already spend today". Asia's Silver Economy is beginning to emerge rapidly with a potential $4.56 trillion market value by 2025 as the demands for eldercare technology, healthy ageing and senior care begin to feed through with Singapore and Japan leading the way and China in hot pursuit. According to the 2020 Ageing Asia Silver Economy Index, governments in China, India and Malaysia are already investing heavily in AI and digital ID, and Asia already has a mushrooming digital market, a wealth of tech-talent, an IT-literate workforce and strong government support and investment not only in existing markets such as smartphones but in emerging fields such as renewable energy and electrified transport. Moreover, most countries and economies in the Asia-Pacific region are emerging relatively unscathed from COVID-19 – a stark contrast indeed to Europe, the United Kingdom and United States.

China is growing old faster than almost any other country. It is emerging as a classic example of the longevity dilemma with nearly 18% of its population over age 60 in 2018, projected to be approaching 40% by 2050 as its working population shrinks and its total population begins to plummet from 1.4 billion in 2050 down to 1.06 billion by 2100. The legacy of a one-child policy designed to halt a population explosion of young in the post-war era has ironically backfired and created a population explosion of old in the first half of the 21st century with a substantial gender imbalance as males heavily outweigh females. China's OADR has nearly doubled and the cost of health and welfare threatens to drain its economy. According to the Chinese Academy of Social Sciences (January 2019), China faces an unstoppable demographic decline after its peak in 2029, resulting in "a picture of China's future that bears little relation to its leaders' dreams of global supremacy: an increasingly unequal society of oppressed women and lonely men, many burdened by the care of elderly parents and grandparents, and an economy crippled by unsustainable debts". Nevertheless, China's ambition to be a world superpower remains undaunted, and besides investing heavily in AI, the government has introduced a wave of age-friendly policy initiatives that have included the passage of the Elderly Rights Law which requires adult children to regularly visit their parents, a 13th Five-Year Plan which sees home-based care as the bedrock of its healthy ageing strategy, a 2017–2020 Action Plan for the Development of Smart Health and Elderly Care Industry and a 2019 policy announcement for creating a multilevel elderly care (social) security system that maintains increases in the basic pension and that seeks to improve integration between healthcare and social care.

Ageing America

The United States is one of the "younger" nations in the developed world and likely to stay so. It is ageing at a much slower pace than Japan and even Europe. But it is ageing, even as it grows from 314 million in 2012 to a projected figure of 400 million by 2050 (US Census Bureau: 2020).

According to the July 2019 Factsheet: Aging in the United States,

★ The over-65 population is projected to nearly double from 52 million in 2018 to 95 million by 2060, from 16% of the US population to 23% in 42 years. The baby boomer generation alone is estimated at about 73 million in 2020 as the oldest boomers reach 74 whilst the youngest will not turn 65 until 2030. Average life expectancy has leapt from 68 years in 1950 to 78.6 years in 2017 while the gender gap in life expectancy has narrowed from seven years in 1990 to five years in 2017.

★ Older adults are projected to outnumber children under age 13 by 2025 – a truly historic event as baby boomers move as a generation into the ranks of the elderly over the next ten years generating, in turn, a dramatic "shift in the age structure, from 13.7% of the population aged 65 and over in 2012 to 20.3% in 2030" (US Census Bureau 2020). Meanwhile, as elsewhere in the developed world, it is the "oldest" old – those aged 85 and over – who are projected to grow fastest; from 5.9 million in 2012 to 18 million in 2050 – a phenomenal rise that nearly doubles the percentage of very old in the United States from 2.5% to 4.5% in the same period.

★ The older population is increasingly racially and ethnically diverse with the non-Hispanic, white population projected to plunge from 77% in 2018 to 55% by 2060; and increasingly well-educated with 29% having completed a bachelor's degree in 2018 compared to only 5% in 1965.

★ The older population is increasingly working longer with 24% of men and 16% of women aged 65 and older still working in 2018 and projected to rise respectively to 26% and 18% by 2026.

★ Older voters still outnumber the young and are still more likely to turnout to vote. However, the ethnic shift across America "will usher in an age of demographic transformation", according to Stef W. Kight (December 2019) as Generation Z, with 24 million eligible voters, comes onto the electoral register and Hispanic Americans surpass Black Americans as the largest ethnic minority voting group.

According to Nora Super (2020), aging America faces three great challenges, namely:

• The health and social care *time-bomb* lurking beneath America's ageing baby boomers as over two-thirds of federal government spending goes on those aged 65 and over. Social security and medicare expenditure is projected to rise from 7.9% of GDP in 2019 to nearly 10% or $3.4 trillion in 2029, as the share of the US population age 65 and over reaches nearly 20%.

• The crisis in care giving as the number of caregivers in America shrinks just as the need for care explodes. Approximately 70% of older Americans are likely to need LTSS later in their lives but as the number of family care helpers declines and the number of care workers recruited from abroad is restricted by tighter immigration rules, then as in the United Kingdom, LTC is going to become "hot-potato" politically that few administrations so far have been willing to handle.

• The geographical age chasm emerging in America as states such as California, Florida, Maine and Vermont and Texas "Go Grey" in a big way and the old age dependency ratios in these states escalates dangerously in terms of both social cost, medical and care facilities and staffing.

As President Joe Biden's Commerce Secretary declared in July 2021, America's ageing population is likely to hit the US economy like a "ton of bricks" without increased federal aid while the escalation in America's dependency ratio or OADR is likely to generate increasing intergenerational tensions. Paul Taylor of the Pew Research Center identified a generational gap emerging in the United States back in 2016: the "young and old in America are poles apart, demographically, politically, economically, socially and technologically… the generations are more different from each other than any time in living memory"; while Harry Dent (2015) predicted an "Age War" as more than half the federal budget by 2022 is predicted to be going to the older age groups in the form of social security, Medicare and the non-child portion of Medicaid, crowding out spending on infrastructure, education and research – the very kinds of investments that would help the young and ensure prosperity for future generations. Although Pew's surveys since have found no evidence that the young or old today are "spoiling for a fight" but instead "tend to like and respect each other", as the *age crunch* bites and as voting for and against entitlement programmes that benefit older voters at the expense of the younger working populations grow, so the potential for generational conflict is likely to increase.

America will soon have the largest number of people aged 65 and over in the western world – over 43 million now and projected to rise to 83 million by 2050, more than Japan but well below that projected for China. However, compared to Europe and even Asia, America is still a relatively young nation, still capable of attracting talented young immigrants and still a culture where responsibility for the elderly is seen to rest squarely with the individual and the family. According to the Pew Global Survey in 2014, Americans are "more confident than Europeans that they will have an adequate standard of living in their old age". Whether that optimism remains today, after the devastation of COVID-19, remains to be seen. As the AARP survey in Nov. 2020 showed, 95% of COVID-related deaths in the United States have occurred in those aged 50 and above with black and ethnic minority groups five times more likely to be hospitalised and twice as likely to die compared to their white counterparts. Older Black Americans are bearing the brunt of the COVID-19 crisis not only because they live in more deprived areas and highly populated housing but also because they are more likely to be key workers having to go to work and are less likely to be able to afford healthcare insurance and so access to good hospital treatment.

Latin America and the Caribbean (LAC) is the world's fastest ageing region. The 48 countries in this "Rainbow Region" of young and vibrant nations is predicted to grow to 790 million by 2060 with the proportion of those aged 65 and over doubling to over 18% by 2050 and exceeding 30% by 2100. Meanwhile, the percentage of those aged 80 and above is set to triple by 2050 to 5.2% across this continent notably in the Caribbean, Cuba and Brazil. As its working age population shrinks and its OADR ratio rises dramatically, the huge health and social care costs are likely to drain the fragile, informal economies of developing economies bedevilled by poverty, gross inequality and extreme rates of violence, criminality, corruption and dictatorships. This is also the region that has suffered some of the worst effects from COVID-19. This is a region containing just 8% of the world's population but accounting for about one-third of COVID-related deaths globally as leaders such as Brazil's President Bolsonaro have dismissed and deliberately downplayed this devastating pandemic. So, while Latin America and the Caribbean may potentially be a boom area for a Silver Economy of its own given its vast natural resources and tourist potential, until this region enjoys much greater political stability – and COVID vaccination – this silver dividend is unlikely to be realised.

Africa

In stark contrast to the rest of the world, Africa is still enjoying a population explosion of Young but this time of young people not just young children; a Youth Dividend that might well save this continent and transform it into the economic super-power that it should be. Africa's median age in 2020 was 20 years, less than half Europe's median age of 43; and 65% of the continent's population today is below age 25. However, even Africa will start to begin ageing after 2050 with a 15-fold growth in the number of older adults later this century and those over age 60 projected to triple from 74.4 million to 235.1 million by 2100 (US Census Bureau Report on Africa Ageing: 2020). By this time, Africa will also be on the "cusp of a major fertility decline" as at least a third of African countries begin to follow a downward spiral from a TFR of 4.3 today down to or below the natural replacement level of 2.1 evident across the rest of the world.

So, while Africa may age much later than the rest of the world and theoretically have more time to prepare for this age-shift than either Asia or Latin America, this continent is about to experience an explosion of working-age populations as sub-Saharan Africa surges to some 1.8 billion by 2070. This is more than the United States, India and China combined and offers a surfeit of young labour for the rest of the century; a huge *demographic dividend* but one that will only be realised if fertility continues to decline, there is a massive investment in education and training and the shift from the countryside to the cities and from informal into formal employment is well-managed and well-regulated. Educated and employed, the young are the future of Africa; unskilled and underemployed they will become a breeding ground for alienation and resentment, terrorism and criminality, maintaining the brutal dictatorships and corrupt governments that have characterised this continent for the last hundred years. Without stability and economic development, the Young in Africa will either join in its endless civil wars or migrate abroad – legally or illegally. So, Africa is at something of an economic, political and demographic crossroads. Its economy, at present, is minute – a mere $2.3 trillion in 2018, a tenth of that in East Asia or Europe and the vast majority of its people live in extreme poverty. Its potential, however, is immense but only if the wealthier societies invest in Africa as an emerging nation; not as one to be exploited or enslaved as in the past but one to invest in, in terms of education and employment, healthcare and transport. Africa is still likely to see many of its ablest and most talented young people emigrate to Europe or the United States, India or China but possibly return later in their careers to help Africa develop its own economy and infrastructure; a "virtuous circle of reverse migration"; a "win-win" scenario that potentially and ultimately will benefit humankind at large rather than leave Africa ravaged as before. As the WEF highlighted in December 2020, if the West doesn't invest in Africa and help build its infrastructure and governance, China certainly will continue to exploit and export its natural resources, not least its oil and valuable minerals, and use Africa's low-cost labour to offset or rejuvenate its own ageing workforce.

Finally, while Africa hasn't been hit as hard as the developed world by coronavirus and potentially has the advantage of learning the lessons from South East Asia in virus control and benefitting from the vaccines developed in the West, mass immunisation of such a huge continent and its diverse and highly dispersed population will prove an immense challenge requiring considerable support and investment from the wealthier worlds and international agencies at a time when nations across the world are only now beginning to recover. However, as the WHO has constantly reminded us, "no-one will be safe (from Coronavirus) until everyone is safe".

POST-TOUR REFLECTIONS AFTER A COOK'S TOUR OF OUR AGEING WORLD

So, Laura's whistle-stop tour of Japan and Europe alongside visits later to South East Asia, the United States and Latin America left her with a panoramic perspective on the ageing world ahead: a picture of its immense challenges but equally, a vision of immense opportunities for generations to come if the All-Age, All-Continent Demographic Dividend on offer can be realised and released, especially for women; "empowering and upskilling the Young will unlock a $1 trillion prize; empowering and employing the old for longer will release a $1.8 trillion prize in the long-term: empowering and getting more women into work will release a $6 trillion prize" (PWC: 2020).

Three themes, in particular, seemed to emerge strongly from Laura's grand tour:

Firstly, the need for a new social contract for the 21st century. As described above, not only are the intergenerational tensions evident in the western world likely to emerge in Asia, Africa and Latin America too as ageing progresses, but also a ***global generation gap*** is also emerging between the developing and developed nations. "By 2050 the average age in Japan will be 53. In Nigeria it will be 23. In Japan there will be 1.5 working age people for every one elderly person. In Nigeria there will be 15". As the Aegon Centre for Longevity and Retirement (ACLR) Report declared in 2019, the social contracts forged during the 20th century seem to be "crumbling under the pressures of ageing populations and rapid social and economic changes" while McKinsey and Co. called in 2020 for a new social contract for the 21st century and the OECD (2021) urged all governments to embed the notion of Intergenerational Justice within all future policymaking in recognition that policy decisions today impact on future generations tomorrow. Numerous governments have responded to this initiative including Finland's Committee for the Future, Israel's Parliamentary Commissioner for Future Generations, Wales Age-Friendly Strategy and Malta's Guardian for Future Generations, although the powers and independence of such bodies often vary, and on occasion, they have been watered-down.

Secondly, the need for a national plan and long-term strategy on ageing. As outlined in Chapter 1, with notable exceptions such as the Dutch and Scandinavian nations, few countries have developed a comprehensive long-term age strategy on ageing. However, the 2019 Global Survey of National Longevity Development Plans did identify distinct *shafts of silver planning* in an increasing number of countries with Japan, Finland and the United Kingdom leading the way in combining ageing with technological development, healthy living and climate change. While Japan, Korea and Singapore are likely to become the "silver laboratories" of the future, countries such as Norway now have embryonic National Plans for Ageing, New Zealand has appointed a Minister for Seniors and agreed a 15 year strategy for "Better Later Life" and the *Scottish Generations Working Together* Manifesto sees Scotland becoming an intergenerational nation by 2030. The UN's 2030 Agenda for Sustainable Development aims to integrate ageing within economic development and put "the torch for future generations" at the forefront of both its economic strategy and its age and climate change programmes whilst the UN75 Future Possibilities Report 2020 identifies six transformational trends that might help countries to reset their economies in the post-COVID world; a world where "growth is becoming less of a priority relative to issues such as climate change and income inequality". The recent debate in the United Kingdom over the funding of social care has dramatically raised the intergenerational issue of "who pays" and whether pensioners themselves might contribute to the cost involved by, for example, giving up their current triple lock pension protection.

Thirdly, whilst the idea of *agelessness* still remains outside most policymaking perspectives and government planning, it certainly is not outside the orbit of today's tech-giants and super-billionaires. As described in Chapter 4, the longevity or silver economy will soon be the dominant economies as ageing sweeps across the United States, Europe, Asia and Latin America in the next 20 years, raising in its path the possibility of the four-five, even six, generation community with a complete restructuring of "normal life" and of today's social institutions from family to work, from healthcare to government. It will put whole new pressures on the environment and natural resources if the world's population is both increasing in number and increasing in lifespan, raising in turn new ethical and existentialist questions about the meaning and quality of life and what it is to be human. Is aging as Brian Kennedy, Director of Singapore's Centre for Healthy Ageing claims, "the climate change of healthcare"? Is senolytics the new science of ageing and senescence the new adolescence? Will healthier, longer life, speculates the Healthy Life Extension Society not only relieve the burdens of dependency in ageing societies but also help ensure that longer lives are better, more fulfill-ing and purposeful lives for all citizens not just the better-off? Will the "fantastic" ideas of transhumanists such as Aubrey De Grey and "the race for endless life" currently being hotly pursued by Google and numerous other tech-billionaires prove that the human body can be endlessly transformed and repaired by technological replacements?

Conclusions and the move towards a new sociology of ageing

So, that's Laura's grand tour of our ageing world; that's her thesis to date. It is still a work in progress. It is still an embryonic sociological paradigm; a long way from the margins of sociology and the footnotes of introductory textbooks described earlier but strong enough now to generate a new sociology, to inspire new academic thinking and inform government policymaking about the new life ahead as nations age, the longevity economy grows, the 100-Year Life becomes a reality and super-ageing societies such as Japan and Singapore become live laboratories for the new life-course and lifespan ahead. Ageing and demography are part of a global revolution, a digital Fourth Industrial and Urban Revolution that more progressive governments and think tanks now recognise and are start-ing to plan for. How far ageing has permeated public consciousness; how far it has attracted and inspired media attention; how far it has radicalised academic thinking and theorising has yet to be seen. The *silver shoots* are certainly there as Japan's Silver Revolution spreads across Ageing Asia and may eventually light up Ancient Europe while Africa, hopefully, manages to convert its forthcoming "youth bounty" from a potential threat into a source of economic and social transformation for all its ages. What this grand tour had particularly brought home to Laura, though, was that that the debate about ageing is not just about ageing generations or even ageing societies. It is about the future of humankind. It is about an ageing revolution within an ageing world where global forces are transforming the world at speeds currently beyond man's comprehension and where artificial intelligence is creating a whole new structure of power and control. Propelling the age agenda to the forefront of human debate, designing a new intergenerational social contract and unleashing generational power as a counterforce to untrammelled globalisation may prove to be one final attempt to re-establish human values and direction on a world apparently increasingly beyond the control of all but the most economically and politically powerful. A theme poignantly encapsulated in an African proverb: *"The world was not left to us by our parents. It was lent to us by our children. What survives of me are the world's children, for whose sake I act today"* (Generativity: 2001).

Realising the gift of longevity, maximising the full potential of the longer life ahead in the 21st century, however, is a huge challenge but one that is vital to the health and future of the United Kingdom if the younger generation is not to suffer all the cost and the older generation – Laura's grandparent's generation – is not to go down in history as a greedy and self-obsessed generation, blind to the burden that they are leaving behind. In this era of *identity politics*, division and sharply polarised political positions, is there not now a need and a desire for reunion and reunification under a new national plan, a new social contract and a new post-COVID vision for all nations if the world is to become a better, fairer and happier place for all ages not just for the old or the better-off? Just as, the New Old, the baby boomers inherited the post-war world after 1945, so, Generations X, Y and Z are inheriting the Digital World of the 21st century and its associated life of longevity and supersonic change. While the older generations may help with this transition, encourage and support it, ultimately it is the Young who will have to lead and design it – as well as pay for it. Time is running out for baby boomers and, as David Willetts has starkly reminded us, January 2017 was the 70th anniversary of the baby boomer boom and soon even more of us will be aged 70 and over than ever before. The 2024 British General Election is only a few years away, and as Professor Laura Carsten (2009) has so forcefully reminded us: "Aging is inevitable. HOW you age is not! … You will very likely spend about three decades of your life as an old person. Deal with it. Death is the only alternative. If you can put behind you the fantasy of eternal youth, you can begin to plan seriously for what comes next. You can think hard about the type of old person you want to be"; a personal challenge presented to me by my loving wife when she "thoughtfully" gifted me the book (illustrated in Figure 8.2) on my 67th birthday.

Finally, as explained in the "Introduction", this reader was written not just in support of developing a sociology of ageing but also as a contribution to what needs to be an urgent national debate as well as a much needed academic one. Ageing is a mammoth issue and a gargantuan task. It is a national debate that Britain hasn't yet had and while the COVID-19 pandemic might just be the spark that ignites this debate; might well be the existential moment in time when all of us look afresh at our priorities in life and how much more we need to support each other, especially the elderly, deprived and young. So far this debate has yet to become part of the British or international political or social agenda. Combatting inequality and ageism, promoting healthier living, nurturing a healthier planet and developing stronger intergenerational relations need to become political priorities as we try to create a better quality of life for all ages and particularly for future generations facing the amazing but hugely challenging century ahead. That would be a suitable legacy after the devastation and

FIGURE 8.2 Cover of *I'm Dead. Now What?*

misery of coronavirus as well as one that any red-blooded baby boomer would wish to leave behind. As Bob Dylan declared back in 1964, "The Times They Are a-Changin'", but even he couldn't have seen how far and how fast change would affect him and his generation some 50 years later. As Carl Bard (2015) is often quoted as saying, "*Although no one can go back and make a brand new start, anyone can start from now and make a brand new ending*"; a very apposite message for any generation but particularly so for a boomer generation that seems to have had it all, and even now can still pay back more. Only time will tell, and hopefully it will tell well before ageing engulfs all of us in the next ten years and becomes the *Grey Nightmare* many fear rather than the *Dawn of a Silver Age*, many hope for.

> To claim one's place at the fire means to live one's life on purpose. When we claim our place at the fire, we enter into a circle of vital elders who have been the source of wisdom in society since time immemorial. We do this by courageously re-examining and rediscovering who we are, where we belong, what we care about, and what our life's purpose is.
>
> Leider and Shapiro: *Living the Second Half of Your Life On Purpose*

Welcome to the World of Ageing. Welcome to the Future: Your Future; Your Family's Future.

Bibliography

AARP: *The Coronavirus Pandemic: Attitudes among the 50+* (November 2020)

Aegon Centre for Longevity and Retirement (ACLR) Report: *The New Social Contract: Empowering Individuals in a Transitioning World* (2019)

African Proverb: Generativity (2001)

Age Platform Europe *Manifesto* (2014); (2019)

Ageing Asia Silver Economy Index (2020)

Bard Carl: Quoteinvestigator (November 5, 2015)

Bodewig, Christian: *Education is the Key to Integrating Refugees in Europe*: Brookings Institute (November 2015)

Buettner, Dan: *Blue Zones Movement*: WEF (2017)

Carsten, Laura: *A Long Bright Future*: Public affairs/Perseus Books (2009)

Cavendish, Camilla: *Extra Time: 10 Lessons for an Ageing Society*: Harper Collins (2019)

Chinese Academy of Social Sciences (January 2019/Charlie Campbell: Time Magazine (February 18, 2019)

Dent Harry S.: *Demographic Cliff*: Portfolio Penguin (2015)

EU Infographics: EU Commission (2018)

EUC: *Active Ageing Index (AAI)* (2018)

European Commission: *AI and the Future of Work* (2019)

European Commission (EC): *Ageing Report (2021)*; *The Impact of Demographic Change (June 2020)*: *Green Paper on Ageing* (January 2021)

European Commission: *Ageing Europe* (2021)

Healthy Life Extension Society (August 2009)

I'm Dead. Now What?: Important Information about My Belongings, Business Affairs, and Wishes: Peter Pauper Press (2015)

Ipsos Global Advisor Survey on Ageing: *Squeezed in the Middle in Super-ageing Japan* (May 2019)

Brian Kennedy, Director of Singapore's Centre for Healthy Ageing Claims, *"The Climate Change of Healthcare"* (February 2020)

Kight S.W.: *Politics & Policy*: Axios (December 2019)

Leider R.J.; Shapiro R.: *Claiming Your Place at the Fire*: Berrett-Koehler Publishers (2004)

Leonardo Quattrucci, in 2018 (Policy Assistant to the Head of the European Political Strategy Centre, EU Commission) Quoted in WEF article (January 9, 2017)

McKinsey & Company: *The Asian Century Has Arrived* (July 15, 2019)

McKinsey & Company: *The Social Contract in the 21st Century* (2020)

MGI: *Inclusive Growth: Six Global Megatrends Testing the EU Model* (2018); *Tackling Europe's Gap in Digital and AI* (March 15, 2019)

NLDP Global Survey of National Longevity Development Plans (2019)

Nuffield Trust: *What Can England Learn from the Long-term Care System in Japan* (May 2018)

OECD: *Perspectives on Global Development 2019* (2018)

OECD: *Ageing: Health at a Glance*: Asia/Pacific (2020)

OECD Briefing (April 2018)

OECD Report: *Delivering Fair Policy Outcomes for All Generations* (2021)

Pew Research Center: *Survey of Global Attitudes to Aging* (2014)

Population Reference Bureau Factsheet: *Aging in the USA* (July 2019)

Portugal Demographic Commission Report: FT (August 2015)

PWC: *Women in Work Index* (March 2020)

Scottish *'Generations Working Together'* Manifesto for the 2021 Scottish Government Elections

Statistics Bureau of Japan (2020)

Super, Nora: The Milken Institute Center for the Future of Aging in Public Policy & Aging Report: Vol. 30 (April 2020)

Taylor, Paul: *The Next America: Boomers, Millennials and the Looming Generational Showdown*: Public Affairs (2016)

The Japan Times: (November 2011)

UN: *Transforming Our World: The 2030 Agenda for Sustainable Development* (2020)

UN75 Future Possibilities Report (2020).

UNDESA: World Population Report (2015) and the Federal Statistical Office of Germany (2016)

UNDESA: *World Population Ageing* (2017)

UNESCAP Report: *Addressing the Challenge of Population Ageing in Asia and the Pacific* (2017)

US Census Bureau (2020)

US Census Bureau *Report on Africa Ageing* (September 2020)

Vítor Constâncio, Vice-President of the European Central Bank, Has Described as "*Collective Demographic Suicide*" (2015)

WEF: *What Do China's New Economic Plans Mean for Africa?* (December 2020)

WHO: World Population Ageing: *Survey of 95 Year-olds Living Near Tokyo* (2015)

Willetts, David: *Sunday Times* (January 2017)

World at Five (January 20, 2020)

INDEX

Printed in Great Britain
by Amazon

41092370R00145